A Rescuer's Story

Pastor Toureille at his desk at the Chaplaincy,
Lunel, France, 1943.

A Rescuer's Story

Pastor Pierre-Charles Toureille in Vichy France

Tela Zasloff

THE UNIVERSITY OF WISCONSIN PRESS

The University of Wisconsin Press
1930 Monroe Street
Madison, Wisconsin 53711

www.wisc.edu/wisconsinpress/

3 Henrietta Street
London WC2E 8LU, England

5   4   3   2   1

Printed in the United States of America

Library of Congress Cataloging-in-Publication Data
Zasloff, Tela.
A rescuer's story: Pastor Pierre-Charles Toureille in Vichy France / Tela Zasloff.
p. cm.
ISBN 0-299-17500-6 (cloth: alk. paper)
1. Toureille, Pierre-Charles, b. 1900. 2. Righteous Gentiles in the Holocaust—Biography. 3.
World War, 1939–45—Jews—Rescue—France. 4. Holocaust, Jewish (1939–1945)—France. 5.
France—History—German occupation, 1940–1945. 6. France—Ethnic relations. I. Title.
D804.66.T68 Z38 2002
940.59'1835'09448—dc21
2002010201

Contents

Prologue   vii
Acknowledgments   ix
Abbreviations   xi

1. Pierre-Charles Toureille, 1900–1976   1
2. To Be a Huguenot   9
3. Pierre Toureille's Early Years and the Ecumenical
   Movement of the 1930s   34
4. The War Years, an Introduction   63
5. The War, 1939–1940   75
6. The War, 1941   106
7. The War, 1942   143
8. The War, 1943–1945 and After   190
Epilogue   232

Appendix: Postwar Tributes and Awards   239
Notes   245
Selected Bibliography   257
Index   263

Prologue

What we have to learn from heroic societies is twofold: first, that all morality is . . . tied to the socially local and particular . . . and, secondly, that there is no way to possess the virtues except as part of a tradition in which we inherit them and our understanding of them from a series of predecessors.

—Alasdair MacIntyre, *After Virtue*

This is a story of a certain kind of hero, who was shaped by the history of his people. It is not his whole story but focuses on the powerful influences of his French Huguenot heritage and the experiences of his maturing years as a Protestant pastor in the 1930s, culminating in the central drama of his life—his role as a rescuer during the Nazi occupation of France in World War II.

Whether a particular cultural heritage produces certain kinds of character, including the heroic, is one of the questions intriguing those studying rescuers and altruistic action. Most studies have focused on individual rescuers, testing for cultural factors like religious upbringing and family role models. Some try to isolate psychological traits that rescuers have in common, like a strong sense of self, or altruism, or a need for praise, or a feeling of well-being.[1] But when a whole people—insistent over centuries on its own history and its differentness from the larger society in which it lives—produces whole communities of rescuers (as in the case of the French Huguenot village of Le Chambon-sur-Lignon, discussed in chapter 2), we also have to look at the broad subject of cultural heritage as a shaper of action.

My attraction to the subject of rescuers started when, as an American

Jew, I was first struck by certain similarities between the Huguenot villagers of southern France and the Jewish people. Both peoples repeated insistently to their children their history of persecution, their covenant with God to act righteously as a chosen people, their deep reliance on the Old Testament, their persistence in maintaining their faith, their special history, and their sense of peoplehood. By a remarkable twist of fate, the horror of World War II and the Holocaust had brought both together as rescuers and rescued.

My own childhood was securely far away from the war, in a close-knit Jewish community in a small railroad town in the mountains of Pennsylvania. I was born on the eve of the war, in 1938. As with most American Jews, details of the Holocaust seeped in slowly, not only because of my family's reluctance to discuss it with children in the 1940s but also because of the hugeness of the task of assimilating information about it. I was made aware, as far back as I can remember, of being part of some large and special story, of ties to other places in the world, of obligations to people far away and in the past. My four grandparents were immigrants from eastern Europe—from Riga, Latvia, and from Ponevez, in Kovno Province, Lithuania. They arrived in America about the same year that Pierre Toureille was born, in 1900, and the stories of their childhood, why they left home, the dangers they had escaped, and their hard work to make it in America were passed around among us all.

So when I first encountered Pierre Toureille's story, I felt it had an unclear but nevertheless insistent connection to mine.

Acknowledgments

I would like to thank Marc Toureille for providing me the inspiration to write this story about his father. My interviews with Marc over a five-year period and the family papers, documents, and photographs he made available are the foundation on which this book was built.

I would also like to thank the following institutions for providing documents and research materials for this book:

The Leo Baeck Institute, New York

Société de l'Histoire du Protestantisme français, Paris

Faculté libre de théologie protestante de Montpellier, France

The United States Holocaust Memorial Museum, Washington, D.C.

The World Council of Churches, library and archives, Geneva, Switzerland

Yad Vashem, Jerusalem, Israel.

Research and preparation for publication of this book were supported by the Memorial Foundation for Jewish Culture, New York.

All English translations of French sources were done by the author unless otherwise indicated.

Abbreviations

AFSC	American Friends Service Committee
CCA	Center for Czechoslovak Aid
CGQJ	Commissariat général aux questions juives (Bureau for Jewish Affairs)
CIMADE	Comité inter-mouvements d'aide auprés des évacués (Committee of Aid to Refugees)
FFI	French Forces of the Interior
FFL	Forces français libres (Free French Forces)
FPF	Fédération protestante de France (Protestant Federation of France)
GTE	Groupes de travailleurs étrangers (Foreign Workers Groups, also identified as TE)
MACE	Maison d'accueil chrétien pour enfants (Christian Home for Children)
ORT	Organisation pour la reconstruction et le travail (Organization for Rebuilding and Vocational Training)
OSE	Oeuvre de secours aux enfants (Agency for Aid to Children)
STO	Service du travail obligatoire (Forced Labor Service)
UGIF	Union générale des israélites de France (General Union of Jews in France)
WCC	World Council of Churches
WJC	World Jewish Congress
YMCA	Young Men's Christian Association

1

Pierre-Charles Toureille, 1900–1976

Pierre-Charles Toureille was born on May 5, 1900, in the sunny, orange–
and–gray-green countryside of Nîmes in the south of France. After he was
received into the French Reformed Church at the age of fifteen, he was
honored by the Royal Serb government for helping wounded Serb soldiers in Nîmes, passed through a religious awakening at age seventeen,
and at Easter 1918, when he was just eighteen years old, received the calling to evangelize among the Slav youth. His career path was no surprise
to his family. There were many pastors among his Huguenot ancestors,
and of his two sisters, Alice and Marguerite, the latter married a pastor.
His interest in the Slav peoples was initiated by both his parents. Pierre's
mother, born Léonie Bastide, had nursed and aided Slavs who sought
refuge in France during World War I, for which she received the *Cheva-
lière de la Légion d'honneur*. It was to his father, Etienne Charles Toureille, a tax-department official for the city of Nîmes, that he wrote this
dedication for his undergraduate thesis on John Huss—"To the memory
of my father who taught me to know and love the Slavs."[1]

Toureille and his father shared the same middle name—Charles—
and his whole life, he used his middle initial and was often addressed by
his friends as P.-C. From his father's side of the family he also inherited a
military tradition, including two *Légion d'honneur* awardees. His great-
grandfather, Paul Toureille, was in the Imperial Guard, fought at Auster-
litz and Waterloo and served in Napoleon's small military force in exile
on Elba. Toureille's first cousin, Charles Pomaret, received the *Croix de
Guerre* in 1919 and then followed a political career. He served as deputy
from Lozère and Secretary of State for Technical Training and was appointed to Pétain's cabinet in 1940, from which he resigned after serving
less than two months.

After entering the Faculty of Theology of Montpellier in 1919,

Toureille at age seven, 1907.

Toureille studied at the Faculty of Protestant Theology at the University of Strasbourg, concentrating in Slavic language and literature. Upon receiving a scholarship from the Czech government to study at the Faculty John Huss in Prague in 1920–21, he learned Czech, traveled through Austria, Hungary, and Serbia, and translated a work by Tomáš Masaryk, first president and chief founder of Czechoslovakia. For the next two years, from 1922 to 1924, he returned to Strasbourg, where he was strongly influenced by the teaching of Jean Monnier, a professor of theology, spent a year of study at the University of Bratislava, then returned to the faculty of Theology at Montpellier to complete his thesis, titled "Jean Huss: Les débuts de la crise religieuse actuelle de la nation Tchécoslovaque" (John Huss: The beginnings of the present religious crisis in Czechoslovakia). He graduated with a bachelor's degree in theology from Montpellier.

That same year, 1924, he married Délie Lichtenstein-Warnery, from a well-to-do Swiss family with ancestors who include both Huguenots and rabbis. Toureille was appointed pastor of the Evangelical Reformed Church from 1924 to 1928 in Bourdeaux, Drôme, then of the same church

Toureille, age ten, with his family, including his mother, Léonie; his father, Etienne Charles; and his two sisters, at his paternal grandfather's home near Toulon, 1910.

in Congénies, Gard, from 1928 to 1934, and in Béziers, Hérault, from 1934 to 1939. During these years, the couple's first son, Simon, was born, in 1925. The next year Pierre Toureille served in the French army, where he was promoted to sergeant, until discharged in 1927; he then resumed his pastorate with a new appointment in Congénies, Gard, from 1928 to 1934. Four more children were born—Francine (1927), Marc (1929), Anne-Marie (1931), and Jean (1935).

The year 1931 began Toureille's active participation in the World Alliance for Promoting International Friendship through the Churches, an international organization that, for the next ten years, tried to cope with the growing threat of totalitarianism among its member countries, particularly Germany. Pastor Toureille was an active member of the Youth Commission of that organization, meeting every few months with colleagues in England, Eastern Europe, Switzerland, and Denmark. In 1938 he was appointed Secretary for France and Latin America of the Youth Commission. He became a good friend and colleague of Dietrich Bonhoeffer, the liberal German theologian who was imprisoned later by the Nazis for involvement in a plot to assassinate Hitler and who was executed by them at the end of the war. Bonhoeffer and Toureille were two of the most eloquent members of the Youth Commission in trying to inspire their the-

Toureille, in back row, left, a volunteer at a
military hospital in Nîmes, 1915.

ologian counterparts around the world to combat the injustices and persecutions spreading in Europe.

Like many other Frenchmen but perhaps to a greater degree, given
his education and family sympathies, Pastor Toureille was devastated by
the Munich Accords of 1938, which he saw as sacrificing Czechoslovakia
to appease Hitler and therefore betraying France's long-term friendship,
mentorship, and affection for the Czechs. In the last year of his life, Toureille said to his son-in-law, "May God forgive us for what we did to
Czechoslovakia." At the request of the Protestant Federation of France,
he went on an information-gathering trip to Prague and Bratislava in 1938
and was appointed secretary-treasurer of a committee supporting the
Protestant churches of Czechoslovakia and a member of the Center for
Czechoslovak Aid (CCA) in France. In September 1939, when France entered the war against Germany, he was mobilized into the French army,
serving at a munitions factory, then mustered out in December, after

which he enlisted as a military chaplain. Among his military parishioners was an infantry unit of the Foreign Legion and a group of Protestants from the International Brigade of the Spanish Civil War, who were formed into Foreign Workers units. It was a short serve since Germany overran France a month after invading Belgium and Holland in May 1940, in what the French like to call *la drôle de guerre* (the so-called war). France became a divided country under the Germans, the northern half the Occupied Zone, and the southern, the so-called Free Zone headed by Marshal Pétain, a World War I hero whom his countrymen hoped would be their protector against German dominance.

Now began the dramatic center of Pastor Toureille's life. Because of his deep roots in the liberal traditions of republican France, his missionary impulses, and the intellectual sophistication gained from his education and international experience among church colleagues across Europe, he saw, from its beginnings, the evils of the Nazi regime and the uselessness of the French's hope that a Pétain could save them. With a fierce zeal and sustained energy, he immersed himself during the war years in what was later called the spiritual resistance, taking on a widespread aid mission that covered 12,000 parishioners and large administrative responsibilities that often sat uneasy with his natural impatience and quick temper. In 1940 he was appointed, by the World Council of Churches (WCC) in Geneva and the Protestant Federation of France (FPF), to be chief chaplain for Protestant Refugees and Camp Internees in the southern zone. He worked in collaboration with the WCC committee for refugees under Pastor Adolph Freudenberg who was based in Geneva, and loosely with CIMADE, which developed an extensive aid mission to refugees and camp internees in France.

These duties were legitimate in the beginning, with willing cooperation from Vichy, overwhelmed by the flood of refugees from northern and eastern Europe and Spain who were being pushed into the southern zone by the Germans. But as the Vichy and German authorities' repressive measures against refugees, especially Jews, grew harsher, and as the detainment camps clearly became deportation and death camps, aid missions became rescue missions. Priorities changed from ameliorating living conditions in the camps to saving lives and helping people to escape the death trains. Toureille's activities became clandestine, focused on bold interventions with the Vichy authorities, helping escapees live in hiding, fabricating false identity papers, including baptismal certificates, and finding people passage and way stations along the escape routes into Switzerland and Spain.

His commitment to Czechoslovakia emerged during the war in several ways. In September 1940, he became vice president of the Center for Czechoslovak Aid (CCA) in Marseille, which provided work and refuge to those Czech military who had not escaped to London after the German victory in France. He also helped found a home in Vence for the children of camp internees, the large majority of whom were Jews, called MACE (*Maison d'accueil chrétienne pour enfants*, Christian Aid Home for Children)—the "Christian" in the name was a cover, which Pastor Toureille reinforced by sending there, for over a year, his youngest daughter, Anne-Marie, and for a shorter time, his youngest son, Jean. In January 1941 he also enlisted in a Franco-Czech resistance network, the Réseau Rossi-Rybak.

He was in constant communication with Freudenberg in Geneva at the newly organizing WCC, whose office was funding Toureille's operations. His trips to Switzerland and reports and speeches on conditions in Vichy France were crucial in marshaling Swiss and international aid. By the fall of 1941, he had moved his family, home, and office from Cournonterral to the small railroad town of Lunel, in Hérault. In December 1941, after the American declaration of war, Toureille moved up from vice president to president of the Committee of Coordination of Nîmes, which grouped together all the aid organizations in Vichy, both Christian and Jewish. He had worked actively with the former president, Donald Lowrie, an American and head of the International YMCA, including many protests to Vichy authorities about their oppressive measures against foreigners and Jews.

This was increasingly dangerous, life-threatening work, as rescue missions, particularly for the Jews, became more desperate. Toureille was arrested and interrogated seven times by the Vichy and Gestapo authorities, and his office raided twice. For his service during the war he was awarded several medals: the FFL (*Forces françaises libres*) medal for his part in the Franco-Czech resistance network (1945); *La Médaille de la résistance française* from the French government (1946); the *Vojenska Medaila za Zásluhy, I, Stupne*, the Czech government's highest military award (1946); the Order of the White Lion, from President Benès of Czechoslovakia (1947); the highest civilian award to a foreigner from the West German government (*Das Grosse Verdienstkreuz*), thanking Toureille for having risked his life to save "German lives, meaning, above all, Jewish lives"; and finally, in 1974, the Yad Vashem Award to Righteous Gentiles and the planting of a tree in his honor in the Avenue of the Righteous in Jerusalem.

At the end of the war, Pastor Toureille's Chaplaincy ceased, and by 1946 he had left his pastorate in the French Reformed Church to go to Czechoslovakia. The immediate reasons for his abrupt departure are not clear but must have evolved from the sometimes contentious relationship between him and the church authorities on the control and organization of his rescue activities, and from the natural deflation that followed his intense spiritual and physical activity during the war years. It appeared that the engine driving him was abruptly shut off, but he continued as a theologian and pastor. He studied for and received a doctorate in theology at the Faculty of Theology, University of Bratislava in 1946–47. He also served as visiting pastor of the French Protestant Church of Czechoslovakia, under the Evangelical Church of Czech Brothers, in Prague. There, the Jewish community of the Old City thanked him, in a special ceremony, for saving Czech Jews.

The rest of his life was spent in restless moving from one pulpit to another after emigrating with his family to the United States, and in teaching and mission work after his return to Europe. In 1947 he was appointed pastor of the French Protestant Church in Washington, D.C., then at a Methodist Church in Simms, Montana, in 1949, then the Slovak Presbyterian Church in Johnstown, New York, from 1950 to 1954. During this same time, Toureille taught at a Bible Institute in Albany, New York, in addition to teaching French at a Presbyterian church summer institute in North Carolina, training missionaries to serve in the Belgian Congo.

After becoming a U.S. citizen in 1955, he served as a missionary and teacher with the American Presbyterian Congo Mission in the Belgian Congo, spending a preparatory nine months in the Colonial School of Brussels. In the Belgian Congo he served in Luluabourg, Kasai (1955–57), and Stanleyville (1957–60). The revolution in the Congo terminated the Toureilles' service there.

The couple returned to France and Switzerland in 1960, where he taught French, history, and geography at several lycées. From 1964 to 1973 he was European secretary for the Evangelical Leprosy Mission, during which time he built a network in western Europe and Scandinavia, operating out of Morges, Switzerland.

In 1973 he retired and lived the rest of his days with his wife at a retirement home in France, in Anduze, Gard. Until October 31, 1976, when he died of kidney cancer after more than a year of illness, he continued to travel and lecture.

In a curriculum vitae he wrote in 1967, Toureille added a personal final paragraph of self definition:

I am a good Reformed Calvinist Evangelical. I have experienced, since 1924, all the current theological movements. The longer I live, the more evangelical I am, that is, positive and steadfast on matters of doctrine, but I am also very open to ecumenism and participate actively in the European movements making ties between Catholics and Protestants. I am, without being narrow-minded, a Reformed Protestant Presbyterian. But I have excellent relations with all families of Christianity (Protestant, Catholic and Orthodox) with whom I converse in a spirit of peace and unity.

The largest photograph I have of Toureille is a portrait, head and shoulders, taken in 1948 when he emigrated to the United States. and served as pastor of the French Protestant Church in Washington, D.C. He is wearing his clerical collar and a tweed jacket. His face is fully fleshed, of a southern Mediterranean type, with dark, neatly smoothed-down straight hair, an unusually broad and high forehead, and bushy brows over dark, intense eyes that look close to anger. He is looking, not at the photographer, but to his left. He is not smiling, but his mouth is turned up to one side, in an expression that combines sensitivity and irony. The other photographs show that his build was short and stocky, with a tendency to put on weight past his teen years, and that his posture was always bolt upright. "I'm surprised—he looks so earthy," a friend of mine remarked.

2

To Be a Huguenot

If you want to understand my father, you must study the history of the French Huguenots, their beliefs, their martyrs, their exiles, how they survived centuries of persecution and separation. You must learn also about the history of the Protestants in the Cévennes, the wars of the Camisards under Louis XIV. Only then will you have a clear view of our atavism and our way of thinking.

—Marc Toureille, son of Pierre Toureille, interview with the author

Marie Durand was nineteen years old in 1730, from the Cévennes mountain region of south central France and engaged to be married. Like many other Huguenot women from that area, she was imprisoned in the Tower of Constance, for the sole reason that her brother Pierre was preaching in "the Desert," a phrase denoting remote places sought by the French Protestants where they could pray in secret, after their public worship had been suppressed. Marie Durand was liberated in 1768 at age fifty-seven, broken by thirty-eight years of incarceration with more than twenty other women, in one room of the stone tower, ninety feet high with walls eighteen feet thick, built as fortification by Philip the Bold in the thirteenth century. This somber pile of rocks was erected in a desolate salt marsh area called *Aigues Mortes* (old French meaning "dead waters"), complete with sluggish streams and canals, and it served throughout the eighteenth century as the major prison in southern France for Huguenot women who held to their faith.

According to one visitor to the Tower in the 1670s the single room holding the women deserved Dante's lines over its entrance, "Abandon hope, all who enter here."[1] The only source of light and air was one circular hole six feet in diameter in the ceiling, through which rain and snow also poured down, with a similar hole in the floor to a second chamber below. This visitor reports that, at his appearance, the fourteen women languishing in the room threw themselves with sobs at his feet, unable to speak. The youngest, over fifty years of age, had been only eight when seized by the authorities while going to hear a sermon with her mother.

By the time Marie Durand was released, her brother had been dead a third of a century; the authorities had hanged him in 1732 for preaching. She herself was destined to greater fame than her other martyred prison mates. Around the stone margin of the hole in the tower room floor was found the single word *Resistez* (Resist) traced throughout a lifetime, according to tradition, by Marie Durand, slowly digging out the crude letters with her knitting needle. A symbol of the inflexible spirit of the Huguenots opposing oppressive royal power, Marie Durand has remained for French Protestants a key symbol of steadfast religious faith in the face of unjust temporal authority, from the eighteenth century to the period of the Vichy regime and German occupation of World War II.

Her family home in Le Bouchet, Vivarais, has been preserved as a monument to the Huguenots who held firm. The house is built into high stone walls, in the style of fifteenth-century fortified villages in France, with narrow vaulted stone passageways, continuous new levels of doorways, windows, and niches, allowing sudden bursts of sunlight into small plazas. The house is situated above two mountain valleys carved out by the Eyrieux and Rhone Rivers, and faces the Alpes du Dauphiné. Unlike the flat hard face of the front of the house, the back opens out through a stone arch to a dirt and flagstone path lined with thorny flower bushes. In the central room, beside the open hearth and near a large Bible open on a table, there is a Huguenot cross on the wall, a third piece of wood encircling the two crosspieces at their meeting point.

The French Huguenot story traces a clear and simple line through the history of France—a stubborn spiritual resistance to temporal authority, a resistance that periodically evolved into military and political forms, as well as religious. This chapter provides an overview of Huguenot history through World War II, to set the cultural context out of which Pierre Toureille became a rescuer. Pierre Toureille learned about his Huguenot history through stories like Marie Durand's, passed from parents to children. In the tradition of the Huguenots, the retelling of their own story was a way of maintaining their identity as a people and their special role in God's plan, in Old Testament style. These stories must have been vivid and present in the mind of Pierre Toureille as he was growing up. His mother was an example of strength through remembering. Although proud of her native village in southern France, she reminded her children and grandchildren all her life that she had been betrayed by the Protestant occupants of her village two hundred years earlier, because they had converted to Catholicism under threat of imprisonment and execution by the king's dragoons.[2]

Such stories must have shaped not only Pierre Toureille's view of his life's role but also his style of writing—narrative was consistently his favorite technique of analysis. To continue that tradition, the following historical overview will include some of the narratives that demonstrate most vividly the periods of deepest crisis in Huguenot history.

Early Years: The Edict of Nantes and the Exodus

The spirit and mind of the Huguenots is Calvinist, maintaining the severe sense of duty and rigorously logical strictures set out by its founder. John Calvin barely escaped with his life, from France to Switzerland in 1534, after giving a lecture at the Sorbonne that purportedly smacked of heresy. After teaching and traveling, he became, in 1536, the spiritual and temporal leader of a Protestant, or Reformed, community/state in Geneva, which rivaled the Catholic church in its merging of religious and political power.

The Huguenot/Protestant community of France was active before Calvin had formally established his religious state in Geneva, but by doing so, he gave the Huguenots a political legitimacy and provided them a source of aid and refuge for the next four centuries. The name Huguenot has been attributed either to the sixteenth century Protestants of Tours, who assembled in a tower haunted by a spirit called King Huguet (or Hugon), or to the word *aignos*, a derivation of the German word *Eidgenossen* (those bound together by oath). Independent of the German Lutheran Reformation, the French Reformation began around 1512 and spread rapidly in France; the first of its martyrs was burned at the stake in Paris in 1523.

At the center of Calvinism is the doctrine of predestination: that God is not only the unique source of salvation for the sinner but that God has, since the beginning and for all eternity, set out all that would happen in creation, including who would—and would not—be saved. We are no more in control of our destinies or can alter them by our actions, good or bad, than is the worm about to be tramped upon by our foot—as some commentators phrase it. Humankind thus is divided into two sets, those of the elect whom God has chosen to save, and the damned. The burning question then becomes, can we know who are the elect? The answer is partial and only probable at best: God has given us a means to sense election, since only the elect can successfully act out God's commandments against all adversity and can be instruments for God's will. Only the pious life of good works implies election, but the good works are the result of election, not its cause.

To the charge that such a doctrine produces fatalism and passivity in human actions, Calvin answered, on the contrary, that this doctrine drives the pious into a lifetime of good works, as reassurance to themselves that they are among the elect and in compliance with their duty to serve as God's vessel. Such a concept of lifetime service and discipline, such demands on oneself to follow duty, together with a sense of being an elite apart, formed a character of people who could survive centuries of persecution and temporal losses and gains, taking on martyrdom if necessary. It was such a character that produced the Protestant church of France, whose adherents, during times of heavy persecution, emigrated by the hundreds of thousands to northern Europe, England, and America, carrying with them and planting in their new lands a fervent belief in their God-given duty to obey God's laws, to work hard, and to prosper.

Persecution, martyrdom, and periodic floods of refugees from France became a consistent pattern for the next three centuries of Huguenot history. Because their battles with Catholic monarchies and church authorities were for independent religious and civil liberties, and despite their insistence on loyalty to the king, the Protestants constantly posed a political threat that became more dangerous than the religious one. The nature of this threat, and the accompanying levels of persecution, waxed and waned according to the level of civil unrest and tides of reactionism within the kingdom.

The first centralization of the Protestant churches in France took place at the Paris synod of 1559, in which Calvin's constitution and representative system of church organization was established. The number of

Protestant churches in France increased from 15 to 2,150 after the conclusion of the Paris synod, which established the Protestant church as a powerful political opponent to the dominant Catholic authorities, both temporal and religious. The years from 1562 to 1598 were among the bloodiest for the Protestants. Alternating with dubious treaties claiming to guarantee religious tolerance to the Huguenots were violent pitched battles and civil disorder. The worst of these and the one most fixed in Huguenot memory was the St. Bartholomew's Day Massacre of August 24, 1572, plotted by Catherine de Medici, Charles IX, and the de Guises. Modern historians estimate that 3,000 Protestants were slaughtered in one day in Paris alone by roving Catholic bands and tens of thousands more killed throughout the country in the next two months.[3]

For the next forty years, the Protestants maintained a militant and often violent resistance to the governing authorities, pushing for full religious and civil liberties. Their champion, Henry of Navarre (Henry IV), had to abjure Protestantism when he took the throne in order to pacify his kingdom, but in 1598 he promulgated the Edict of Nantes, which established for the Huguenots their religious and political freedom. This charter lasted eighty-seven years, amid chronic tensions and sporadic violence between the Protestant communities and governing authorities. Following the civil war of 1620, the Huguenots' military and political advantages were destroyed by the final defeat of their military forces. Despite this setback, by 1650 there were over one and a half million Protestants in France, about one-ninth of the total population, concentrated in the Nîmes-Montpellier area.

By 1681 they were forced to undergo Louis XIV's system of "dragonnades," by which soldiers were quartered in Huguenot homes with license to persecute them, in order to force them to convert to Catholicism. This led to the forcible conversion of thousands. Following the attrition of the Huguenots' rights to religious practices, property ownership, and civil liberties as guaranteed by the Edict of Nantes, and the large number of forced conversions, Louis XIV revoked the Edict in 1685 as "unnecessary," thereby committing what some French historians call one of the largest royal blunders in French history. An estimated 300,000 of France's most productive citizens emigrated to northern Europe, England, and America, taking with them resources in business, crafts, and manufacturing.

Jacques Fontaine, 1658–1728

Born during this era, one of the worst periods of persecution against the Huguenots, Jacques Fontaine was from a middle-class Huguenot family from Normandy, with some lines to nobility. He wrote a memoir in 1722 that tells of his odyssey from France to England and Ireland after the Revocation of the Edict of Nantes.[4] This memoir demonstrated the Huguenot, Calvinist impulse to trace the paths of Grace carved out in the seeming arbitrariness and coincidences of one's life—to see one's life as a demonstration of Election. It was also an eloquent expression of the moral toughness and confidence, activism, and ingenuity of his character, mixed with an arrogance, as others may see it, in considering oneself chosen by God to do good works. In his memoir, Fontaine reminded his descendants of this chosen-ness in his first paragraph: "I would fain hope that the pious examples of those from whom we are descended, may warm your hearts and influence your lives. . . . You cannot fail to notice, in the course of their lives, the watchful hand of God's Providence, supporting and preserving them through hardship and suffering."

He insisted that his life had had special blessings on it, which made him remorseful for his "frailties and sins." His strongest hope was that this memoir, in "recording the past mercies of God" for the benefit of his descendants, would increase and strengthen his own gratitude and confidence in God, and secure God's continuing "fatherly protection during the few days I have yet to live." These introductory remarks encapsulated the Huguenot perspective on life, an uneasy, even paradoxical combination of arrogance and humility, which produced a dissatisfied, restless, passionate spirit continually productive and doing good, as an assurance that the source was God's Grace.

He recounted his own story in swashbuckling style, full of narrow escapes from pursuers, astounding flouting of authority, even from a prison cell, and a string of commercial successes as a refugee and entrepreneur in Ireland and England. His entire family experienced the violent conflicts of this era in France. The Edict of Pacification of 1561, in granting Protestants rights of worship, took the adjudication of heresy out of the hands of the courts and placed it into the hands of anyone who had a grudge against Protestants, including murderous, pillaging armed mobs, encouraged, Fontaine claims, by priests, monks, and bigots. His great-grandparents had their throats cut by such a mob, and his minister father was forced, in

1595, to convert to Catholicism when the king's dragoons occupied his house.

One of his adventures about which he was most proud was his flouting of the French justice system. During Protestant rebellions in 1684, he was imprisoned for presiding over clandestine meetings of the cult in his family home, then, once in prison, exacerbated his situation by leading prayers among the other Protestant prisoners (65–98).

In August, when his case was taken to court, he argued in his own defense with such intelligence and eloquence that he persuaded a good number of the judges. His key tactic was to destroy the credibility of the witnesses to both the original, illicit prayer meeting and the praying inside the prison. Then followed another series of hearings, in which Fontaine amazed and exasperated his judges with his stubbornness and loquacity. By this time the court recognized that he was not at the illegal meeting of the cult under question and could produce a good alibi, and that no one could verify that his speaking in prison had actually been praying.

The President had no more questions to ask Fontaine as an accused, but, "as a matter of curiosity," asked him if he thought a mechanic could understand Holy Scripture as well as "the learned doctors and councils." Fontaine answered that if the mechanic were blessed with the Holy Spirit and the councils not, then the mechanic would understand the Scriptures best. "Our blessed Lord and his poor fishermen found themselves opposed by the Scribes and Pharisees at Jerusalem. To come nearer to our own days, I certainly think that Luther and Calvin understood the Scriptures better than all the popes, cardinals, and councils put together."

The judges got the invidious comparison. Fontaine wrote, "At these words they all arose, crying out, 'Jesu Maria! What infatuation!' 'Ere long, gentlemen,' said I, 'we shall all be summoned to leave this vain world, and we shall then see whose has been the infatuation.'"

It is easy to imagine Fontaine telling this story, in just these overblown terms, to his grandchildren. And perhaps not so hard to imagine that it might have happened just about as he said it did.

All this occurred a year before the Revocation of the Edict of Nantes and the beginning of the most bitter persecution the Protestants had undergone since the St. Bartholomew's Day Massacre. The justice system ceased to function, and the dragoons ravaged and pillaged Protestant homes mercilessly, encouraging lawless mob violence. Fontaine urged that the Protestants of his area around Rochefort take up arms, but the elders urged passivity and oaths of loyalty to the king, in the spirit of patience and long-suffering taught in the Gospel. These same leaders proved to be "arrant cowards" (102) when the dragoons appeared at their homes. They fell all over themselves, as Fontaine tells it, trying to get into the church first to recant their religion. He decided, then, that the real "courageous and unshaken faith" resided among the poor and rural people.

Fontaine concluded that he must emigrate, which launched him into a peroration of love, grief, and accusation toward his country (104), a clear expression of the tensions within the Huguenot mind between two fierce loyalties—God and native land. He saw the formidable army of France experiencing its gloomiest defeat in becoming an army of torturers. King Louis XIV, "the Great," who aspired to rule the world, lost all his glory when he raised his hand against "the people of God," and was deservedly despised in his old age. Famine, plague, and poverty ruled, and gold and silver disappeared, replaced with "a species of enchanted paper" that had turned to nothing. Fontaine finished, "France! miserable France! my dear native country, wilt thou never open thine eyes, and unstop thine ears, and understand the language in which God has spoken to thee? . . . God is not mocked, he will protect his faithful servants, and preserve his holy religion from destruction. Never canst thou, O France! enjoy thine ancient prosperity, whilst thou art the persecutor of God's elect."

The Camisards, 1702–1710

The eighteenth century began, in 1702, with the war of the Camisards, a band of Huguenot guerrillas in the Cévennes mountains, who were defeated by 1710.[5] Despite the fact that they lost their short-lived battle for religious liberty, the Camisards added martyrs and heroes to the Huguenot cause with such vividness that, more than 200 years later, during World War II, those supporting the French Resistance against Vichy and the German occupiers reminded each other that it was a very short step from Camisard to Maquisard. The Camisard battles took place in Languedoc, which contained one-fourth of the French Protestants (about 200,000), and surrounding regions of the Cévennes mountains, covering the four present-day departments of la Lozère, l'Ardèche, le Gard, and l'Hérault.

A book of small, mostly silhouette illustrations of Camisard history executed by Samuel Bastide (1879–1962) represents well the qualities of romance, drama, and eighteenth-century revolutionary bravura that infuse the French Protestant popular view of the Camisard story. The cover illustration, all in silhouette, shows royal troops and cavalry charging up a hill with fixed bayonets, their officer with shapely mustache, long wig, plumed hat, and sword raised, leading them up the crest toward a line of bareheaded men down on one knee, shovels, axes, spears, pitchforks, rifles all raised straight up, their heads bolt upright and eyes straight ahead, their hands clasped around their weapons in a position of prayer. An overarching tree droops finely etched branches over the scene, with sharp mountains in the background, all framed within a series of Baroque panels containing laurel wreaths, pistols, sabers, pitchforks, and spears clustered behind a drum, and an oil lamp with the words *per lucem* emanating from the flame.

Each Huguenot hero, and enemy, has his or her individual story and dramatic silhouette. There is Intendant Baville, strict administrator of royal orders in 1685, who seized infants for conversion, forbid Protestants a legal marriage ceremony, and condemned them to the galleys or the gallows, dragging their corpses through the streets, past jeering crowds, to the sewers. Among the Huguenots who remained passive to this persecution, there arose a strange series of mysterious and mystical experiences, including light and psalm singing emanating from heaven, tears of blood appearing on women's cheeks, and children falling into trances, issuing prophesies, and running through the streets crying, *Repentez-vous!* (Repent!)

Among the more militant, there was the shepherdess Isabeau Vincent, locked in the Tower of Crest, who told a royal official, "You can kill me, but God will raise up others in my place," and Gabriel Astier, who inspired nearly 4,000 followers before being hanged at Baix. There was the royal army massacre of 300 young "prophets and prophetesses," gathered in a crowd of 800 on a hillside to pray. The colonel had sent messengers to warn the crowd to disperse, but the messengers were so moved by the prayers that they joined the group instead of threatening it. There was the simple farmer, Corbière la Sicardie, who, while giving an inspirational sermon to a crowd in 1689, was murdered by royal troops who dashed his head against a rock and, according to local testimony, the blood from his fatal wound could never be effaced from the rock on which he was killed.

Du Ferre (or Du Serre), from Geneva, trained a "school of prophets" who exhorted their followers through the Psalms and such lines from Revelation as "Reward Babylon even as she rewarded you, and double unto her double according to her works" (Rev. 18:6). They prayed before every battle, forbade drinking, quarrels, and swearing, and were followed into battle by the prophetesses to preserve their moral scrupulousness.

Abraham Mazel, one of the few to escape later from the famous and dreaded Tower of Constance, was eighteen years old in 1685, when he watched the burning of his temple and then the forced conversion of the congregation. Sixteen years later, at night, at the base of a rock wall in the mountains, where the Camisards had their first assembly, Abraham Mazel had a prophetic vision, in which God commanded him to take arms against the persecutors. Like Moses, he hesitated at first, pleading that he was not a warrior, but then obeyed. His band's first victory was saving four boys and three girls who had been arrested while fleeing to Geneva, by Abbé du Chayla—infamous as policeman, judge, and jailer, and Inquisitor without mercy. The torture bench to which he chained his victims is still on display in the *Musée du Désert* (Museum of the Desert) in southern France, where relics of Huguenot history are collected.

The Camisard bands distinguished themselves in guerrilla warfare and in ambushes that furnished them more weapons and clothing, which they sometimes wore in order to enter enemy territory in camouflage. There were, at times, formal pitched battles, like the one in the Valley of Banes in 1703, when royalist Captain Poul, at the head of sixty dragoons, charged a group of Camisards. Their leader, Ravanel, ordered them all to fall to their knees in prayer and to chant psalms, then answered the charge with a hail of rocks and musket shot. Captain Poul was killed and his dragoons fled. "When they sing their damned songs, we no longer have control of our soldiers," one royal officer is quoted as saying. By the end of 1702, Intendant Baville wrote, "The whole country is in revolt—a revolt without precedent."

The royal authorities tried a new policy—burning the villages and forest lands of the Cévenols so that the Camisards would have no base. But, for a while, this seemed to push even more people to join the rebels. The Camisard army moved to the mountains in caves and grottos known only to the local people, where they kept their arms and supplies, making powder out of the saltpeter they had dried in the sun, and musket balls with the iron taken from their churches and their hospitals. After a royalist victory near Nages, where the royalists, with 3,000 soldiers encircled and squashed the Camisards, a traitor revealed to the royalists one of the largest Camisard grottoes, full of supplies, arms, and wounded, which the royalists destroyed completely, including killing all the wounded.

The Camisards were finally defeated by the most brilliant of the royal officers, le Maréchal de Villars, who began, in 1704, by promising the Protestants amnesty and freedom to worship as they wished. Cavalier, one of the Camisard leaders, discouraged by their recent defeats, promised they would lay down their arms if they would be granted, in turn, liberty of conscience, the freeing of their fellow Huguenots now imprisoned and slaving in the galleys, and the right to emigrate.

However, these promises from the royalists were only a trick to disarm the Camisards. Some of their leaders realized this and fled to Switzerland, failing in a few subsequent invasion attempts, while others, particularly Pierre Laporte, known as Roland, continued the fighting. De Villars tracked down Roland, who, after meeting with his lieutenant and their wives at the Château of Cornelly, near Lasalle, was finally taken and shot at point blank range.

In one of the silhouettes in the Bastide book, Roland presses his back against a tree, pointing his pistol at a line of royalist rifleman about to fire on him, and saying, "My mission is to sustain and cherish, to my last breath, my religion and my country." A monument marking the spot reads: "In this valley was killed, April 14, 1704, at the age of 24, Pierre Laporte, called Roland. To the memory of all the victims, in expiation for all the hatred." Two days after his execution, the body of Roland was dragged through the streets of Nîmes and burned in the central square. His five lieutenants were burned alive at the stake.

De Villars left the province covered with glory. By 1705 the Camisard revolt had lost its force, and more than 500 Camisards left the country. De Villars' replacement, the Duke of Berwick, resorted to burning and hanging all remaining Camisards who could be captured. Abraham Mazel, after his miraculous escape from the Tower of Constance, took up battle again in 1709 but was killed near Uzès; his head was put atop a column and burned near his last battle. Although fighting continued sporadically for the next few years, the War of the Camisards was virtually over.

The author and artist of this silhouette history of the Camisards, stretching mightily to place them in a position of importance in French history, tried to draw linkages between the Camisards and the ideals of the French Revolution of 1789. The French monarchy, he argued, cannot congratulate itself on defeating the Camisards. If it had granted them their rights, it would have spared the lives of its own troops and those who fought against it. The monarchy would not have encountered the defeats and economic disasters coming in the future, and the children of the Camisards would have defended the monarchy that they loved—and the people would not have decapitated the least blamable of its kings. On July 14, 1789, the people established the right to think and live according to their conscience, for which the obscure peasantry of the Camisards had earlier given their lives, in "the most selfless battle the world has ever known."

In 1715, Louis XIV, on his deathbed, declared Protestantism eradicated from the kingdom, contradicted by the first meeting of the "synod of the Desert," the Huguenots' reorganization of their churches in remote, secret areas. The growth of this underground movement revived a new period of virulent persecution of the Protestants, encouraged by the monarchy and the powers of the Catholic Church. One famous case was that of Jean Calas, in 1762, tortured and condemned to death on the false charge that he killed his son for wanting to become a Catholic. Voltaire became his defender and raised public indignation at the injustice of the case. The edict of 1787, supported by Lafayette, and the Revolution of 1789 restored to the Protestants full rights of religious worship and entry into all professions.

The White Terror, 1814–1816

Under Napoleon, the Huguenots were granted state subsidies in return for state control of their churches, which had been reduced in numbers due to long persecutions of previous regimes. At Napoleon's fall, the 1815 "White Terror" of reaction that reestablished the Bourbon monarchy opened up the Protestants again to outrageous persecution, mob violence, and forced emigration, particularly in the southern area around Nîmes.

Mark Wilks was an English Protestant pastor in 1820, sent on a fact-finding mission by the Committee of the General Body of Ministers of the Three Denominations in the area of London and Westminster. His task was to investigate the wave of persecution of Protestants in France. The title of his book, published in 1821 in London, lays out his task in all its ponderous seriousness: *History of the Persecutions Endured by the Protestants of the South of France, and more especially of the Department of the Gard, during the years 1814, 1815, 1816, &c. including a defence of their conduct from the Revolution to the present. In two volumes.* The Committee had presented Wilks with mountains of documents recording stories of the victims and witnesses of these persecutions, and directed him to authenticate these and put them in a larger political context.

Wilks set out a framework in his short preface, which represented the combination of religion and politics that had always characterized the Huguenots and had been their chief dilemma. He berated those who tried to dishonor the Protestants by claiming that their rebellion and recalcitrance was political rather than religious. He argued that their behavior was, rather, a mixture of religion and politics, and always had been: "The principles of the Reformation, must ever expose their professors to the hatred of those who advocate, either from interest or inclination, the cause of mental slavery," and that it was the independent spirit of the Reformation rather than the religious doctrine that challenged kings, priests, and the courts of Europe. Wilks, like his counterpart pastors in France, found his lesson in the Book of Daniel but, in this case, as the model for the political motivations behind what was ostensibly religious persecution: "Daniel was not really persecuted for his faith: his faith was the secret cause of his advancement; but it was because he governed, not because he prayed, that he was attacked; and his enemies found occasion against him in his religion, because every other pretext failed." (vi)

That much established, Wilks launched into more than 600 pages of detailed, first-person testimony on the persecutions under the period of the White Terror in France, keeping enough in touch with the political climate to present the kind of Daniel-like mixture he is arguing for. Like all long and detailed listing of atrocities, this one became mind-numbing with extended reading, but one well documented case seems the best way to demonstrate Wilks's message.

One of the most notorious events of this period of Protestant persecutions began in November 1815, in the area of Lunel, a small town on the main road between Nîmes and Montpellier. A local Catholic group, while gathering to meet with a royal emissary, the Duke d'Angoulême, so harassed the Protestants in the area that the latter were forced to arm themselves with scythes and pitchforks in self-defense. This kind of mob violence was continually fomented by bands of reactionary vigilantes who, in this period of political instability and in the name of the king, were trying to seize power by forming their own army and terrorizing public officials. The Protestants were the natural targets of inchoate public rage. They were depicted as unrepentant enemies of the monarchy and the church, and thus the source of all disorder and violence.

Following the local outburst near Lunel, and even though order was quickly restored by gendarmes, eight Protestant fathers were dragged to jail for defending their families, and 200 troops and a brigade of gendarmes were quartered in Protestant homes.

This outburst of violence occurred despite the fact that the duke had just appeared in Nîmes a few days before and heard testimony from the Protestant leaders on the sufferings their people had undergone. They had to gain his audience secretly, through a back door so as not to enrage the populace. The duke told them he was astonished at the civil disorder and closing of the Protestant temples by local officials. He assured them that the royal family guaranteed freedom of worship and wished the temples to be reopened, and ordered the area military commander, Général Lagarde, to take every measure necessary to secure civil order during this period of reopening.

Unfortunately for the Protestant community, Général Lagarde would not appear in the region for a few more days, so the local officials, egged on by the armed vigilante groups and the mobs, continued their policies of repression of Protestants. When Lagarde finally appeared in Nîmes, he promised the Protestant community that he himself would protect the opening of the temples the next day, a Sunday morning. The president of the consistory and its pastor, Juillerat Chasseur, took the precaution of opening only one small temple on a narrow side street, omitting the ringing of the bell and playing the organ so as not to alert the mob.

The congregation began to assemble quietly at 10 A.M., almost as if they were committing a crime rather than exercising their rights. Although Pastor Chasseur would be performing the service he begged his wife and parishioners to stay at home, so that the opening would be symbolic only, and, in case of a mob break-in, he would be the only victim. But none of them agreed to that. As the pastor walked to the temple that morning, he passed groups of people giving him ferocious looks and shouting "What! do they still have the nerve to pray to God?" and "This is it—time to squash them, and neither women nor children must be spared." One man was heard to shout, "If they dare come by again, I'll get my musket and get ten of them for my share."

When the pastor reached the temple he found the concierge so terrorized that he couldn't open the heavy front door, so the pastor did so himself. Then the congregation started to arrive. They were blocked in the street and at the front steps by an angry mob growing increasingly larger, shouting "Kill the Protestants! Kill the Protestants!" Général Lagarde tried to calm and disperse them, and he placed guards at the most vulnerable points. The apparent order this achieved prompted him to leave the scene.

The church was now filled, and Pastor Chasseur started the service. In a few minutes, a small number of the mob entered the church shouting, "Long live the King," and "Death to the Protestants," but the gendarmes were able to remove them and close the doors. The noise outside increased; the mob started banging on the doors trying to break them down. Once they succeeded, there would be no defense against a massacre. The congregation pressed together, some crying out and groaning, and others not speaking, remaining pale and motionless. The pastor tried to lead them in Psalm 42, but he could not be heard.

This state of siege continued for nearly forty-five minutes. The pastor's wife hid under the pulpit, holding their daughter, and was soon joined by the pastor himself. She recalled later exactly what was going through her mind: "I remembered that it was the anniversary of my marriage. After six years of happiness, I said, I am about to die with my husband and my daughter. My baby son whom I had left at home was, I confess, almost forgotten. We shall be slain at the altar of our God, the victims of a sacred duty, and heaven will open to receive us and our unhappy brethren. I blessed the Redeemer, and without cursing our murderers, I awaited their approach" (482).

The gendarmes outside could not control the growing mob, and the national guard refused to act, saying they would not put themselves in danger "for such villains." An additional detachment of soldiers appeared and promised the congregation refuge if they opened the doors. Some few were able to escape the church this way but the crowd got to most of them in the street, showering them with stones, beating and whipping them, and dashing them against the pavement and walls, without regard to age. The pastor, his wife, and daughter were chased with rocks and his mother almost killed with one of the blows to her head. Some were trampled under horses' hoofs, others whipped and cut, others dragged along the stones, many of whom died of their injuries. The total number of people so treated amounted to about eighty.

The fanatics were then checked by the sudden news that there had been a murder attempt on Général Lagarde. He had returned indignantly to the scene on horseback, after hearing of the violence. A rioter named Louis Boissin, a sergeant in the national guard and a member of one of the vigilante bands, had approached when someone had seized the bridle of the general's mount, pointed his pistol at the general's face saying, "You are going to make me retreat?" and he fired. When Boissin saw that the general was still mounted, he called out with disappointment, "Ah! I haven't killed you yet." Many witnessed this but no one arrested him, and he escaped easily.

Général Lagarde ordered his officer to protect the Protestants and galloped back to his hotel, fainting on arrival. When he came to, before letting the doctor examine him, he insisted on writing a letter to the government, establishing, in case of his own death, who the murderer was, so that no one would dare accuse the Protestants. He died after a few days.

The king, this time, had to react to the turmoil in the south—this was a murder of one of his officers. He issued an ordinance that publicized the scandal to all of Europe, calling it "an atrocious crime . . . in contempt of the constitutional charter" (494), and set out measures instituting legal proceedings against the assassin and accomplices, quartering more royal troops in Nîmes, at the residents' expense, and disarming those who were not regular members of the national guard. But, as Wilks pointed out, this ordinance threw a veil over the whole event. It did not address all the other crimes being committed in the south in the name of the king and, most importantly, said nothing about the source of the violence, which was oppression and mob attacks against the Protestants, fomented by the terrorizing groups that the assassin represented.

The trial was obviously rigged. Boissin's lawyer was a major in the same national guard in which Boissin had served as sergeant, and the chief witnesses were members of the national guard and the police. The audience was an enthusiastic mob, which drowned out any attempt at maintaining order and rationality. Boissin was found not guilty to attempted murder, and the court maintained he had been provoked to using his weapon by both an attack on his person by a public law enforcement officer and threats from the Protestants themselves—"the enemies of legitimacy . . .

[who] returned, and in November displayed their wonted audacity" in practicing their religion, as his lawyer put it.

Boissin's acquittal not only cleared him but pronounced Lagarde and the Protestants as the guilty parties. Despite the fact that moderate Catholic legislators and royal representatives were outraged at this outcome and defended the Protestants as victims of murderous civil disorder, the minister of justice could not bring Boissin back for a retrial since the vote of the jury was the final authority. Although invited by the mayor to leave Nîmes, Boissin remained free. Civil order was gradually established in France, and there were increased demands from moderate forces to protect the Protestants rights and bring the murderous elements to trial. But by 1820, when Wilks finished his book, the future still looked alarming for the Protestants, especially when their enemies were being elected to the legislature, and their safety was still tied so precariously to political fluctuations.

Pastor Chasseur, who after involvement in the Lagarde incident at Nîmes, fled to a pastorate in Paris, commented later to Wilks on the aftermath of the incident. He claims that the number baptized in the portion of his congregation in Nîmes that remained, amounted to only fifty or sixty, "which can only be ascribed to the combined influences of misery and terror" (509). Chausseur deplored those who, years later, questioned the authenticity of such reports as Wilks's, thus denying or distorting the facts: "Charity demands mercy and pardon even for the most wicked, but not at the expence [*sic*] of truth and innocence" (509).

After order was restored on the national level, the French Protestant church reorganized and throughout the rest of the nineteenth century, under more enlightened national governments, developed schools and religious societies. The church eventually separated into two parts, an orthodox and a liberal wing.

The Twentieth Century and World War II

The 1905 law granting separation between church and state was welcomed by the Protestant church, thus requiring it to provide for itself. By this time, the Protestant population of France was estimated at one million out of a total population of thirty-seven million. After much regrouping and subdividing, the churches joined together after World War I, under the Fédération Protestante de France, which has remained the major unifying body. In 1938, within the larger Federation, all Protestant denominations, with the exception of the evangelical churches, became members of the Reformed Church of France. Some historians argue that this process of subdividing and regrouping has been a basis for the vitality of the Protestant church in France, which seems to renew itself by airing theological and political differences at all levels of its organization.

During World War II, the Protestant rescue networks were enabled by the fact that control of clandestine operations resided with pastors at the local village level. Protestant church spokesmen were prominent as one of the earliest, as a religious group, to protest the Vichy and German repressive measures, particularly those directed against Jews. It was not only the pastors who actively protested: At the village level, whole communities bonded together as rescuers, particularly those Protestant villages in the Cévennes mountains of south-central France, stretching from the west bank of the Rhône River opposite Valence to Nîmes.

For centuries, this area provided a haven to those fleeing oppression. Mark Wilks, the English pastor reporting in 1820 on The White Terror period, characterized these villages: "The inhabitants were deeply afflicted by the knowledge of continued evils which they could not prevent; by the presence of numerous fugitives whose distress they could not adequately alleviate; and, finally, by a cruel proscription [government repression of religious observance, and quartering of troops] which they did not in the slightest degree merit. As the inhabitants had avoided all ground for reproach and persecution, so they endured, with exemplary patience, the constant provocations to which they were exposed" (410–11).

One of Wilks's informants, a member of a distinguished Catholic family from the area of Le Vigan, made several observations about the character of the people:

I saw multitudes crowded together, and suffering the most dreadful anxiety; but every door was open to them. For a time labor was suspended, and no occupation was thought worthy of attention, but that of rendering assistance to the unhappy. The most affecting care and hospitality was afforded to all whom danger or fear had driven to the mountains.

I observed that in their commiseration there was less of softness and more of solemnity than in ordinary pity;—religious principle mingled with the impulse of humanity, and gave it a character more serious and august. There were no tears, no effusions, no complaints. A gloomy silence and a severe sort of virtue was observed by the hospitable hosts, and they received, in return, from the fugitives, but few expressions of gratitude. An immoveable attachment to the persecuted, a pious and heroic firmness, and a simple and unostentatious generosity distinguished all. This religious feeling, which cannot have escaped those who have visited the Cévennes, even in a season of prosperity, was especially impressive in a period of alarm and consternation. (411–12)

Marie Brottes, 1906–1996

I was fortunate to have spent three days with a rescuer from the best known of these Cevenol villages, Le Chambon-sur-Lignon. Marie Brottes' testimony about her war experience explained much about what drove Pierre Toureille during the war. Her rescue activities, guided by the village pastor, were typical of those taking place in the entire cluster of Protestant villages through which Toureille formed his network. Not only was Mme. Brottes serving in the same effort that Toureille was managing at a higher level, she also shared with him the particularly Huguenot notion that resistance to political authority and need to provide refuge to the oppressed was a religious duty.

During World War II, Marie Brottes was part of a total village effort to give refuge to thousands of foreigners escaping Nazi and Vichy persecution. The entire village of Le Chambon was given the Yad Vashem award by the Israeli government. In *Weapons of the Spirit*, a documentary film on the wartime rescue work of the villagers of Le Chambon-sur-Lignon, someone said of Marie Brottes, "Hugging her is like hugging a tree."[6] In 1994, when she was eighty-eight years old, she still reminded one of a tree, a small mountain spruce. Her face was narrow, the deeply cut lines all verging into a sharp chin, her voice, harsh and husky. She was not tall but held her head and neck upright, at attention, even though her posture was bent and she needed a cane when she walked me through the village cemetery with slow determined steps. Her dress was the same as the other women of her age in these mountain villages: flowered skirt to her ankles, black shawl, black stockings, and black leather oxfords with heavy heels, iron white-gray hair parted in the middle and pulled straight to the back, covered by a flowered kerchief. In the last photo we had taken together, she had put her arm around me and I held her hand, which was dry and warm.

She was born in the Plateau Vivarais canton of Failly-sur-Lignon, and her family name was Soubeyran—an old name in the southern regions of France. She and her husband, who sold construction material (and who died in 1970), had settled in Le Chambon and had one son.

It is not hard to imagine how Le Chambon looked during the war. The dominant look, the traditional rough, light brown-gray stone farmhouses with orange tile roofs and plain facades, repeated itself from village center to outlying farms. The Lignon River takes a sharp corner turn around one edge of the village. Down the hill from Marie Brottes's apartment and across from the Protestant temple, there is a plaque on the wall: "'The righteous shall be held in everlasting remembrance' [Ps. 112:6]. In homage to the Protestant community of this Cevenol land and all those inspired by its example, believers of all faiths and nonbelievers, who during the War of 1939–1945, blocking the crimes of the Nazis, have, at the risk of their lives under the Occupation, hidden, protected, and saved thousands of the persecuted. The Jewish refugees in Le Chambon-sur-Lignon and the neighboring communities."

Here is an excerpt from Marie Brottes's written account to Yad Vashem in 1986, of her wartime activities:

Dr. Mautner had to hide on a farm. The owner of the farm had prepared a hiding place in his barn, and each time there was a round-up of Jews, the family of three hid there. Sometimes his wife and son had to hide in a hole. When the gendarmes came, the owner, M. Russier, would say to them: "What do Jews look like?" banging on his anvil—he was also a blacksmith. Then he would say, "It's hard to find iron these days, when we have to save metal and coal—but come on, you're probably a little thirsty, let's go see what my wife has put out." Eva, who fully understood, brought out a bottle with a little wine, served the police a glass, and they left without further questions.

The refugees had to keep moving, again and again, and each time, I took them food at their new place. We absolutely had to share and exchange goods with each other to get enough to eat for ourselves and the people we were hiding. My husband, for example, didn't smoke but we exchanged a packet of tobacco we got from a farmer, for some butter and cheese.

When I finally was able to get false identity cards for them, the Mautners, and others, left for Switzerland. But, sadly, they were arrested near Annemasse and interned in the camp at Gurs. They were starving there, so every week I sent four potatoes, a little flour and some sugar, if I had it (one kilo total). Even when I was harassed by the gendarmes, I kept sending the packages, so I saved the lives of these dear friends.

They returned to Le Chambon at the end of the war, and it was here that their son Eric was born. He later came to see the house where he was born and visited me. It was hard to understand him since I don't speak German, but luckily my son, with his English, could interpret for both of us. . . .

I can say that not only the village of Chambon has helped save more than 5,000 Jews, but the surrounding villages showed great solidarity in rescuing people. Our Cévenol land has a heritage of rescue from our ancestors who have suffered for their faith, and they have set us an example to follow—although we're not always faithful to it.

Everything that was done during these times of trial will not go unrewarded because our God, who is the same as the God of the Jewish people, renders to each of us according to our works.[7]

Grete Mautner, the wife and mother of the three-person family Marie Brottes rescued during the war, wrote the following testimony in 1987, to Yad Vashem:

Without knowing us at all, Mme. Brottes, risking her and her husband's lives, came to one of my hiding places one day and offered me and my family her un-selfish help. . . . She insured, by collecting items in the neighborhood, that we had enough food and clothing. And it was thanks to her that I could work as a tailor since she made a sewing machine available to me. Whenever we had to go into hiding she took the sewing to the customers and collected their payments for me. I owe a special debt of gratitude to Mme. Brottes for providing us with food and clothing packages during the six months we stayed in the concentration camps of Rivesaltes and Gurs in 1942. She also made sure that our four-year-old son, who fortunately escaped deportation, could return to Le Chambon, where he lived a relatively happy life until our release.

We might not have survived without her commitment. Again and again she put her life and the life of her family on the line, including her son who was born during this time.

Marie Brottes told other stories of that period.She talked about the passionate pacifist and charismatic but difficult Pastor Trocmé, and other local pastors, who risked their lives urging and organizing their parishioners to abide by the holy commandment to help their neighbors, even if it meant defying temporal law. She spoke of the code words the pastors used when they were sending Jewish refugees to each other's parishes. Often it was, "I'm sending you three Old Testaments," and sometimes it was in Morse Code on the lyrics of a songbook page.

She claimed that, despite the presence of convalescing German soldiers in the village center (who might have even been aware of the secret hiding and feeding going on around them), no villager betrayed the others' rescue efforts. There was one French militiaman who denounced one Jew, and that informer was shot, probably by the local Résistance. When a journalist recently said to Mme. Brottes, "You must know who killed the informer," she replied, "I don't know, but if I did, I wouldn't tell you." Once, during the war, a gendarme had warned her, "Be careful, Madame, you're being watched," to which she replied, "But not by you! I am guarded by God above [pointing upward]."

She retold the story of Oradour-sur-Glane, the village in south central France that the Nazis set up as an example of how they handled resistors. An SS detachment of 200 men routed all 652 inhabitants from their homes, drove them into barns and the church, barred the doors, and set fire to the entire village, shooting those who tried to flee the fire. There were only ten who survived, by feigning death. The gutted church and cemetery have been left as a memorial. When asked why Le Chambon was not destroyed in the same way, since there were suspicions that the Germans knew about the spiritual resistance going on there, Mme. Brottes gave an indirect answer: "We are people of prayer. Our ancestors were persecuted. Marie Durand was kept for thirty-eight years in the Tower of Constance. Our people were burned at the stake. So when we were young, we didn't read novels; we read our own history, and the Bible."

Her favorite biblical character was Deborah, a prophetess of Israel and one of the Israelite judges. She saved her people during the period when Israelite history alternated violently between victories over the neighboring tribes when the Israelites were faithful to God, and defeat and slavery when they worshiped their neighbors' idols. Deborah inspired Barak to lead the Israelites in victory against Sisera, the mighty captain of the Canaanite armies. Another heroine, Jael, enticed Sisera, who was fleeing Barak, into her tent, then, while he was sleeping, hammered a tent pin through his temples to the ground underneath. Mme. Brottes particularly loved "The Song of Deborah," the epic poem in Judges that celebrates this story, not, she explained, primarily for its account of the Israelites' victories over their enemies, or the fact that the two heroes are women, but for the constant signs of the hand of God in human affairs. She read the poem aloud to me, with vigorous voice, her finger jabbing at the text.

"People are more egotistical today," she said reflectively when she had finished reading. "I don't think the villagers today could have done what we did, under the same conditions."

The last village landmark Marie Brottes pointed out was the Protestant temple of Le Chambon, where, in August 1942, the whole community defied a visiting Vichy minister and prefect by refusing to turn over the Jewish refugees being hidden there. At the end of the religious service in the temple, preceding this confrontation, someone shouted "Vive Pétain!"and someone else shouted "Vive Jesus Christ!" then the whole congregation burst into song with the Cevenol Hymn, its last stanza catching the mood of militant spiritual defiance:

Cevenol, is not the God of our fathers, our God forever?
Let us serve Him in days of prosperity
As they did in days of pain:
And let us be valiant as they were,
Nourished like them by the bread of the strong,
Let us give our lives to our Master
As our ancestors gave theirs![8]

Huguenots and Jews

The Bible, primarily the Old Testament, was the bedrock of Marie Brottes' speech and consciousness, and its particular kind of eloquence has shaped her own speaking and writing style. When writing to the director of Yad Vashem to explain why she and her community helped Jews, she quoted "Is it not to deal thy bread to the hungry, And that thou bring the poor that are cast out to thy house?" (Isa. 58:7) and added, "It's been fifty years since, in the greatest secrecy here on the Plateau, we shared our bread and gave asylum to all the homeless. We did not do it for a certificate, or for a medal, or for a tree planted along the Avenue of the Just! We have simply followed the word of God. What greater glory than to help one's neighbor."

Marc Toureille accounted for an affinity between Huguenots and Jews this way:

One of the reasons my father saw so clearly what Hitler was about was because my father was a French Huguenot. We have a history of persecution for 400 years. The persecution is over but it stays with us. That's how we were drilled. You know what it is to be a minority. As a kid, you say, "Why am I different?" And you're told why you're different.

We have a kind of empathy with those who are persecuted. The Jews were the same, in the same place where we used to be. If you look at French history, the Revolution, Protestant and Jew were always on the same side. The Dreyfus case: Look what side the Protestants took. They knew very clearly why Dreyfus was persecuted. If it happened to a Jew, it's going to happen to you because you're Protestant.

The French Right was very much against Jews, Protestants, and Masons—
and there still is such prejudice today. The Masons are suspect because it is a secret society and probably critical of the Catholic Church. I remember, in 1941,
how the Vichy government expelled teachers from the schools because they were
Jews or Masons.

I remember that the Germans wanted us to hand back to them the people we
took in as refugees, Jews and non-Jews. This is what's morally wrong, and this was
my father's attitude—this was *wrong*. And there's something about Jewishness,
the Old Testament. Every persecuted people—the Huguenots, or Black people
in this country—look back at the time of Moses, the liberation from Egypt. The
Prophets are also very important for us.

An Israeli historian, originally a French-born Jew who hid in Le
Chambon during the war, offered, a few years ago, an interpretation of
Marie Brottes's words and actions, and those of the refugees.[9] Referring
to a paper he was about to give on the war, titled "The Banality of Good,"
he drew a comparison between rescuers and rescued. The inhabitants of
the Plateau Vivarais and the Jews, he asserted, had in common the view
that what was being done to the Jews in France was profoundly disgraceful. The major difference between the two groups, he continues, was that
for the Protestants, these events made sense in a religious context—the
testing of man by God. For the Jews, the historical events of the destruction of the Temple and the expulsion of the Jews from Spain in 1492, also
made some sense—they were horrible but could be explained historically.
But for a Jew, not sharing with the Huguenots the notion of divine election, the genocide of the Nazis was not only a disgrace to humanity but
worse, was absurd. "My grandfather died at Auschwitz," continued this
historian, "because he could not understand why he, a French citizen
without stain, should hide in the forests of the Vivarais!"

He continued his comparison between the two groups by asking why
these French Protestant rescuers tended to minimize their actions, as
Mme. Brottes did. The Council of the French Reformed Church had tried
to explain to Yad Vashem that distinguishing people by awarding them the
medal of the "Just among the Nations" makes questionable the profound
sense the rescuers had that they were acting spontaneously. Such an award
implied the extraordinary—that the rescuers were an exception to general
human nature, that mean-spirited action was the norm. Jews take a different view, the historian continued:

You must understand that if sometimes we make too much of this and at other times, not enough, it is because we have lived through an inner shattering that does not heal easily, for this generation at least. We first must try to forget, to separate ourselves from those years of dread and absurdity, at the edge of a yawning abyss that swallowed up two-thirds of the Jews of Europe.

But perhaps now we are ready to accept a certain concept of election, not of an "elite people" but, on the contrary, "people up against the wall," defending themselves. That is why it is we who need, for ourselves and through you, to perform a ceremony and present a medal, to say to our children so they do not lose faith in humanity, that in the worst moments of human degradation, we were not totally alone. What else is there to do if, from the Atlantic to the Urals, there is no other place besides the Plateau Vivarais-Lignon, where this human dignity was the norm and not the exception?[10]

Today the French Protestants are productive members of their society, and little seems to remain of the hostility and tension that existed historically between them and Roman Catholic authorities. The Protestants of France today number about 1.1 million, or 2 percent of the total population. As a comparison, the Jews in France number about 578,400, or one percent of the total population.[11]

3

Pierre Toureille's Early Years and the Ecumenical Movement of the 1930s

May God forgive us for what we did to Czechoslovakia.

—Pierre Toureille

We are not an organization concerned with action in the church; we are a particular form of the church itself. . . . The World Alliance is the church of Christ, terrified, sharp of hearing, and anxious, which calls out to its Lord.

—Dietrich Bonhoeffer

The Influence of John Huss

John Huss (1369–1415), a central figure and religious martyr in the history of Czechoslovakia, was a model of spiritual heroism for the young Pierre Toureille.[1] At age twenty-five, he wrote his thesis for a bachelor in theology degree from the University of Montpellier, on Huss's criticism of the abuses of the Catholic Church, for which Huss was burned at the stake as a heretic. The combination, in Huss, of refusal to recant the religious beliefs of his own conscience, and of representing the particular spirit of the Slav peoples, was a powerful attraction for Pierre Toureille, with his own combination of ancestral Huguenot stubbornness of faith and the strong attachment toward Slavs inherited from his parents.

Special bonds of affection between France and the peoples of Czechoslovakia have, historically, predated Pierre Toureille's own. In several sections of his thesis, he paid tribute to a distinguished French scholar of the Slav peoples, Ernest Denis (1849–1921), born, like Toureille, in Nîmes.

Toureille, a student, in front of monuments in Prague, 1922.

Author of a number of works on Bohemia and cofounder, with Tomáš Masaryk, of the journal, *The Czech Nation,* Denis had been considered, by Czechs, to be one of the founders of the independent state restored to them in the twentieth century

In the preface to his thesis on Huss (titled "John Huss: The beginnings of the present religious crisis in Czechoslovakia"), Toureille explained why he got involved in the project, including his admiration of the immediacy of Slav history in the minds of its peoples:

Brought up in the knowledge and love of the Slav peoples and desiring to devote myself to the youth organizations in Slav countries, I had the honor and privilege, in 1921, of being chosen by the Minister of Public Instruction, after being proposed by the Institute of Slav Studies in Paris, to go to Prague on a scholarship to study the government of Czechoslovakia. The initial proposal was to do a study on the religious crisis facing the young republic, which would lead to a thesis for a bachelor of theology degree.

But during the course of my stay (September 1921 to July 1922), placed daily in the presence of the profound "sense of history" of the Czechoslovak nation, I felt it imperative that I devote myself, above all, to a minute study of what one might call the underpinnings of the present crisis.

Toureille paid respectful, but puckish, tribute to the historians whose attention to scholarship he adopted— "[those professors] who used this method with so much confidence, clarity and zeal. And if some of us do not achieve the level of confidence, clarity and zeal of our professors, who would wish it otherwise? What kind of disciple is it who is greater than his master?"[2] Toureille did not seem to feel comfortable in the role of budding scholar and the anecdotal, narrative quality of his thesis bore that out.

While asserting that his project was based on original documents and research work of the best quality, his deeper purpose was inspirational, of a religious and patriotic kind. He tried to "put in relief this splendid figure, so purely Christian and so nobly Czech, the Master, John Huss." He hoped to revive interest not only in Huss but also in "the valiant and glorious nation of which he remains the purest and greatest hero." Toureille's thesis became a look inside the mind of a young, passionate pastor wrestling with the tensions in his own background, between spiritual and political loyalties—and with a restless urge to heroic spiritual activism. This early writing on Huss, then, stirred a number of themes that remained important to Toureille for the rest of his life, particularly at his moment of greatest challenge, World War II.

Toureille characterized the Slav peoples as particularly fit for adopting Christianity: "By their manners, their patriarchal structures, their poetic and simple religion that appears to have been dominated by a belief in the divine Unity, the Slavs, more than all other peoples, were predisposed to the advent of Christianity among them." On the other hand, he asserted with equal admiration, their independent nature made the incursion of Christianity difficult when it was imposed as an instrument of propaganda or conquest. His thesis proceeded, with obvious relish for writing about religious-political battles, through the story of the implantation of the Catholic Church in Slav lands, with a focus on German political and religious intrigue as the greatest threat to an independent Slav church and state.

By the fourteenth century corruption was rampant in the church, with the sacraments, confession, and ritual becoming endless sources of revenue for the clergy. It was from this church corruption that the early reformers emerged. They fought for an indigenous church separate from Rome and one promoting a more independent interpretation of Scriptures, which led to the eventual martyrdom of Huss, their most influential member.

Toureille clearly found Huss to be an exemplar, with a temperament quite different from his own more volatile one. Huss was, from youth, a person of "deep piety and great courage," strongly attracted to the history of the martyrs whom he emulated by applying hot coals to his body in imitation of Saint Laurent, an early Christian burned by the Emperor Valerian. Huss's nature was "more passive than active, quiet and modest, his speaking manner fluid and persuasive, his moral character elevated and austere." On religious doctrine, Huss appealed to Toureille's own. Although Huss declared himself, to the end, a faithful Roman Catholic, he clearly aligned himself with the growing Protestant Reformation, admitting himself entirely in agreement with Wycliffe on three points: (1) that Sacred Scripture is the infallible authority; (2) that discipline must be restored to the clergy; (3) that spiritual authority resides, not in a sacramental rite but in the proper conduct of those who want to exercise it.

In the political realm, also, Huss appealed to Toureille as a man of pure principle. Huss was caught at the center of a struggle among the local Catholic Church authorities to establish independence from growing domination by the Germans. The popular appeal of Huss's reforming doctrines increasingly became a threat to church efforts to squelch the growing Protestant movement. Although Huss had a number of substantial reasons, both political and spiritual, for cutting himself off from papal authority, he could not do it. Toureille was particularly interested in Huss's dilemma in deciding which battles he should fight on principle, and which he should flee. He quoted Huss's letter to a friend: "I burn with ardent zeal for the Gospel and my soul is sad. I have meditated on these words of the Savior: 'The good pastor will give his life for his flock.' But the mercenary, when he sees the wolf coming, deserts his lambs and flees. I have also meditated on the words of Matthew: 'When they persecute you in the city, flee to another.' Two such different precepts. Which should I follow, which should I obey? I don't know."

Accused of heresy from several quarters at once, Huss could no longer resist. The emperor of Hungary, who saw the anarchy in the Church and attributed it to Huss's doctrines, convoked the Council of Constance to put Huss on trial for heresy. The Council was dominated by Huss's enemies, to whom he had to justify his faith. Huss was imprisoned for months during his trial proceedings and denied the right to an advocate. His former supporters in power now considered him a dangerous fanatic. Each time he was asked to retract his ideas, he replied that he would do so, if he could be convinced that he was in error.

Toureille dramatized Huss's final days. In a last letter to his friends, Huss explained that God would neither permit him to deny the truth nor to retract errors that he had never advanced, that his last prayer was that they love one another, and, finally, that no one should be prevented from witnessing the truth and the faithful should never be oppressed by force. When Huss was tied to the stake, he repeated that his sole aim in his teachings and writings was to rescue souls from the tyranny of sin. "That is why I will sign with my blood today, with joy, this truth that I have taught, written, published and confirmed by the divine Law and the Sacred Fathers."

Toureille's choice of final spokesman on Huss's martyrdom, was Voltaire—"The ironic Voltaire whom some consider deprived of a heart," a man historically remote from Huss but with a viewpoint on heroism probably close to Toureille's own. Voltaire compared Huss's death with Socrates': "What a difference between the customs of Athens and those of the Council of Constance, between a cup of sweet poison that, far from horrible, infamous machines of execution, let a citizen die peacefully among his friends—and the dreadful torment of fire, into which priests— ministers of mercy and peace—throw other priests, who are too opinionated no doubt, but living a life of purity and remarkable courage."

The point of view that most interested Toureille about the political repercussions of Huss's doctrine was that Huss as a spiritual hero was also a national one. However, the primary reason for Huss's condemnation, Toureille argued ("as would argue any thinking Protestant," he added), lay in Huss's particular religious doctrines, which challenged the authority of the Church and established liberty of conscience and the right of all believers to be guided by the Word of God. He quoted with admiration these defiant words from Huss that demonstrated the militant nature of his doctrines: "They think they can strangle the truth, not knowing that the essence of truth is that the more it is obscured, the brighter it shines; the more it is suppressed, the more it rises and is believed. The pope, the priests, the scribes and the pharisees, Herod and Pilate, the inhabitants of Jerusalem, once condemned the truth; they crucified it; they enshrouded it, but truth, rising from the tomb, has conquered all."

Huss's establishment as a national hero during the period when Toureille was writing his thesis posed a theological and political dilemma for the new nation. The Czech Roman Catholic Church claimed that it could not renounce its decision that Huss was a heretic. From the perspective of Czech Protestants, there were also problems, Toureille reflected, in considering Huss one of the fathers of the Reformation. Huss was not a Protestant. But the Czech Protestants whom Toureille observed affirmed that they were only continuing the path set out by Huss, although the attachment to Huss was tighter than they claimed, since the Hussite chalice, like the Huguenot cross of the French Protestants, has been their chief symbol. "To deny that Huss is the greatest of Czech heroes," Toureille finished combatively, "is to fly in the face of the facts, and is the supreme insult to the man who said, 'Love one another and allow to each the liberty of his own truth.'"

Consecration to the Ministry

The same year that Pierre Toureille finished his thesis on John Huss, he preached in public for the first time on the day of his consecration to the ministry, November 11, 1925, in Cournonterral, Hérault. He explained that his decision to become a minister did not come easily to him—and his work on his thesis and the year spent in Czechoslovakia contributed powerfully to the eventual direction he chose for himself. In a speech of strongly expressed sentiment, he narrated the process he went through. He began with his beliefs and his family. His heart was "overflowing with gratitude toward God" who had sustained him, led him past "temptations without number" and now had taken him into service.

He paid homage to his deceased father who, after "living and dying a Christian," gave his son the grand example of hard work, professional integrity, hope for the future, and devotion to social service. On his deathbed, Toureille's father set the "beautiful example" of forgiving his enemies and expressed his joy that his son had entered the Faculty of Theology.

Toureille paid tribute to friends and teachers, "all devout Christians," in school, in the Scouts, the YMCA (Union chrétiennes de jeunes gens, UCJG) and other youth organizations, and to three wounded soldiers he befriended during World War I, who died shortly afterward. Toureille spoke confidently of the hand of God who guided his own fate and determined his future. He said of his experience working with soldiers: "You would find it hard to believe how much the memory of these young men, who died for my sake, and yours, inspires me. All the encouragement and force to move ahead that one usually receives in life, do not match those blessed experiences that promise us that the future will not be all obscurity and uncertainty." He refers to November 11 as a date of special significance, commemorative of the War (World War I) and also of the present consecration of a son of that War.

He also paid tribute to his mother, who taught him how to pray and spoke to him "of Godly things with so much love and delicacy." He remembered well how often he made her cry, but also knew how, each time, she turned to God to express her misery and powerlessness. God did what men could not do—opened her son's heart, as He could the hearts of other sons whose mothers cried for them. He thanked his two sisters and his brother-in-law for all their encouragement—and sensed that God was also moving through them. Finally, Toureille mentioned with gratitude his grandparents who stepped in "with so much tact and love" when his father died.

To his wife, "the last to enter" his life, he owed gratitude for "all the treasures of affection, encouragement and tenderness" that she lavished on him. He thanked God for her, "a Christian mother prepared to a remarkable degree for the sometimes heavy and thankless task of being the wife of a pastor."

His first intimation of a future religious vocation occurred in 1914, inspired by hearing a pastor in Nîmes, followed by his conversion and simultaneous choice to serve in February 1917. "From the instant God said to me: 'Come!', I knew that he was also saying, 'Go serve!'" At first, it wasn't the pastorate toward which he was attracted, because it seemed to him an obsolete vocation. He felt the call was to work in the Balkans, among the youth there. It was a hard blow when, during the year he spent in Central Europe, he saw clearly that evangelizing among the Slavs had to be left to the Slavs themselves. When Toureille returned to the Faculty of Montpellier to complete his thesis, he had decided to be a pastor in the

Evangelical Reformed Church of France and accepted, without the slightest hesitation, his first post in Bourdeaux. He ends with this affirmation:

My convictions are, I repeat, very clearly evangelical. Each of you will understand, I hope, what that means. I adhere without any reservations to the confession of the faith of 1872, especially to the statement: "the sovereign authority of Holy Scripture in matters of faith, and in salvation through faith in Jesus Christ, only Son of God, who died for our sins and who rose again to save us". It is in this spirit that I have worked in Bourdeaux during the past year—it is in this spirit that I shall work as long as God will give me breath and life. May God hear my prayer! May God grant me help and a ministry that is faithful, fruitful and blessed. That is the grace I ask him to accord me for the love of Jesus Christ, my Savior and my Master. Amen.

For the next six years, Toureille was pastor of the Evangelical Reformed Church in the Drôme and Gard areas of southern France, began raising his family, and served for two years in the French army. He then was ready to launch himself into Protestant ecumenism on an international scale.

The World Alliance and Toureille's Activities

The World Alliance for Promoting International Friendship through the Churches was founded after World War I as a Protestant ecumenical organization. Toureille developed lifelong contacts among his colleagues in the World Alliance, which gave him the crucial experience he needed to operate as a rescuer. He first met Dietrich Bonhoeffer at the 1931 World Alliance Conference, and they became friends and colleagues. Both men were members of the World Alliance Youth Commission and Management Committee, and leaders of its ecumenical movement among young pastors throughout the world. In 1931, Bonhoeffer warned the World Alliance meeting in London that "nationalist professors of theology" in Germany opposed the World Alliance.[3] By that time the political winds in Germany were blowing strongly against the ecumenical movement, which was denounced for being internationalist and pacifist. By 1932 the movement ceased to exist in Germany at the national level.

In a letter to a friend in 1936, Bonhoeffer described his own development during his service in the ecumenical movement, from a theologian to a Christian, as one biographer called it. Bonhoeffer's home setting was Germany, which was becoming Nazified, not southern France, and the propensities toward pietism and martyrdom that had already appeared may not have been part of Pierre Toureille's mental makeup, but Bonhoeffer expressed a stringency of self-analysis about his own beliefs, and a frame of mind about the church and issues of the 1930s in Europe that Toureille, as his friend, must have admired and associated himself with. Bonhoeffer wrote:

I threw myself into work in a very un-Christian and arrogant way. A crazy ambition which some people have noticed in me made life difficult for me. . . . At that time I was terribly alone and left to myself. That was very bad. Then something else happened, something which has changed and transformed my life to the present day. I discovered the Bible for the first time. It is also very bad to have to say that. I had preached often and seen a good deal of the church, . . . and yet I had not yet become a Christian. The Bible and especially the Sermon on the Mount freed me from this. Since then everything has changed. . . . It became clear to me that the life of a servant of Jesus Christ must belong to the church, and it became even more clear, step by step, how that must come about.

Then came the 1933 crisis. That strengthened me in this. Now I found others who shared this purpose with me. Now I was concerned above all for a renewal of the church and the pastorate. . . . All at once Christian pacifism dawned on me as being a matter of course, though shortly beforehand I had passionately fought against it. . . . And so things developed, bit by bit. It took over all my perception and all my thought. . . . Before me lies my calling. I do not know what God means to make of it. . . . But this is the way I must go.[4]

It was only after the advent of the war that Bonhoeffer became an activist rebel against the State and eventually its victim. He was executed by the Nazis in April 1945 for being an accomplice in a plot to assassinate Hitler.

The World Alliance was grappling, in the 1930s, with the spread of totalitarian regimes across Europe, trying to find its proper place as a religious body that had to respond to a new and dangerous situation in the political realm. Its ultimate ineffectiveness in dealing with fascism during the 1930s was part of what historians generally saw as the failure of the Church to stem the Holocaust. Throughout the 1920s and until 1936, the World Alliance adhered to pacifism, but in 1938 the Reformed Church of France withdrew on the pacifist issue.

During the entire decade of the 1930s the French Protestant church itself was embroiled in debate between those defending pacifism and those wanting to prepare for an eventual "just war." Marc Toureille remembers his father was an activist on this issue: "When my father came back from a trip to Germany in the late '30s, I remember he told us, 'Things are so dangerous over there, we should attack them now, before they get too strong for us.'"

The World Alliance also had internal problems, particularly between its French and German members. From the beginning of their relationship in the Alliance, the German Protestant Church spokesmen did not have the same political tendencies, nor considered themselves a church responsible to the world, as did their French counterparts. The German Protestant Church was fragmented into three groups, each with its own reaction to the establishment of a German fascist state in 1933. First, the majority, the German Evangelical Church (DEK, or Deutsche Evangelische Kirche) and the Lutheran wing of the Confessing Church, claimed that the state could demand complete obedience by divine right. The Barthian wing of the Confessing Church urged complete separation between the Church and the State but did not urge active resistance to the State regime. Finally, the smallest group, the Dietrich Bonhoeffer circle within the Confessing Church, called for verbal protest against evils of the state, although such protest was too passive in doctrine to challenge a totalitarian state or withstand its suppressions.

Toureille was among the French representatives at the 1931 World Alliance conference in Cambridge, England, who reported their dismay at the differences between themselves and the majority of their German colleagues:

[The struggle] would certainly have been less hard if the attitude of the German Evangelical Church had not filled the French Reformed Church with deep concern and painful surprise. When war mania had disappeared, our churches expected from the German churches some gesture of regret about what had happened and a desire to lead their people along the path of justice and fraternity. No act of penance was expected from them, only a word of sympathy for our plundered and destroyed churches. But nothing came. The German churches bewailed only the suffering of their own people, whose complete innocence they proclaimed. Hence one can understand the mistrust and suspicion that filled our churches in view of this attitude of their sisters in Germany.[5]

Toureille's participation in the World Alliance during these precarious and increasingly darkening years of the 1930s in Europe turned him from being an idealistic young pastor to a sophisticated spiritual activist at the crossroad between religion and politics. His beliefs took on a militant form against the growing injustices imposed by totalitarian regimes against their own people and, and, as he met with knowledgeable coreligionists from other countries, he learned their languages (he could speak nine by the late 1930s) and addressed himself to their ideas and the national issues with which they were grappling, with an eager and fertile intelligence.

His deepest affections were still focused on the new Czechoslovakia and on Tomáš Masaryk, its national hero and first president, who was the subject of several Toureille articles and a book project, which, evidently, was never completed as the impulse toward active participation in world events took over. As mentioned earlier, there was a tradition among French intellectuals of a kind of romantic attachment to the peoples of Czechoslovakia, particularly Moravians. This was part of Toureille's mindset, through the influence of his parents and his student work on John Huss.

In the early 1930s, while a pastor in Congénies, Gard, he published *Les Protestants de l'Europe Centrale et les Missions en Terre Païenne* (The Protestants of Central Europe and missions to pagan lands).[6] This was an exhortation to Central European, particularly Czechoslovak Protestants, to join with the Missions Society of Paris in its evangelical work. Toureille was speaking as a zealous missionary here, a duty that he himself did not fulfill until twenty-five years later, in a very different frame of mind, darkened by the war experience.

Toureille's emotional and spiritual ties to Czechoslovakia were apparent in the style and rhetoric of this article. He began by quoting with approval an earlier article that bemoaned the fact that of the nearly twelve million Protestants in Central and Eastern Europe, almost none joined in missionary work with their French brothers. One of his central arguments was that the Czechoslovak Protestants were the most appropriate for this work, because of their culture and recent history. The country accomplished an admirably bloodless revolution of 1918 and created a new free state that, without a doubt, "is viable. It will survive . . . with a very expert Minister of Foreign Affairs, M. Bénes. It is truly facing the most brilliant future."

Then, he wrote a tribute to the Czechoslovaks themselves and the large mission he assigned to them:

In assessing the potential of Czechoslovakia, it is important to note that, among all the Slavs, the Czechoslovaks presently, and for a long time have held first place. Older brother of a race that totals in the world population more than 225 million representatives (compared with the number of Germans, for example, which is less than half of this figure), the Czech, more refined, more civilized, more advanced in all aspects than his younger brothers (because of his ethnographic location and his history of submitting for five centuries to the yoke of Germanic peoples and culture), the Czech has a truly cultural, civilizing mission to fulfill. . . .

It is placed in the very heart of Europe as a sentinel for the Slav world. . . . Czechoslovakia is being summoned to play a role of the first order in what is often called "the equilibrium of Europe," on which depends the equilibrium of the world, universal peace.

After describing the distribution of the more than one million Protestants in Czechoslovakia (out of a population of fourteen million that includes Czechs, Slovaks, Germans, Magyars, Ukrainians, Jews, and Poles), Toureille discussed the special relationship between Czechoslovak and French Protestants. He especially recognized one man with whom he clearly empathized and whose work he had studied: Ernest Denis. Denis was a historian of Czechoslovakia, a native of Nîmes, like himself, and an instrumental figure in the formation of the Czech national consciousness and the new state, about whom Masaryk said, "He has understood our history and penetrated our character." Ties were established by exchanges between theology students—Toureille himself was one during the 1920s—and among intellectuals, which planted among the Czech Protestants the idea of missionary service.

Pierre Toureille's first appointment to the World Alliance was as Secretary of the Youth Commission, representing France. He was assigned to coordinate work in Latin America, the Balkans, Poland, and Czechoslovakia. (The other two secretaries were the representative of Germany, Dietrich Bonhoeffer, and Great Britain, W. T. Craske). Disarmament was the central issue on the minds of the World Alliance members, particularly since a conference on disarmament was about to convene in Geneva. The World Alliance issued a manifesto from Cambridge, making several general points that show its active participation in European politics.[7] First, the Church should educate and warn its members to further work in "political, social and civic work," as "the highest duty for the conscience of the followers of Christ." Specifically, the "disquieting

economic crisis which is sweeping through the world is a decisive warning." The present wartime economic systems and "the immense social
forces which are struggling together in the social storm and setting the nations at variance with each other" must be abandoned in favor of systems
that promote disarmament—otherwise, "the entire work of civilisation
will be threatened with shipwreck."

Secondly, the World Alliance reminded the governments taking part
in the Pact of Paris of 1928 that the Pact declared "all war of aggression in
future [to] be branded as infamous and stigmatized as a crime." Further,
it appealed to all Church authorities under these governments "to declare
in unmistakable terms that they will not countenance, nor assist in any way
in any war with regard to which the Government of their country has refused a bona fide offer to submit the dispute to arbitration."

Finally, the World Alliance urged the upcoming disarmament conference to be courageous in bringing about a substantial reduction of arma-
ments in accordance with the League of Nations, defining its own attitude
as being in the activist spirit "of Him who said: 'I come not to be minis-
tered unto, but to minister.'" It was under such directives and through
such insertion of the world Protestant church in the thick of political affairs, that Toureille spent the next nine years in constant travel and meetings across Europe.

1932

The World Alliance was well informed, in 1932, of the events and issues feeding the growing power of the Nazis and totalitarian regimes in
Europe. The Secretary of the Austrian Council of the World Alliance,
Franz Fischer, sent a memorandum to the World Alliance Geneva meeting in August, demanding the revision of the peace treaties signed at the
end of World War I. He argued that Central and southeastern Europe
were condemned to a chronic low standard of living and political and social discord, and that the forced disarmament among the defeated powers
was matched by a "psychosis of militarism" among the victors. Finally, he
argued that the peace treaties were a gross infraction of international law
defending human rights, and that the victors had no right to hold the vanquished responsible for the war.

The World Alliance Management Committee reacted to this memorandum with restraint. The Committee first justified the role of the World
Alliance in this issue: it argued that Fischer's arguments demanding revi-

sion of the peace treaties and the resentment he expressed at their perceived injustices were growing among the public worldwide and therefore claimed the attention of the churches worldwide. Finally, the Committee set up a group to formulate a World Alliance resolution on the whole issue.

Pierre Toureille was not so restrained as the Management Committee on the issue of Church activism in the growing tensions in Europe. He attended three World Alliance Youth Commission conferences in 1932, which strongly influenced his state of mind. In April, at a Franco-English Conference at Epsom, he commented in his report:

Not so much . . . by the knowledge that the individual Christian should, in spite of everything, consecrate his life to the establishment of the Kingdom of God on earth, but by the sudden gleams of insight, by contact with a positive realism and an optimism which had nothing to do with reason, by this great influx of experiences, I feel that the Conference has increased my faith, renewed my hope, and enlarged my understanding of others, not only other nationalities, but all "others."

World forces seem to crush and overcome us every day, but we do not combat them alone, and God who from the beginning has willed the victory of good over evil, changes our enemies into friends, and at the same time works miracles in us. How can one doubt, fear or hesitate? How can we escape or refuse to act when we know that our only real satisfaction will come when we are doing the will of our Father?

Toureille attended a Franco-German Conference in July 1932 at Westerburg, which he cochaired with Bonhoeffer. The subject was "The Unity of Franco-German Protestantism between Catholicism and Bolshevism." There were tensions at this meeting because of the unyielding position of the French at the ongoing Geneva disarmament negotiations, from which the Germans withdrew—but debate at Westerburg was lively and informative. The German representative from Dresden told the French what was to be expected of the Nazi victory predicted for the coming year. Bonhoeffer later described himself as being strengthened by this conference, especially by "a young Frenchman," who was most probably Toureille: "I shall never forget the day on which this text [Daniel 10:12] first made its impact on me. It was at a meeting of young Frenchmen and Germans; we had met on the common ground of the Church and wished . . . to submit ourselves to the commandment . . . of 'peace on earth'. . . . We were all full of fear and dismay about our task . . . and when we were together, and somewhat alarmed in this way, a young Frenchman read out these words . . . and when he came to the words [spoken to Daniel] 'fear not, peace be with you,' we all felt that afterwards we could say, 'Let my Lord speak, for you have strengthened me.'"[8]

While the Conferences on Disarmament and Reparations continued in Geneva, the World Alliance held an International Youth Conference in Gland, Switzerland, in August 1932, organized by Toureille, Bonhoeffer, and Craske. About sixty participants attended, from Europe, America, and Asia, including C. F. Andrews, a close friend of Gandhi. The chairman of the World Alliance, Bishop Ammundsen, described the conference, with a light British touch, in the *Church of England Newspaper*, September 23. Toureille's talents as an entertainer, are an added feature:

Here, in a setting of orchard and garden, with a wooded slope descending to a bathing-beach, some four or five rather heterogeneous buildings house "The Fellowship School". . . founded eleven years back by an English Quaker lady, . . . for education in an atmosphere of Christian international fellowship, and on somewhat original lines.

It was thus an apt meeting-place for the International Youth Conference . . . organised by the International Youth Commission of the World Alliance. . . . The whole Youth Secretariat of the World Alliance was also present: M. Toureille, a French Protestant pastor from the "Midi"; Dr. Bonhoeffer, a Lecturer and "Student Chaplain" at Berlin; and the Rev. F. W. T. Craske. . . . All three are young men, with very obvious gifts for their World Alliance duties, including remarkable talent as musicians and entertainers when an international social evening was decreed.

Toureille's report of the French group's discussion at this international youth conference provides a view of his state of mind at this period. The group listed the following questions for consideration, "in spite of great mental differences and in a veritable spirit of comprehension": "1. What is the message to be presented by the Church? 2. What is the Will of God and can we perceive this Will? 3. Must our old economic system disappear and what would be the essential features for a new and better system? 4. What are our ideas of the Kingdom of God?"

On the first question, the group determined that the foremost task of the Church was to give the world a religious message, but one that insisted on individual social action "to establish the missing balance in our society." God was speaking to them, they decided, but their egotism made them deaf to Him. On the very different kind of question, on economic systems,

World Alliance meeting, Gland, Switzerland, 1932. Toureille is seated in the second row from the front, second from right; Dietrich Bonhoeffer is in same row, second from left.

the group agreed that the world economy must be "controlled centrally," that nationalism prevented improvement, and that the best remedy resided, not in economics, but "in the human heart." Lastly, after much dissension, the group agreed that the Kingdom of God began in the heart, where painful personal denials make it possible for the Will of God to act through humankind. But individuals, not content with only their own salvation, must then, Toureille wrote, "give [to others] the wherewithal to live, protesting against the great social injustices, . . . Let us concentrate all our forces to give to each man the power to approach God, in procuring for him a minimum of well-being, so that on the day of judgment he may find a place in that Kingdom which our intellect cannot conceive."

In another article on this youth conference, by Bishop Ammundsen in the *Yorkshire Post,* Toureille was characterized, in his giving of one of the keynote addresses of the conference, as being typically French in his approach with no further explanation for this remark. In defining the Church's role, the Bishop reported that Toureille "emphasized that there are no cheap remedies for such a condition as we have to face." Bonhoeffer's address was described as "pessimistic, verging on pacifism," and Dr. Zernoff's, a Russian speaker, as "more constructive," of working to establish an "organic society," based on the "creative principle of love."[9] In a letter to Henri-Louis Henriod, Secretary-General of the World Alliance, based in Geneva, Toureille praised the contribution of Zernoff to the conference, at the same time complaining that the French delegates did not take an active enough part. Subsequent letters between Toureille and Henriod in 1932 spoke of a Commission on Minorities that Toureille evidently suggested setting up within the World Alliance.

1933

The advent of the Nazi Party to power in Germany at noon, January 30, 1933, fundamentally altered the World Alliance's plans for further contact with its German Protestant colleagues. While the dean of one of Germany's most prominent churches explained that the swastikas surrounding his altar were "the symbol of German hope. Whoever reviles this symbol is reviling our Germany," Bonhoeffer's first sermon that same month included, "The Church has only one altar, the altar of the Almighty . . . no other faith, and no other will than the will of God, however well-intentioned,"[10] and he and his family agreed that this meant war for Germany. The World Alliance's official reaction to the events was reticent, as stated in its Annual Report of its meetings in Berlin that year.

In June 1933, Toureille and other World Alliance members met with Bonhoeffer and other Germans in Basle, Switzerland. Immediately before this conference, Bonhoeffer had met Martin Niemöller and they began organizing a movement to separate "the Church of Christ" from the established German Evangelical Church, which was swiftly being nationalized under the Nazis. The Basle meeting did not live up to the optimism with which it had been planned. Controversies over disarmament and the revision of the peace accords were not resolved, the allegiance of the German participants to the Nazi State remained ambiguous, and mistrust was rekindled on the French side. A British church society member who attended a Youth Peace Conference at Gland during the summer of 1933 characterized a similar kind of conflict among Europeans, as both ideological and theological:

We from Britain were astonished at the complete unanimity of the Germans on the present regime. Here were German students, ministers, and journalists in a foreign country, where they could say what they liked without fear—National Socialists every one. It was amazing! . . . In the exposition of their creed, we were warned that any event so recent as the German revolution could not be judged for some years yet. . . . to describe it in words was like trying to describe a thunderstorm. If it could be compared to any other, the Cromwellian revolution was its only parallel.

The Jewish persecutions, the only aspect of the revolution touched on in other countries, were but one small part of the mighty revolution. Most of it was private vengeance on middlemen and others who had incurred deep hatred by their wrongdoing: the part played by the State was to mete out retributive justice. In a revolution, as Luther himself said, the devil stirs up the dregs of the soul. . . . And so the Conference progressed. . . . Right to the end the difference remained and was never avoided, nor could it be ignored.[11]

The next World Alliance conference, attended by both Toureille and Bonhoeffer in Sofia, Bulgaria, September 1933, set out a more activist role for the organization. The major political issue the conference addressed was treatment of "racial minorities." After establishing its position that racial discrimination anywhere, on any basis "constitutes a great danger to peace and the welfare of humanity" and disavows "the super-racial character of the Gospel," the World Alliance referred specifically to the treatment of Jews and of Protestant ministers in Germany: "We especially deplore the fact that the State measures against the Jews in Germany have had such an effect on public opinion that in some circles the Jewish race is considered a race of inferior status. We protest against the resolution of the Prussian General Synod and other Synods which apply the Aryan paragraph of the State to the Church, putting serious disabilities upon ministers and church officers who by chance of birth are non-Aryan, which we believe to be a denial of the explicit teaching and spirit of the Gospel of Jesus Christ."

A Commission on Minorities was set up under the liberal German theologian Siegmund-Schultze as chairman, with Toureille as his assistant. The stated aims of the Commission were to deal with the minorities issue in an "orderly, continuous and effective" manner, and from a primarily religious standpoint. The Commission was to be the agency for receiving all complaints and charges made by minorities to the Alliance, and would make "a scientific study" of the minority question "in relation to the ideals of Christianity."

On this burning question of treatment of racial minorities, Toureille, Ammundsen, Henriod, and others had met with Bonhoeffer the evening before the Sofia conference, when he informed them about the situation

World Alliance meeting, Sofia, Bulgaria, 1933. Toureille and Bonhoeffer are seated next to each other in the second row, far right.

under the Nazis in Germany and attacked the repressive measures of the new regime. Henriod wrote later of this meeting: "[Bonhoeffer spoke] on the real situation in Germany and the brutal and intransigent attitude of the official German Church. We asked him to tell his friends: (1) that they could count on deep sympathy and help from the international Church, and (2) in principle it was now necessary to send to Germany a delegation to determine if the Church could recognize the new Protestant church in Germany."

The group closed with a prayer that very much moved Bonhoeffer. He wrote that evening to Siegmund-Schultze: "On this occasion I spoke very frankly about the Jewish question, the Aryan clause in the Church, and the General Synod, and also about the question of the future of the minority, and met with a great deal of understanding." The next day, when the Resolution on Racial Minorities was adopted, Bonhoeffer took active part in the wording. A participant later observed of the discussion, "Bishop Ammundsen was moved almost to tears by the proceedings in the plenary session. . . . Perhaps the finest and deepest religious experience was the occasion when Bonhoeffer conducted morning prayers."[12] Toureille and

Bonhoeffer must have felt in a celebratory mood after this conference. The latter's biographer reports: "Serious though the situation was, Bonhoeffer and Toureille did not miss the opportunity of exploring the Bulgarian markets where they bought Eastern antiques."[13]

1935

In August 1935, Toureille attended a Youth Commission conference in Chamby, Switzerland, at which he presented a report on Christian conscientious objectors in France—Henriod commented that Toureille's report made a deep impression on his audience. His activity with the Youth Commission was growing. He had been appointed president of the French section of the Youth Commission, and he reported of increased correspondence with Spanish, Italian, and Polish friends of the Alliance. He also asserted, at this meeting, that the Alliance must not forget about the Protestant minorities in the Balkans. The Commission members heartily agreed and proposed sending him to Czechoslovakia and Poland to stimulate support among the church youth in those two countries.

It was at this conference that Bonhoeffer began to cut his contact from the Youth Commission of the World Alliance, sending a substitute to Chamby. His biographer suggested that he no longer had hope that these conferences could find solutions to the problems facing the Church in the heated political atmosphere, particularly its having to decide "between heresy and truth."[14]

The most important aspect of the Chamby World Alliance conference, for Toureille's activities, was the Conference on Minorities. As Secretary of the Alliance's Commission on Minorities, Toureille wrote a report of this meeting that focused on the problem of the growing swell of refugees from Germany (largely Jewish, although identified at this conference sometimes as non-Aryans and sometimes as Christian non-Aryans.) Toureille insisted, and the members agreed, that something must be done to provide homes and education for the young refugees, who were in despair and had lost the "joy of living," chased out of every country they flee to. The Commission members also heard reports on Protestant minorities in Hungary (27 percent of the population but "autonomous and free"), Romania (no churches recognized outside the Roman Catholic Church), and Czechoslovakia (the Protestant churches were able to revise their constitution, but the government had not yet given its approval).

By 1936 it was evident that the World Alliance was collaborating

energetically with other international church organizations to deal with
the alarming increase of displaced and oppressed peoples in Europe. At a
joint meeting that year of the youth commissions of the World Alliance
and the Universal Christian Council for Life and Work, the participants
were planning ahead for a World Conference of Christian Youth in 1938.
Toureille listened to Tracy Strong of the international YMCA outline that
organization's policy and plans, including a push for "a worldwide cooperative effort . . . [combining] the forces of all Christian youth organizations
for united study and witness to the pressing problems of Christian youth
in its responsibility to Church and to State."

1936 and 1937

In March 1936, the World Alliance Commission on Minorities met
and instructed Toureille, as its secretary, to address a letter to the governments of Germany, Poland, Lithuania, Sweden, Norway, Denmark,
Czechoslovakia, Italy, and Switzerland, listing its concerns on treatment
of minorities, as established in the Chamby conference of August 1935.
At this same March 1936 meeting, the group made plans for a second
Chamby conference of the Commission on Minorities, in August of that
year. The program was to include reports on activities aiding refugees, including identification papers, work permits and visas, and full reports of
Toureille's work in behalf of minorities in Central Europe. The Commission also urged him to carry out the activities he had suggested for his own
and the Commission's work: that he focus on gathering information on one
country, probably Czechoslovakia; and that he put out a quarterly bulletin
that would collect information on the Commission's activities.

A final issue addressed at this meeting was how to provide schooling
for the refugees, above all those "non-Aryan refugees obliged to send their
children to Jewish schools." Toureille, Henriod, and one other Commission member agreed that they should not focus only on issues of German
refugees, because the Commission was formed to help all minorities. By
1936 Toureille's colleagues at the World Alliance clearly appreciated his
zealousness in working for the church and his political savvy in building
networks to aid oppressed people. A letter to him in November 1936, from
a British colleague in the World Alliance, mentioned with gratitude Toureille's work for the organization.

The last World Alliance conference that Toureille attended with Bonhoeffer, according to Alliance records, was the London meeting of the

Youth Commission in February 1937. Bonhoeffer had been less active for several years in the Youth Commission of the World Alliance, and at this conference he sounded as if he were saying goodbye, according to the minutes of the Youth Commission. Within his own Confessing Church in Germany, he was still allowed to lecture to students and could discuss questions regularly in private, although only in small groups. He added that the differences between the factions in the German Protestant church—between those supporting the government and those against— were so great that he could not put together one German youth delegation representing everyone.

At a July 1937 meeting of the Youth Commission, Toureille's report makes it clear that he was busy and productive. He reported that young Protestants in France showed increased interest in the ecumenical movement and that he had formed a "strong and representative" French Committee, which focused on World Alliance issues and those issues facing other churches, including the churches in Hangchow. A national Church committee had been created in Czechoslovakia, but Spain and Italy could no longer send representatives to World Alliance Youth Commission meetings, due to "political circumstances" in those two countries. Both Hungarian and French-speaking Swiss members of the Alliance asked that they become a part of Toureille's church network.

Toureille's Articles on Masaryk and Minorities

A few months later a 1937 issue of *l'Avant-Garde (Journal populaire du christianisme social)*, a liberal Protestant newspaper published in Marseille, featured two long articles by Toureille on the two subjects of keenest interest to him on the eve of the war—one on Tomáš Masaryk, a heroic example of political activism, and the other titled "The Problem of the Minorities in Europe." There was also a notice of a public lecture by Toureille on a related subject, "Christianity and International Justice."

The Masaryk article was prefaced by the editors' tribute to "our friend Toureille, who knew Masaryk personally and who talked to us for a full hour on the work and religious thought of this extraordinary man." They mentioned also that Toureille intended to publish a large work on Masaryk, "and it is from the pages of this future book that he has gleaned many rich insights on this molder of men."

Tomáš Masaryk must have been a powerful inspiration for Toureille, particularly at this period in his life, when the tight intertwining of politics and spiritual belief was making such demands on his conscience. Despite his editors' compliment that he had gleaned "rich insights" into Masaryk, Toureille chose, in his *Avant-Garde* article, to pass those insights onto the reader only indirectly. He elected to pay tribute to Masaryk by telling stories about him, stories that he apparently collected himself, for he called them "authentic anecdotes from a good source." He revealed, in the obvious relish with which he recounted these tales, what he admired so about the Czech leader, beyond the general praise that he "was not only a convinced democrat but also an excellent Christian socialist."

There was Masaryk's common touch, in his refusal to change to a fancier tailor upon his assumption of the presidency of the Czech Republic in 1918 [The word "Czech" is used here to mean "Czechoslovakian," referring to the whole country]. There was his remark, "A good blacksmith is not less admirable than a good president"; and his pithy advice to a master shoemaker measuring his foot for a new pair of slippers was that he himself went barefoot at home and recommended that the shoemaker do the same.

There were also anecdotes showing the personal affection Masaryk evoked from the Czechs. On his eighty-fifth birthday some Moravian children send him a pot of honey with the note: "Little father, this honey is for your bears but don't give it all to them. Keep a little for yourself!" When a seven-year-old ran out from a crowd, grabbed Masaryk's hand and kissed it, saying, "Mr. President, I love you so much!" Masaryk replied, "Me too, I love you!"

Toureille's second *Avant-Garde* article, "The Problem of the Minorities in Europe," was grim and thus an important documentation for the Church and relief organizations, not only of the general state of minorities but also of the German refugees from government oppression who were then flooding all of Europe. It was also an eloquent document of the breadth of his humanitarian concerns. He began with an apocalyptic assessment:

Extreme uncertainty spans Europe. The League of Nations, on which we had relied with too much hope, is defunct, since events in Manchuria, the withdrawal of Germany, and the war in Ethiopia. This is a crisis that seems to grow worse day by day. Whatever we say or do, Europe is now divided into two camps that grow more and more hostile, ideologically and politically. And looking at the two—the total-itarian fascist states and the democratic states, it is very difficult to stay neutral—at least for those of us who are not "the head of the Church" and who do not adopt a "balanced" point of view on the two camps so as not to lose too much. Which means, in reality, that on the approaching day of settling accounts, all will be lost.

In a Europe more and more uncertain and enfevered, a Europe that has lost not only the mastery of the world but also the mastery of itself, it is not sur-prising that the problem of minorities is, again, the order of the day. It is the prob-lem that dominates all European politics, in our century and perhaps even the next one.

The problem of the minorities, he continued in a kind of parable, is like the problem of bad family households: "If there is enough money (in political terms, 'prosperity'), everything still works. But as soon as the smallest difficulties arise, there is a crisis, each side pulling the blanket, and sometimes they rip it. At this point, if, by chance the two sides make peace and want to live together again in harmony, they perceive, with ter-ror, that the pieces of the blanket can no longer cover the same surface as before. The cover has become too small. So they fight again to determine which one will have control and possession. And often this battle ends with the death of both parties. Peace is thus made by death, in death."

The present immense diversity of races and civilizations in Europe, he asserted, was masked, up to 1914, by the three empires of Austro-Hungary, Russia, and Germany. But the truly observant knew that there were, in Central and Eastern Europe, a mass of more than sixty million minorities belonging to twenty nationalities and speaking as many diverse languages. The map of Europe, after World War I, became more com-plex—there arose new states with odd names, a multiplication of eco-nomic, judicial, and political regulations, and many protestors thereof. The peace treaties of 1919–20, he argued, had the merit of reducing sub-stantially the number of those protesting. But there were still twenty-six million people who were still referred to as minorities in Central Europe. If these have not been liberated, it was mainly because they could not be, and we must be more patient, he added. "The mills of God work slowly but surely," he quoted Masaryk as saying. "It is impatience that causes discon-tent in politics."

Toureille then presented some important facts that he had gathered. There were twenty-six million minority peoples living in Europe who

cross national boundaries: Germans and Hungarians living in Czechoslovakia; Germans in the Baltic states and Poland; Slovaks in Hungary; Serbs
in Alsace and Germany; Turko-Tartars in Macedonia and Bulgaria. "To say
nothing of the problem of Jewish minorities, that any adjustment of national frontiers will still never resolve." He then listed the geographic and
numerical information he had gathered on minorities within each country
of Europe.

It is impossible to tell, without footnotes or references in the article,
how Toureille acquired this information, why information was missing
(like figures on the Jews in Austria, Hungary, Yugoslavia, Albania), why, if
the study was of Central and Eastern European minorities, he included
Italy, Greece, and Denmark, and finally how he distinguished between
German Jews and other Germans among those German-speaking people
living outside Germany.

His figures and his comments indicated that, in the latter case, he
probably could not make clear distinctions. This would have been a problem for anyone doing a study of European minorities at this time, since
Jews were sometimes distinguished in the data as a separate nationality,
with lower rankings in privileges and citizenship claims—as they were in
the Soviet Union; and sometimes as citizens of one nationality defining the
whole country, but suffering particular oppression from their own government—as they were in Germany. It was the Holocaust of World War
II, soon to begin, that sensitized the world to the Jews as one, distinguish-
able minority people, no matter what country they were living in.

World Alliance minutes indicated that Toureille had been gathering
information on minorities for at least two years and probably more. It was
clearly a major project for him in these few years before World War II began, and it deepened his understanding of the central problems humanity
faced in the mid-twentieth century. Reading Toureille's lists of the identifiable Jews in these countries, gathered by a church organization for the
enlightened purpose of extending help and refuge, was a wrenching reminder of the same lists gathered a few years later by the Nazis, for their
own dark purposes.

As a comparative check on Toureille's findings, his figures on Jewish
populations are followed, in brackets, by those given in a 1992 book on the
Holocaust (Block and Drucker, *Rescuers*). In most cases on Jews, he un-
derestimated the numbers, probably as a result of availability of informa-

tion at that time and the way he set up his categories: "Estonia, 5,750 [see USSR]; Latvia, 95,000 [see USSR]; Lithuania, 154,000 [see USSR]; Poland, 1,550,000 [3.5 million, pre-World War II]; Germany, 600,000 [500,000 1937]; Czechoslovakia, 186,000 [350,000]; Greece, 100,000; Bulgaria, 43,000 [48,000]; Romania, 828,000 [see USSR]; Turkey, 82,000; USSR, 2,800,000 [3,000,000, with 50% in the Ukraine]." He listed the total number of Jews in Europe as 7,403,000, including those in the USSR.

What conclusions did Toureille draw from his statistics? One was that the problem of both Jewish and German minorities seemed insoluble because both peoples were so widely dispersed. He warned, presciently, that the rest of Europe needed to understand the present 6,763,000 German minorities living in other nations, their fidelity to their race and Führer, their whereabouts, numbers, and importance, their politics and its effects on the rest of Europe, particularly the threat of being a springboard for German expansionism.

Except for the Jews and the Ukrainians, he continued, the national minorities of Europe were, in general, segments of peoples living outside their own nation states. Their satisfaction or their discontent would, without doubt, have repercussions in international relations, in the peace of Europe and the world. They would react according to the signals or advice of the nations to which they belong. They thus could become instruments for satisfying political or economic ambitions, which explained, in part, the attitude of Hitlerian Germany toward Poland and Czechoslovakia.

Toureille saw no solution to the minorities problem, short of realizing a European Union. Discontented minorities, he warned, were a powerful predictor of war and a constant anxiety for Europe. The alternative to war, an exchange of populations, would be impossible to finance for twenty-six million people, he asserted, and even if possible, how could "we Christians" have agreed to that? His assessment of the paralyzing effect on the rest of the world in dealing with discontented minorities was prescient, since German armies were permitted to march across Czechoslovakia and Poland two years later, claiming their rights to those lands because they had large German minorities. Toureille ended his bleak conclusions with a halting, uncertain exhortation to the church: "In the case of minorities, more than in any other issue, don't we believe that Christianity, Social Christianity, with its practice of the great principle of love of one's neighbor, will have a role to play one day?"

The War Approaches

In March 1938, Germany began its military expansion by absorbing Austria. Hitler then demanded that Czechoslovakia surrender the Sudetenland to Germany, because its people were German-speaking. Czechoslovakia counted on its allies, France and the Soviet Union, to protect it, but in September 1938, the British and French signed the Munich Pact with Hitler, agreeing to give him the Sudetenland upon his promise that he would make no further claims. A few months later, the Germans took all of Czechoslovakia, demonstrating the futility of Munich, the now-classic model of "appeasement."

The Munich Pact was a disgrace particularly to the many French who considered Czechoslovakia their protégée nation, which they had made possible at the end of World War I and to which France had had cultural affinities and attachments for centuries, particularly with Bohemia. Although the Protestant community as a whole, like the rest of France, breathed a sigh of relief that war had been avoided, certain among them were outraged at the betrayal. Their words must have found many reverberations in Pierre Toureille's consciousness.

The Christian Socialist movement led by theologian Karl Barth of Switzerland mobilized in protest. Barth wrote a letter to the Czechs, published a few months after Munich, which pictures them as martyrs for the church militant: "On the liberty of your people depends the liberty of Europe. . . . [If Czechoslovakia must face the Nazis alone,] I dare hope that the sons of the old Hussites will show Europe, become too weak, that men still exist today. . . . Every Czech soldier who fights and suffers, will be doing it for us and—I say this without reservation—he will also do it for the Church of Jesus Christ. . . . What a unique time to live in, dear Friends, when, if one has good sense, one must know that we are commanded, by the love of our faith, to put in the second rank the fear of violence and the love of peace, and to put resolutely in first place the fear of injustice and the love of liberty."[15]

About the same time writer Suzanne de Dietrich exploded in another Protestant journal: "We have shown neither the courage of peace (1920–33) nor that of war (1933–38). We have misunderstood the fundamental Christian doctrine that there is no peace without justice." She preceded this statement with her assessment of the moral dynamics that produced such a terrible mistake:

This unraveling of the acts of grace, to a moment when justice is thrown to the ground, when a small nation must suffer, she alone, the errors of all of us . . . makes me squirm. . . . [A French newspaper, in offering condolences to Czechoslovakia and thanking her for sacrificing herself, and the French press in general,] licks the boots of Hitler. . . . We must now admit that for all the nations of the world, the word of France no longer counts. Because, up to now, it counted. If Czechoslovakia had been invaded, we would have marched. I truly think so. But Czechoslovakia was not invaded: the aggressor was content with holding a knife to her throat: her two good friends, one holding her wrists, the other, her ankles, said to her: let us amputate and that will save your life. Then they cut off her hand and said: nothing will separate us ever again.[16]

Some days after the Munich Pact, the French Protestant Committee for Aid to the Czech Churches was created, under Pastor Marc Boegner, of the FPF (Fédération protestante de France) and A. Legal, a law professor at the University of Montpellier who had studied in Prague.[17] Toureille was secretary and treasurer of this Committee, and in this role contacted about 100 French communities and gave around eighty speeches in France, England, Belgium, Holland and Switzerland on behalf of the Czechs—both the refugees to other countries and those being oppressed within Czechoslovakia itself, even after the German occupation there in March 1939. From its beginnings the French Protestant Committee set up aid centers and places of worship for Czechs within France, with the Committee of Paris as the center, for the flood of Czech refugees produced by the German expansion. Some of these refugees in France were members of the Czech army, mobilized by the Czech government-in-exile in London, after the war against Germany began in September 1939.

In the summer of 1939, Toureille received this letter from Pastor J. B. Sochor, from Miroslav, Moravia, and a member of the Synod of the Church of Czech Brothers in Prague:

Dear Friend,

Thank you for asking about our friends here. The three professors are still at liberty. J.L.H. tried to leave, but, as of today, in vain. All our friends are still working in their parishes. . . . Our Church as such has not suffered. But the future is still uncertain and no one knows what will happen tomorrow.

The number of refugees grows day by day and the bulk of them come from Slovakia and sub-Carpathian Russia. All tell stories of mistreatment by the Hungarians. Even their rings have been taken off their fingers by force.

That is all that can be written in brief, but our hearts are full from these unexpected and surprising events. I want to express to you the thanks of the Synod Council for your letter and I add my own. We pray that you think of us in your prayers. It is always comforting to know that we are not alone and abandoned and that there are friends and brothers with whom we are united in faith.

4

The War Years, an Introduction

Pierre Toureille's rescue activities from 1940 to 1945 took place against the vast backdrop of the world at war and the infernal Nazi attempt to destroy the entire Jewish people. To clarify Toureille's role and the obstacles and dilemmas he faced, this chapter focuses on three aspects of that larger setting: the political context in France, including Vichy anti-Semitism; rescue groups and the spiritual resistance; and the struggle within the French Protestant Church on rescue issues.

Political Context and Vichy Anti-Semitism

France was defeated ignominiously by Nazi forces that, in a matter of months in the spring of 1940, swept over Denmark, Norway, the Netherlands, Belgium, Luxembourg, then France. The war had begun the year before when Germany broke the Munich Pact by invading first Czechoslovakia in March 1939 and then Poland in September. France had been caught in a weakened state because of the economic depression during the 1930s and the political fragility of its newly elected governments, battling conservative and reactionary forces and its own inadequacies.

Adding to the stresses of this period for France was the fact that the Nazi buildup of power in Central and Eastern Europe, their political repression, and preparation for war during the 1930s had created a flood of refugees into France, including those fleeing the Franco victory in the Spanish Civil War of 1936–38. By one estimate, in 1933 alone, there were 25,000 German refugees in France, two thirds of them Jewish.[1] By 1936 there were almost 2.5 million aliens on French soil. By the end of the 1930s, France had a larger proportion of immigrants than any other country in the world—515 for every 100,000 inhabitants, compared with 492 per 100,000 in the United States. This influx of refugees during the 1930s included 180,000 who were still not naturalized by the summer of 1938.[2]

These émigrés had been welcomed during the need for labor in the 1920s but were considered a burden during the depression years. The refugees were the most vulnerable targets of a growing xenophobia among the French, who saw these newcomers as a threat to their jobs and native culture, as well as a provocation toward an unwonted involvement in the aggressive and fascist policies of France's neighbors Italy, Spain, and Germany.

The Jews were a special case among this refugee population in France. Between 1933 and 1943 an estimated 55,000 Jews of all nationalities fled to France—not a great number compared with, for example, the 720,000 Italians who lived in France in 1936.[3] One of the largest single groups of Jewish refugees was the surge from Germany and Austria following the Nazi occupation of Austria in March 1938 and the Nazis' repressive measures after *Kristallnacht* of November 1938, which amounted to 30,000 Jewish men deported to German camps, women jailed, and children expelled from schools and public institutions. More important than the numbers of Jewish refugees to France was the reaction these measures provoked. A virulent form of traditional French anti-Semitism rose to the surface, emerging from reactionary forces against the socialist governments of Blum and Daladier and fostered by a popular anti-Semitism that focused on the Jewish refugees as the cause of the nation's problems—as job-stealers and foreign influences threatening to manipulate and destroy French culture.

When the Nazis defeated France in the spring of 1940, they divided the country into a northern Occupied Zone and a southern Unoccupied Zone (or so-called Free Zone), the latter under a new government based in Vichy and headed by the old World War I hero, Marshal Pétain. The Vichy government was at first supported by most French as saving them from German domination and as offering a kind of moral rearmament after defeat, but within a year of Vichy rule it was increasingly evident that the government was a puppet of the Germans.

Vichy, however, was not completely passive. It passed legislation of its own choosing, for which it needed no encouragement from the Germans relating to the one attitude they both shared: a desire to rid themselves of Jews. For the Vichy authorities, the first priority was to deal with the mostly Jewish camp internees, who threatened France's sparse resources and reactionary political climate. Vichy instituted two Statutes for Jews that applied to both refugees and French citizens (the latter category provoking some public protests among the French), squeezing Jews from public life and depriving them of individual rights. The first Statute, of October 1940, instituted one of the most deadly aspects in using a criterion for registering Jews that cast a net farther back into family roots than even the Nazi one. These Statutes, and the regulations that flowed from them, promulgated the Vichy authorities' system for policing the Jewish foreigners on its soil, most markedly in the setting up of the internment camps.

In January 1939, before Germany had defeated and occupied France, the French government under Daladier responded to the "refugee problem," as the French press often referred to it, by setting up its first internment camp at Rieucros, in Lozère. The camp was intended for foreigners from enemy lands who were under suspicion and who had to be "under special, permanent surveillance, in the interest of order and public security."[4] When the Vichy authorities became the French government in the southern zone in 1940, they continued this policy of setting up camps, with the difference that they were targeting foreign Jews in particular, and in considering the camps as a way to permanently isolate the internees from the rest of France.

By 1942—the year of the largest number of deportations from France—there were eleven camps in the Vichy zone, most of them clustered along the southern border between Les Milles in Aix, and Gurs at the edge of the Pyrenees Mountains. By comparison, there were six internment camps in the Occupied Zone.[5] One historian cites the following figures on these camps, which show the large percentages of Jewish internees among the totals. By the end of 1940, out of 40,000 total internees in the southern camps, 28,000 were Jewish; by February 1941, out of 47,000 internees, 40,000 were Jewish. By April 1941, the camps were emptied out to some extent through liberation of inmates to aid centers, forced labor battalions, or, in a few cases, emigration abroad. Out of the 22,000 internees remaining, 16,000 were Jewish. In November 1941 and February 1942 there were 15,000 internees, of whom 11,000 were Jews. This number accounts for the bulk of the estimated 13,000 Jews deported by Vichy in 1942.[6]

Vichy's active collaboration with the Germans on deportation of Jews played a significant role in the "Final Solution," the term commonly used to denote the Nazi plan to exterminate the Jews. The Germans were short on manpower and would not have been able to accomplish the task alone with the same efficiency. The internment camps, some of which were first considered transit areas for those awaiting emigration papers, all became, by the summer of 1942, camps of deportation to the death centers in German-occupied Poland and other countries in Eastern Europe. The Vichy vice–prime minister, Pierre Laval, explained to those protesting Vichy's collaboration with the Nazis that deportation of these refugees would solve several problems at once. It would satisfy the Nazi appetite for rounding up Jews and therefore protect the lives of French Jews, and it would solve the refugee problem in France. Predictably, this statement was not only vicious but also empty. After the German total occupation of France in November 1942, French Jews were hunted down as well.

By the end of the war, more than 75,000 Jews had been deported from France.[7] Most were gassed upon arrival in the camps in Poland; others were put to a not-much-slower death in forced labor battalions. About 2,500 survived. One third of the total Jews deported were French citizens, the rest, about 50,000, were foreign refugees. Almost 2,000 were under the age of six, more than 6,000 were between ages of seven and thirteen, and 8,700 were older than sixty. The Vichy government fully participated. During the black summer and fall of 1942 alone, Vichy deported over 13,000 Jews from the south of France, including internees and those living outside the camps, many of them former internees. The number of Jews deported from all of France in 1942 alone was 42,500. The 15,000 Jewish children killed or deported in France during the entire German occupation represent one-half of the Jewish children in prewar France. Two thousand Jewish children were from the Vichy-ruled zone.[8]

The Spiritual Resistance

French resistance to the German occupation took two general forms: armed resistance, which grew slowly and with little effect until the latter half of the war, and what is sometimes called the "spiritual resistance," which ranged from noncooperation with the enemy to active rescue work. (The term *spiritual resistance* also refers to resistance efforts sponsored specifically by the church.) During the early period of the German occupation in France, the general public offered no active resistance to the repressive measures of Vichy and of the occupiers, not even to the two Vichy

Statutes for Jews that were issued in 1940 and 1941. The Catholic Church had officially embraced Vichy in 1940 and remained silent. The few public statements against the Statutes, made by some Catholic and Protestant Church individuals and by citizens' letters to the newspapers, protested mainly against the fact that the Statutes applied equally to French and foreign refugee Jews—not against the fact that the Statutes were unjust altogether. Many of these letters also expressed sympathy with Vichy's need to handle what was commonly accepted as "the refugee problem," or in reality, "the Jewish problem."

As thousands of refugees were confined in the internment camps across France under inhuman conditions, the effects of Vichy anti-Semitic policies became clearer to the public. When the mass deportations to the death camps began in the summer of 1942, groups across French society were shocked into action—although it was a clear case of too little, too late. One group was the lower-level administrators in the French bureaucracy, some of whom were lukewarm in arresting Jews, some even helpful in finding them refuge. Catholic authorities, in the summer of 1942, disseminated letters of protest that encouraged individual Catholic clerics to hide Jews in religious institutions, to issue baptismal certificates, and to help refugees escape across the Swiss border.

During that same period, the head of the French Protestant Church, Pastor Marc Boegner, issued two letters that became public, denouncing the Vichy roundups and deportation of Jews. This action galvanized those Protestant communities of the south, in particular, who were already aroused by their local pastors. In addition, Protestant aid organizations were instrumental in prolonging the lives of the refugees and attempting to rescue them from deportation. These organizations joined with other religious and nonreligious groups, national and international, including the Quakers, the Unitarians, the YMCA, the American Friends Service Committee, the Swiss Red Cross, and French and international Jewish organizations. The latter soon had to go underground, as did all the aid groups eventually, as the deportations and roundups of Jews intensified, as the Germans took complete control of the south in 1942. The Committee of Nîmes, with Pierre Toureille as vice-chairman, then chairman, was established in 1940 as the coordinator of all these aid groups working with the Vichy authorities until the groups were officially disbanded at the end of 1942.

From 1940 to 1942, French and international groups trying to aid the refugees cooperated with the Vichy bureaus set up to handle the refugee population. Vichy needed their help in dealing with thousands of unwanted foreigners whom the government had to police, isolate, and feed at a time when France's resources and food were fast disappearing into the German war machine. The aid groups sent representatives, who were to live in the camps themselves, to provide food, medicine, clothing, libraries, training, and arts and crafts in an effort to foster a more humane social and religious life. They tried to speed up the process of emigration and pressure the government to liberate people from the camps, particularly to get the children to homes and aid centers. Many more people would have died in the camps without the help of these aid groups.

Up to the summer of 1942, the camps seemed to have had various and shifting purposes: some, like Les Milles, as transit camps for potential émigrés to other countries; some as forced labor camps; some as detention facilities holding German political resisters to Nazism. Even during that time, chances for emigration had shrunk to a near impossibility because of Vichy red tape and its fear of operating independently of the Germans. The chances of liberation from the camps to an aid center in a town or institution were also diminished, and all the camps had become equally deplorable as sites of starvation, illness, deprivation of clothing and shelter, and exposure to harsh climates, and indifferent or hostile authority. By one estimate 3,000 people died in the internment camps in France, most of them from 1940 to 1942, after which the remaining inmates were deported. In Gurs alone, during the first months of the arrival of Jewish refugees from Germany in 1940, more than 1,000 out of a total of 13,500 inmates died of starvation, dysentery, and typhoid.[9]

By the summer of 1942 it was obvious that Vichy's mission was to provide foreign Jews to fill the German demand for deportees to be sent to "the East," as the German and Vichy authorities called it, meaning the death camps in Poland. The cover story for these mass deportations, which Vichy authorities repeated to those protesting Vichy compliance with German demands, was that these Jews were being sent to start a national homeland in the East, or, alternatively, that they were being sent to fill the forced labor battalions there. The aid groups now worked in desperation to keep as many people as they could off the deportation trains—but given the tens of thousands of deportees who perished, the hundreds saved seem pitifully few.

There was one burning question that some members of the aid organizations began to ask themselves during the war, which continued to fester in their postwar reflections: in choosing to spend their energies and resources ameliorating the conditions in the camps, in collaborating with the Vichy authorities, were they normalizing and perpetuating the camps as death traps? Shouldn't they have seen ahead, were they not suspicious, even forewarned, about the fatal purpose behind this brutal way of isolating and ostracizing people? Shouldn't they have worked from the beginning to get people out and hide them, to fight against the very existence of the camps as destroying essential principles of liberty, justice, and religious belief?

The Church Struggle

According to André Encrevé, historian of French Protestantism, among the general population of Protestants in France during the 1930s, political positions varied along the same lines as the rest of the country. "But," he continued, "when it came to anti-Semitism, meaning Christian anti-Jewish attitudes . . . one can assert that the great majority of French Protestants declared themselves against it. Outside of the theological argument against anti-Semitism presented by most of the pastors, there was the tormented past of the Huguenots and the traces these persecutions left in the collective memory."[10] Another historian, Asher Cohen, commenting on the denunciations of Jews collected by Vichy agents, claimed, "Among the Protestants, informers were rare, and in all cases, badly informed."[11] Even a member of the Protestant Right, René Gillouin, confidant and advisor to Pétain, wrote in August 1941: "I am ashamed for my country, because of the policy on Jews that it has borrowed from Germany, and I don't know any Frenchman worthy of the name who has not condemned it in the secret of his heart, as being neither Christian, nor humane, nor French."[12]

The French Protestant Church held a unique position among churches during the Nazi occupation of France. Its Huguenot history placed it as an uneasy minority church, which in certain periods had been repressed as an enemy of France by reactionary French governments and the Catholic Church. Its spokesmen over the centuries had to not only assert its loyalty to France but also maintain its right to independent religious belief and practice. Unlike the German Protestant Churches, the majority of which championed Nazism (as discussed in chapter 3), the

French church had historically followed a liberal and internationalist politics, with strong ties to the international seat of the church in Switzerland.

The Catholic Church in France, by comparison, fully supported Pétain initially, as it was the church empowered by the advent of the Vichy regime. The French Catholic Church's eventual protests against Vichy came from individuals throughout the church hierarchy, rather than being as unified a church effort as was that of the French Protestant Church.[13] As mentioned in the previous chapter, the decentralized structure and intellectual tradition of the Protestant Church provided a network of local pastors and lines to Switzerland that was crucial to Toureille's rescue efforts.

One church-related influence on Toureille, was the traditional French—and French Protestant—ethic of the *intellectuel engagé,* that is, the notion that the best educated have the personal duty to involve themselves in social issues. This ethic was particularly influential within the church, with its history of combining religion and politics, in dealing with both the state and with international ecumenical issues. Toureille and Boegner were named, among others, as prime examples of this type of Frenchman by several historians who made the additional point that the French Protestant lay public whom these pastors represented were also well read, particularly in the Christian socialist press before and during the war.[14]

Two Protestant pastors—Marc Boegner and Adolf Freudenberg—directed Toureille's wartime rescue activities. Boegner was spokesman for the French Protestant Church and head of the Protestant Federation of France (PFF). Freudenberg was director of Ecumenical Aid to Refugees at the WCC, in formation in Geneva. The WCC was the seat of international Protestant organizations and the major outside support to French aid to refugees. Freudenberg and Boegner set the political and moral parameters within which Toureille could act. Toureille was not always in concert with these organizations, nor they with each other. In particular, they disagreed on control of aid funding and administration, the church's responsibility for the Jewish refugees, and the historical issue of how to define the church's fealty to French government authority. The highest point of crisis for the church on this question of fealty was Vichy's collaboration in Nazi persecution and extermination policies, particularly during the black summer of 1942, with the massive deportations of Jews to the death camps.

The points at issue between Boegner and Toureille are not as clearly documented as they are in Toureille's correspondence with Freudenberg, but they must have involved administrative control of aid to the refugees and general posture in working with the Vichy authorities. And, true to the nonhierarchical nature of the Protestant Church structure in France, the public reactions of church spokesmen in general covered a wide range of spiritual resistance, dramatized in the difference between the fiery resistance of Pastor André Trocmé of Le Chambon and the careful diplomacy of Boegner. A main point at issue between Freudenberg and Toureille was whether rescue efforts should concentrate on ameliorating camp conditions, or on trying to liberate people from the camps altogether.

Freudenberg's background gave him special insights as administrator of aid to refugees. He was born in Germany and served in the German diplomatic corps until the Nazis' rise to power in 1933. In 1935 he became a theology student and joined the Evangelical Confessing Church. Freudenberg and his wife, Elsa Liefmann, fled Germany in March 1939 because of her Jewish origins. The Freudenbergs went to London, where he directed the refugee commission for the WCC. In August 1939 the couple moved to Geneva, the new WCC headquarters.

This organization was guided by an ecumenical committee that included representatives of the Red Cross, the World Alliance of YMCAs, the European Bureau for Inter-Church Aid, and Henri-Louis Henriod of the World Alliance for Promoting International Friendship through the Churches—the organization in which Toureille had been active in the 1930s. Freudenberg spent the war in Switzerland directing the Committee for Ecumenical Aid to Refugees, which became the major source of funding for Toureille's rescue activities.

Freudenberg's office was also the only window to the outside for a refugee agency in Berlin still allowed to operate, up to its closing in December 1940. After strenuous attempts to get people out of Germany at great expense, only 71 of the 400 to 500 on the waiting list had emigrated under the auspices of this office and the WCC, at a total cost of $10,800: "Little enough in comparison to the hundreds of thousands destined to die; and yet for 71 fellow human beings, everything!" Freudenberg was quoted as remarking, in a postwar article about his wartime activities.[15] After the Nazis had deported thousands of German Jews to the Gurs camp in Vichy France in October 1940, Freudenberg concentrated his rescue mission there, working with Protestant aid groups and Toureille.

Because of his own forced emigration from Germany, first-hand knowledge of the nature of Nazi repression, and residency in a neutral country, Freudenberg was more outspoken, fervent, and aggressive than Boegner in trying to free the refugees from their internment in France. Freudenberg worked at the WCC under Secretary General Dr. Visser't Hooft, with whom he shared the same theological mentors, Karl Barth and Eduard Thurneysen.

In his 1968 memoir, Freudenberg explained his and Visser't Hooft's philosophy for action as theologians: "In the daily tension between the Christian life and that of the world, we founded our faith upon the experiences and the trials of the resisting churches in Germany, the Netherlands, and Norway. . . . It was up to us now to try to return freedom to those who had been deprived of it."[16]

He was in touch with pastor friends in Berlin, many of whom were arrested and perished in the camps and gas chambers, and also with a small Protestant group in the Warsaw ghetto, until they too perished. When Dietrich Bonhoeffer visited the Freudenbergs in Geneva in March 1941, Bonhoeffer impressed upon them his own spiritual resistance (for which he was later executed) by saying, "I must say that I pray for the defeat of my country for I believe that is the only possible way for it to pay for all the suffering it has caused in the world."[17]

WCC aid to the refugees in France gave Freudenberg some measure of accomplishment. In his memoir, he wrote of his wife's aged Liefmann cousins interned at Gurs, about whom he exchanged several letters with Toureille and whose story made him aware, on an individual level, of the inhuman conditions in the camps in France. The Swiss reaction to aiding these French internees and refugees was warm and immediate, as Freudenberg described it: "One thing was sure: our French friends could not, in their own distress, support this additional responsibility [the refugees and internees] alone. Switzerland was the neutral neighbor from whom they had every right to expect the first fraternal assistance. . . . Solidarity with the suffering brother in the crucial moment was demonstrated throughout all Switzerland with comforting simplicity." Large sums to help the refugees in France started flowing in from the Swiss parishes, he reported.

According to Freudenberg, except for the International Red Cross, which "was in a more delicate position because of its traditional work in the prisoner of war camps, which it feared would be endangered by working for the Jews," the bond was unbreakable among the rescue groups with whom he worked: "I can only be amazed at the mutual confidence that reigned among all of us—Swiss, Dutch, Swedes, French, British, Americans, Germans, Christians and Jews. . . . In the midst of the struggle of ideologies, of the abolition of freedom, we felt, wherever we came from, completely free in a common service to the victims of terror. It was ecumenism in action."

On the delicate question of how far the World Council of Churches could go in aiding the refugees, Freudenberg defined the mission as not only answering religious needs but also fighting the battle against human misery. The mission also officially limited its aid recipients to those in "the Protestant and Orthodox [Eastern Orthodox Church] communities"— which leaves in the dark the question of how and when they widened their rescue net to Jewish refugees, a question that looms over much of the Freudenberg-Toureille correspondence. Given Vichy censorship, they probably could not discuss openly their awareness that their aid recipients were, by a large majority, Jewish, since these refugees were outside the ecumenical boundaries allowed them by Vichy.

At the end of the film *Schindler's List,* Schindler is seated in a car driving away from the hundreds of Jews he has saved from the death camps and sobbing, "I could have saved more." The remorse that often haunted wartime rescuers grew out of their nagging doubts about whether the choices they made during that desperate period were the right ones. Most of us who have never taken on such responsibility in a time of national trauma assume that rescuers must feel good for performing acts of goodness that look heroic to the rest of the world. But the responsibility they took on, of choosing whom they could save and therefore necessarily sacrificing others, was a heavy and permanent burden for the human mind and heart, at least for the type of human being who became a rescuer.

There is no direct written evidence that Toureille suffered this kind of remorse about the triage he had to perform. He may have guarded himself against it in order to act most effectively—but the weight of such decision making took its toll on his spirits nevertheless. In addition, rescuers like Pierre Toureille were acting not only as individuals but also as representatives and decision makers for whole groups—in his case, the Protestant Church, the Committee of Coordination of Nîmes, and his own immediate family. The necessary constraint of having to work with the Vichy government in order to reach those who needed help, presented an extreme and profound challenge to one's sense of duty and loyalty and to one's ability to make choices that meant life or death for others.

For Toureille, then, the wartime events in France presented him with these moral questions: How should he choose whom to help? By working with Vichy as an officer of the Committee of Coordination, was he helping to perpetuate the internment camps as an acceptable institution, and the internees as guilty, subhuman beings? By working clandestinely, through his position as chief chaplain and his network of pastor rescuers, was he endangering the church itself, opening it to the threat of being taken hostage by the authorities? Finally, by working illegally and clandestinely, was he endangering not only himself but also his family? The following chapters on the war years offer glimpses of how Toureille faced these questions as he reacted to the accelerating pace of events.

5

The War, 1939–1940

Chronology

November 9–10, 1938: Nazis burn synagogues and loot Jewish homes and businesses during *Kristallnacht*. Nearly 30,000 German and Austrian Jewish men deported to camps. Jewish women jailed.

November 15, 1938: All Jewish children expelled from public schools in Germany; segregated schools created.

December 2–3, 1938: All Gypsies in Germany required to register with police.

March 15, 1939: German troops invade Czechoslovakia.

June 1939: Cuba and the United States refuse to accept Jewish refugee ship SS *St. Louis,* which is forced to return to Europe.

September 1, 1939: Germany invades Poland: World War II begins.

October 1939: Hitler extends power of doctors to kill mentally and physically disabled in "euthanasia" program.

Spring 1940: Germany invades and defeats Denmark, Norway, Belgium, Luxembourg, the Netherlands, and France.

> **June 1940:** France agrees to turn over German refugees to Nazis; Marc Boegner, President of Reformed Church of France, urges saving German refugees.

> **July 1940:** Vichy government, under Marshal Pétain, established in Unoccupied (or Free) Zone, the southern region of France.

> **July 1940:** Boegner meets with the Grand Rabbi of France.

> **Sept. 27, 1940:** German military command orders a census of all Jews in Occupied Zone.

October 1940: Warsaw ghetto is established.

> **October 3, 1940:** Statute for Jews, written by Vichy officials, broadens German definition of who was Jewish (anyone with two Jewish grandparents, including any married to a Jew) and excludes Jews from public service, armed forces, journalism, teaching, film, radio, and theater. Prefects are authorized

to intern foreign Jews or send them to forced labor camps; a subsequent law deprives all Algerian Jews of citizenship.

October 4, 1940: 40,000 Jewish foreigners interned in the Unoccupied Zone, at Gurs, Noé, Récébédou, Rivesaltes, Brens, Rieucros, and Les Milles.

October 23, 1940: CIMADE (*Comité inter-mouvements d'aide auprés des évacués*) becomes active at Gurs camp—650 Protestants helping 17,000 refugees.

October 25, 1940: Boegner opposes Statute for Jews, at Vichy-sponsored meeting in Unoccupied Zone of all Protestant leaders.

November 20, 1940: First official meeting of Committee of Nîmes, a group of 25 national and international religious and aid organizations, to help the camp internees. Donald Lowrie, American, YMCA, selected president; Pierre Toureille, vice president.

December 23, 1940: Letter from Boegner to eight church presidents in Unoccupied Zone on the Jewish laws. "For the Church, there is no Jewish problem."[1]

In April 1939, a month after Hitler invaded Czechoslovakia, four months before World War II began, and a year before Germany defeated and occupied France, Pierre Toureille attended several meetings in Germany on church business for the World Alliance.[2] In a report dated April 21, 1939, to Henri-Louis Henriod, secretary-general of the World Alliance, Toureille wrote that only a few of his French colleagues attended these meetings, making it necessary for him to give more speeches than he had planned. The German Church representatives greeted him warmly and assured him of their attachment to the work of the World Alliance. The report continued in this restrained manner, requiring some reading between the lines to find the troubling issues that were on the minds of the people Toureille met.

During one session in Heidelberg, Toureille reported, he had raised "certain questions relative to non-Aryans." In Dresden he had called on a Dr. Edelmann, whom he had known since 1933, "a man devoted to the church and its work for peace." They discussed "the situation in the Sudetenland" and the Serb minority. In Berlin, "full of people and festivities," he was introduced to several pastors and notables. He learned that the official German religious press was attacking Pastor Boegner, the head of the Reformed Church of France. He commented, in his report, on the liberal German theologians who were feeling increasingly oppressed by the Nazi government: "Our German friends very much need these visits, which have to be undertaken systematically." The Berliners did not seem to appreciate "the gravity of the situation," he noted. They did not believe that Germany would take military action but agreed that Germany would ally itself with Italy.

By this period in his career, Toureille had experienced first-hand, through church politics and his long-term study of minorities, the powerful forces in Germany building up for war. Marc Toureille remembers, "My father saw the German threat from the beginning. In 1938, when I was nine, he came back from a World Alliance trip to Germany and said, 'We should march in there right now. This is the time to go.' He knew right away, when they were rounding up the Jews a few years later, that they wouldn't come back, they were going to be killed. 'All you have to do is read *Mein Kampf,*' he told us."

Under the assumed name of Pierre du Touat, he published an article in *Revue du christianisme social* in the late 1930s, informing his colleagues of the scurrilous anti-Semitism in Nazi propaganda books he had collected on his trips to Germany and had brought home to show his family. After his introductory warning, "We must be aware of the hatred for Jews that the Hitlerians want to inculcate in children," he lets the written word speak for itself, by translating passages from a 1936 book for children and describing the pictures. The article ends with two paragraphs quoted from the book. The first reads: "The Hitler Youth are proud and handsome, from the oldest to the youngest. These are the nice boys, clean and strong. They love the Führer—they fear God high above. They hate the Jews, who are not like them in any way, and who, because of that, have to sneak away!" The second describes the Midi (the south of France) as "the birth-place of the Jews. . . . They must go there, with their wives and children, as quickly as they came." Toureille noted that the accompanying illustration shows six Jews, one of whom was a woman and another a little boy, loaded with suitcases and packages, hurrying toward the train station. The caption reads: "March! March! The Jews are our misfortune!"

With this image of harassed people in his mind, Toureille committed himself to helping the masses of refugees created by the growth of Nazi power, refugees who, clearly by 1939, would soon overwhelm France.[3]

Aid Organizations under Vichy

After the French defeat in June 1940, the Vichy government encouraged aid organizations, both French and international, to help deal with the overwhelming flood of refugees into the south, primarily through administering aid to the internment camps. From the beginning, working with Vichy administrators was precarious for these aid organizations. The Vichy government kept changing the rules and retracting promises to ameliorate conditions for the refugees and internees. Its own view was that the refugees were hostile foreign elements and a burden to be gotten rid of. Although the international organizations, particularly those from the United States, were able to work legally under Vichy in this early period, the hiatus lasted only until the end of 1941, when America entered the war against Germany.

Toureille was an active participant in three of these aid groups—the Center for Czechoslovak Aid (CCA) in Marseille, the Committee for Ecumenical Aid to Refugees at the WCC (in formation) in Geneva, and the Committee of Coordination of Nîmes (CCN). The bureaucratic center for all his activities was the Chaplaincy, which he set up in his home.

Center for Czechoslovak Aid (CCA)

At the defeat of France by the German army in June 1940, the majority of the Czechoslovak troops in France managed to flee to England. Eight thousand of them remained in France, along with 2,000 Czech civilians who had neither family nor friends. About 1,500 of these Czech refugees were put into internment camps set up by Vichy.[4] Others were incorporated into the wartime forced labor battalions, the GTE (*Groupes de travailleurs étrangers,* or Foreign Workers Groups). The plight of these Czech refugee thousands was of special concern to Toureille throughout the war.

At this time, Toureille became vice president of the CCA, based in Marseille, with Donald Lowrie of the International YMCA as president. The CCA, with Oldrich Dubina as director, set up a population of nearly a thousand men with jobs and lodgings, establishing the majority in farm work that turned out to be remarkably productive. In an article published in a Prague journal in 1947, Toureille remembered the gratification they all felt from the enterprise of this group, in a period of wartime scarcities:

We had to find work for these Czech refugees. Then the idea came to Dr. Dubina, native of a Moravian village, with the heart of a peasant, to make them farmers. We rented, near Marseille, the Château la Blancherie and transformed it into lodgings for 100-some people at a time, as well as providing a small school and medical and dental services, all free to Czechoslovaks. . . . How we were to feed them, presented a greater problem. Agricultural produce was never abundant in the Mediterranean region. What's more, the food that we were starting to cultivate was requisitioned, in increasing amounts, to sell to the Germans. We had to plant our vegetables for the refugees, in the public park.

After a certain time, people started to say to us that if vegetables were a good thing, meat would be even better. Dr. Dubina bought a cart and horses and entrusted them to a Slovak cabdriver who, every morning, toured the restaurant and hotel kitchens of Marseille collecting scraps. We combined these with the meat from the 100–120 pigs and 500–600 rabbits we were raising. This is how everyone was able to have meat. A Prague butcher built a little cottage at one end of the garden and put up a sign: "Now the only producer of authentic Prague ham in France." So, in the dining room of the château, we could serve our visitors smoked pork with cabbage. The odor and taste transported them in an instant, to Czechoslovakia.[5]

World Council of Churches (WCC)

In 1940 Pastor Adolf Freudenberg was appointed director of the Committee for Ecumenical Aid to Refugees at the World Council of Churches (WCC) in Geneva. This organization had absorbed the World Alliance in which Toureille had been active in the 1930s. Pastor Marc Boegner, as head of the French Protestant Church, appointed Toureille in the fall of 1940 as *Aumônier des protestants étrangers refugiés et internés en France* (Chief Chaplain of Protestant refugees and camp internees in France). Toureille's office was to be coordinated with the WCC under Freudenberg's direction, together with the French Protestant Church under Boegner and with CIMADE (*Comité inter-mouvements d'aide auprès des évacués*), the agency providing aid inside the internment camps.

Toureille's lines of contact with Freudenberg at the WCC were more unwieldy and frustrating than those with the Committee of Nîmes, mainly because he was working so much through official Vichy channels in dispensing aid. His job required him to compose his frequent correspondence in oblique style to hide from the Vichy censors and to make decisions in haste in response to fast-changing conditions.

Freudenberg was his strongest ally. He was Toureille's most crucial source of funding for rescue activities in France; he was his main counsel and, at times, his protector. He fully empathized with Toureille's sense of urgency and passion in these efforts but from a cooler and broader administrative and diplomatic perspective. Their frequent letters to each other over the next four years illuminated both the large issues and small details with which they had to cope.

Toureille's earliest letter to Freudenberg existing in the WCC files registered his eagerness to work with the WCC in aiding the refugees flooding into France. It was dated September 12, 1940; the Vichy government under Pétain had been set up for over a month, and it had been three months since the French government had agreed to turn over its German refugees to the Nazi victors. "It is clear that our work is necessary and urgent," Toureille wrote. "It is no less clear that the situation in France will be more and more difficult. Proof of this lies in the Vichy government decision, announced by its Council of Ministers on Sept. 10: 'The presence in our territory of great numbers of people who emigrated or were expelled from their country, foreigners or natives, Jewish or non-Jewish, constitutes a certain danger to tranquility and public order. The Council of Ministers has decided to apply certain precise measures to safeguard the nation.'" Toureille proposed himself for the position of chief chaplain, to act as a liaison with the WCC in its aid to the refugees. "I respectfully point out that, being presently without work, I would be fully ready to take on the refugees, as representative of the WCC committee on refugees. I have substantial experience on this question and am not without resources. I put myself at your service, if you think I can be useful."

Committee of Coordination of Nîmes (CCN)

The other large organization through which Toureille worked on refugee aid was the Committee of Coordination of Nîmes, most often referred to as the Committee of Nîmes, so called after the place where most of the Committee meetings were held. This organization, founded under Vichy in November 1940, grouped together a large number of nongovernmental aid groups—Christian and Jewish, French and international—with the American Donald Lowrie, of the International YMCA, as its president, and Toureille its secretary, later vice president and then president.[6] The membership organizations and some of their representatives[7] with whom Toureille had particular contact, ranged widely in their backgrounds and interests, which kept Toureille energized and gave him, for a time, a sense of effectiveness.

The Committee of Nîmes was most productive up to the German occupation of southern France in November 1942, after which the internment and deportation of some of its members crippled its activity. However, most of its subsidiary organizations, even some of the Jewish ones, continued their work for another year since the authorities saw them as useful for managing the camps and refugees remaining after the mass deportations of 1942.

The Chaplaincy and Dealing with Vichy: A Moral Dilemma

Toureille used his Chaplaincy headquarters in his home in Lunel, as the base for his rescue activities. Jean Boisset, president of the Chaplaincy Executive Committee, in a postwar attestation, summarized how Toureille coordinated his aid activities through this office:

At first, in October 1942, the office of the Chaplaincy, which employed six people, was part of the Toureille home. The office was then installed in another place to allow Pastor and Madame Toureille to have a more normal family life. After the events of June 1940, as successor to Pastor Forell who had to flee to the United States, Pastor Toureille received one list of Protestant refugees in France, comprised of only about 20 names. Upon leaving the Chaplaincy in September 1945, he left several lists and a folder containing several thousand names and addresses.

The work and organization required to achieve this, was accomplished in extremely difficult and often dangerous conditions. M. Toureille, with great fidelity, visited the internment camps in France and North Africa, the Groups of Foreign Workers, the aid centers, the isolated and those in hiding, carrying to the Christians in the churches belonging to the World Council of Churches, moral and necessary material aid and comfort. This meant incessant moving around, in all seasons and by all means of transportation (even going by bicycle and on foot were made difficult by the administrative formalities required in this period). . . . The considerable fatigue that resulted was exacerbated by the regulations on the opening hours of restaurants and hotels. M. Toureille had to skip meals and spend the night in station waiting rooms, or on public park benches.

Pastor Toureille's task was facilitated by his profound knowledge of several languages and by his great memory. . . . He presided regularly at the religious services held in the most diverse and remote communities. . . . Several thousand books were collected in a circulating library. The benefits of this literature in all languages were incalculable for a population almost entirely dominated by the psychosis of fear. . . . A very heavy correspondence required that the Chaplaincy employ 12 people, which allowed M. Toureille to devote himself to administration.

In the course of the summer of 1942, the anti-Semitic measures became more and more grave, and M. Toureille, since a great number of his parishioners were racially Jewish, worked hard to protect them, contacting other aid organizations for help, in France and abroad.

Pastor Toureille had to undergo surveillance from the Vichy police and from the Gestapo. His home and his office were searched in his presence and his absence. He was even required to report to the authorities in Montpellier on two occasions, although it would have been possible for him to take refuge in Switzerland—he had a permanent permit to do so. By this choice, he showed openly that he would not abandon those for whom he was the ONLY connection to life. . . . Thus, to foreigners of all nations who fled to France, M. Toureille devoted himself to showing them "the true face of France," and to those French inexperienced about foreigners, he made them known, and often, loved.[8]

Some historians of this period ask a demanding question of aid groups: Did they help perpetuate the camps and therefore act as tools of Vichy by providing aid through official channels? Why didn't they apply more pressure against the camp system itself and get more people out?

Toureille must have been attuned to these issues that were being raised early at Committee of Nîmes meetings, with no general agreement on the answers. As an officer of the Committee, he debated actively on many grounds, but his view on how much to cooperate with Vichy at each decision point, is not clear.[9] Toureille's comments and tone in the Committee of Nîmes minutes, compared with his correspondence with Freudenberg, show a greater determination to put pressure on the Vichy authorities, on such issues as liberation from the camps and emigration for the refugees. One major reason has to be that the letters to Freudenberg were accessible to the Vichy censors, while the Committee minutes were presumably not. Another reason might have been that Toureille was of several minds about the crucial lifesaving issues of how to achieve liberation and emigration, but he was clearly from the very beginning not a supporter of the Vichy regime and, from his ecumenical experience abroad, savvy about the long-term evils and injustices of such a government.

Certainly after the mass deportations from France of 1942, the aid groups must have felt betrayed by Vichy. One wonders which of the following remarks made by his colleagues Toureille might have agreed with, at the time or in hindsight:

We were too inclined to respect a certain legality, in the hope of better serving the interests of the internees. . . . We should have acted as we did beginning in 1943, when we had to shelter the Jews who were outside the camps, to save them from Hitler's clutches. If we had known that the deportees were all being sent to their deaths, we would have reacted differently, we would have adopted a system of defense and rescue. (Rabbi René Samuel Kapel, camp chaplain and member of the Committee of Nîmes.)[10]

It is *at the start* that one must refuse to become accustomed to something, so that your yes is really yes, and your no is really no. (Pastor André Dumas, CIMADE representative, Rivesaltes internment camp.)

It was not the internees' existence in the camps that had to be helped, it was the very existence of the camps themselves, that had to be wiped out, for God's sake! (Nina Gourfinkel, member of aid team of Abbé Glasberg, member of Committee of Nîmes.)

Again, a comment from another of Toureille's colleagues on the Committee of Nîmes, passing a harsh judgment on the choices aid groups were making and their failure to recognize the political realities:

Whether one wishes it or not, however pure be the intentions and serious the situation, as soon as one collaborates in an enterprise in which the liberty and dignity of the human being are undermined by arbitrariness and cowardice, one becomes a tacit accomplice. . . . To work toward ameliorating the camp conditions, even if one is exclusively preoccupied with the internees' best interest, is to arrive, little by little, insensibly, at a tolerance, then an acceptance of the camps as the life condition of a certain category of human being. . . . One no longer sees who has put up the barbed wire or who has committed crimes. The wire is there, put up by an anonymous force, symbolizing those in power on one side and those who are weak and diminished on the other, a judicial authority on the good side, a guilty group on the other. The value of liberty is so profoundly anchored in men that no one, including the prisoner himself, can escape from the suggestive force that a prison represents. (Dr. Joseph Weill, representative of OSE [*Oeuvres de secours d'enfants*], a Jewish group aiding child refugees.)

Aid groups, continued this same commentator, do real social service only if their actions are political, fighting social injustice, which is their essential purpose. This means separating out the essentials from the mass of details, imagining farsighted policies, and knowing how to make effective choices.

In his memoir, *The Hunted Children,* Donald Lowrie wrote of his version of the Committee of Nîmes's mission. He contended that they were not a political organization and, in their social service mission, had to work within the authorities' structure to fulfill their goal—which was to relieve the internees' suffering as much as possible. And in that effort, the Committee, he claimed, were a unified group: "Although the Nîmes

Committee sedulously avoided politics, the overriding sympathy of all its members was whole-heartedly with the Allied cause. . . . This fact of both organizational and spiritual unity gave the Committee, with all its international connections, a prestige and influence with French authorities that proved to be of even more significance than coordination of effort" (86).

What's more, he continued, the Committee was the "sole defender of the interests of a hundred thousand otherwise defenseless refugees" and could act effectively with the Vichy authorities who were overwhelmed with the task of dealing with these refugees. "Happily, most of the Committee's relations with Vichy were not in the form of protests," he added, and "by viewing the situation from the internees' standpoint and collecting data on one or another problem," the Committee was able to propose cooperative efforts with Vichy that kept many people alive in the camps.

The issue of the Committee's unanimity and the question of whether the members were most effective in saving people by cooperating with Vichy, reappeared in a different light in the minutes of the Committee's meetings. Of the few members who objected to the Committee's procedures, Daniel Benedite, one of the American members of the Committee, must have been one of the harshest and the least persuasive to the others, at the time. He wrote in 1984: "I was present at an academic discussion, an exchange of superficial views, vague and timid proposals. Each member counted on resolving the problems case by case through courteous negotiations with the Vichy authorities. No one seems to have envisaged vigorous and concerted actions to ameliorate the camp system. . . . I proposed launching a vast press campaign in the US denouncing this scandal dishonoring France, in order to disgrace a government inflicting inhuman treatment on tens of thousands of individuals and to threaten a stoppage of all assistance (which was far from negligible) to the French people if no solution was reached to this inexorable situation."[11]

Benedite noted that his proposal was met with "stupor" and, with a few exceptions, with "disapproval," as if he were ranting. Objections were that "we will make defensive those whom we must persuade and whose good faith is not in question." Lowrie ended the discussion, Benedite reported, with "Monsieur, no politics here."

French Jewish Aid Workers

French Jews working in aid organizations faced a special dilemma. In the first two years of the war, the Vichy Statutes for Jews made no distinction between foreign Jewish refugees and Jewish French citizens. Nevertheless, in the first years of the war French Jews, although concerned about the new limitations on their professional and personal lives, by and large felt themselves protected by their French citizenship and loyalty to the French nation. In general, they identified themselves as French, not as members of the foreign Jewish community who, as refugees from the Nazis, were flooding France and creating great distress among the local population. Especially after the mass roundup of 1942, which included French Jews in its nets, the Jews of France were shocked into the realization that they, too, were Nazi targets for deportation.

Jewish aid organizations remained active as long as they could, some members working to save the refugees long after it was possible to save themselves. Toureille was a close friend of one Jewish aid director whose story epitomizes the dilemma faced by French Jewish aid workers.

Raymond-Raoul Lambert was a French Jew whom Toureille had known since 1933, when Lambert was involved in helping refugees to France by serving vigorously in French Jewish agencies. During the war, Lambert was one of the earliest members of the Committee of Nîmes, representing the Committee of Assistance to Refugees (CAR), and later accepted the post of President of the UGIF (*Union générale des israélites de France, or General Union of Jews of France*), an organization imposed on French Jews by the Nazis and by Vichy. In 1943, he was denounced by the chief of the CGQJ (*Commissariat général aux questions juives,* or Bureau for Jewish Affairs) and deported to Auschwitz with his wife and children, where they all perished.

Toureille was intensely interested in the dilemma of identity Lambert faced, of being, as Toureille put it, "both passionately French and passionately Jewish," in an historical period that fatally split apart these two loyalties. Toureille wrote a tribute to Lambert after the war in which he picked out those aspects of Lambert's character that he most admired, and thus associated himself with Lambert's story and with the difficult choices he had to make.[12]

Toureille wrote that Lambert was a scholar of German language and culture, an admirer of Germany's poets and philosophers. He was a third-generation Parisian and distinguished by his World War I military record that earned him the *Légion d'honneur.* He was a social activist in the national and international Jewish community, establishing contact with the German Jewish communities during World War I, then serving as president of the Jewish war veterans organization and the Jewish Universal Alliance in France.

He was a fine writer, an editor-in-chief of a Jewish journal, and among the earliest generation of French Jews to become a Zionist. When Toureille met him, in the early 1930s, he was active in an association of Jewish emigration organizations. As a member of Prime Minister Edouard Henriot's cabinet, he enriched his already developed political sophistication and could intervene with the French authorities in dealing with the flood of German Jewish refugees beginning in 1933. He could "speak as an equal" to the Vichy authorities, Toureille commented, and was "the heart and the brains" of the CAR. Toureille chose the following story to demonstrate Lambert's patriotism:

The General Commissioner of the CGQJ, Xavier-Vallat, once let it slip, at the end of a meeting, that he, R.-R. Lambert, although a hero, was, after all, a foreigner in the French community. Lambert replied immediately, in an impassioned tone, pain expressed clearly across his whole face and in the deep sadness of his eyes: "I am French with my whole being. For three generations my family has fought for France—my grandfather in the Crimea and at Solferino, my father in 1870, myself in 1914–18 on the Marne, the Somme, at Verdun. And I am now being told that even though I won the *Légion d'honneur* on the battlefield for France, I am not French! What, then, would I have to do, to be considered a Frenchman?"

Vichy feared Lambert's frankness, Toureille claimed. Lambert once called the second Vichy Statute for Jews, a cold repeat of the St. Bartholomew's Day massacre.[13] It was during the massive roundups of Jews in the summer and fall of 1942 that Vichy authorities felt the heat of Lambert's passion, Toureille continued, including the Secretary of the Interior, whom Lambert told, "Now your hands have been dipped in Jewish blood." And Lambert slammed the door on Laval after an office conversation, saying "You are worse than the Boches!"

In his war diary, Lambert wrote a long, moving account of how he, as a representative of a French Jewish agency in August 1942, had to make choices about which internees he should try to keep off the deportation trains at the camp at Les Milles.[14] He told of spying a Viennese editor internee who, like himself, was a *Légion d'honneur* awardee. "I can no longer be quiet! I dash across the courtyard like a crazy man." He grabbed the man and made him stand behind him, keeping him out of the sorting process. "Such scenes demonstrate the dishonoring of a regime," he concluded, with apparently no conscious awareness that the next year, he would meet the same fate as these people.

But another event brought him closer to such a realization, shattering the distinction he had made in the past between French and foreign Jews. In November 1941 the Germans insisted that Vichy disband all the Jewish organizations and create one, the UGIF, which title translates ominously into "General Union of Jews in France," rather than "French Jews." The next year the authorities asked Lambert to be director, a further sign of entrapment of the community leaders by the authorities, who persuaded those leaders that by cooperating, they would be avoiding the worst. Toureille played an important role in Lambert's decision. Toureille wrote:

Before he accepted the heavy and fearful burden of being the administrator of this organization, R.-R. Lambert did me the honor, as a friend, of asking for my advice. He hesitated to accept, knowing well what this had meant for those who had been willing to accept the same positions in Germany. He also knew and seemed to fear that many would criticize him and accuse him of spying on them and of betraying them. We considered all sides of the question.

I hesitated to tell him my deepest thoughts. How could I do so, knowing that such advice, once followed, affects that person's whole life. Finally, looking him straight in the eye, as he liked to be looked at, I said, "If I were you, I would accept. We must maintain to the end the positions we adopted before the war and the defeat. What was true then, is still true, and always will be." "That is exactly what I said to myself. Thank you. I will accept," he replied. And he accepted.

Toureille did not see Lambert much after that conversation, although he heard criticisms of Lambert from his Jewish friends, who were also friends of Toureille. But Toureille asserted, "No one could ever say that R.-R. Lambert had not done all that was possible, and impossible, to save the most insignificant and least known of his brothers. He taught me the meaning of Jewish solidarity."

Toureille had one more chance to save Lambert's life, but this time Lambert refused outright: "One of the last times I saw him was on a train. We were talking casually about those we had helped cross into Switzerland. . . . I well knew that R.-R. Lambert had numerous acquaintances who could help him and his family flee to Switzerland. Nevertheless, moved by the sincere affection I had for him, I offered him my personal services. He put his hand on my shoulder and looked at me in astonishment: 'How come you, too, make me this offer? You wouldn't do it in my place.'"

That last interchange proved to be an inspiration to Toureille when he himself was summoned for interrogation by the Gestapo. When they warned him that failure to respond would mean that his family would suffer, he thought of R.-R. Lambert in answering the summons. He adds, "During the long interrogation, every time there was mention of a "dirty Jew," it was R.-R. Lambert I thought of, telling myself how foolish they were to pass judgment on a whole race, on a faith that had produced individuals, character, men like him."

Toureille continued: On August 21, 1943, Lambert, his wife and four children, and his in-laws were arrested and deported to Auschwitz. Upon arrival there, on December 10, 1943, the whole family were sent to the gas chambers, "where he died holding his son Tony, aged four, in his arms."

The Spiritual Resistance

At the beginning of the German occupation, a close colleague-in-aid to Toureille, Pastor Jean Cadier, began urging spiritual regeneration in fiery sermons that at first seemed to approve the moral rearmament promised by Vichy, but by the summer of 1941 urged resistance to the authorities. Cadier was a theology professor and later dean of the Faculty of Theology at the University of Montpellier, where Toureille was trained, and regional president in the Reformed Church of France. At Toureille's death in 1976, he published a tribute expressing his admiration and gratitude toward Toureille (see Appendix). It is hard to know how closely Toureille associated himself with Cadier's sermons, particularly those before the summer of 1941, but it is significant that these sermons had a powerful impact among the Protestant communities in Toureille's home area.

In June 1940, at the defeat of the French, Cadier invoked Marie Durand, who "carved only one word on the stone of her tower, but this word is enough. . . . No one can imprison the soul."[15] On August 18, 1940, before enactment of the first Vichy Statute for Jews, Cadier denounced the oppressive measures against Jews and Freemasons already in place: "We are the neighbors of the Israelites, whom we are still burdening with the censure traditionally attached to their people."[16] A week later his tone was aggressively militant against totalitarianism. He urged "not the pious quietude of the Church of Christ. . . . but a battle, the battle that took place before the creation of the world, between God and Satan, the battle for which humanity was created to defend, against chaos and death, the sovereign rights of God . . . [against] those incarnations of Satan named Pharaoh, or Nebuchadnezzar, or Pilate, or Herod, or Nero."[17]

Marc Boegner's public statements at this time were not so militant but had a much larger effect than Cadier's. Before and during the war, Boegner held several leading positions, including president of the National Council of the Reformed Church of France since 1938, president of the Protestant Federation of France since 1929, and vice president of the committee directing the newly forming World Council of Churches in Geneva since 1939. He has been described as formal and dignified in manner, even haughty and imperious, with a gift for eloquence, as his writings and speeches demonstrate.

On November 30, 1944, three months after the liberation of southern France, Boegner published an article in *Figaro*, entitled "Silence is impossible." This article expressed the traditional French Protestant position on the relationship between the church and the state, and summarized the position Boegner took on behalf of the church and its spiritual resistance throughout the war. The article combined political and theological subjects in the old French Huguenot tradition, newly clothed in the experience of the war. Boegner's subject was justice. He asserted the church's independence and differences from the state on that issue, and mapped out the consequences, wrapped in an ardent patriotism and Old Testament severity. The state must respect the person, Boegner asserted, including those who were accused of disloyalty and who had to defend themselves.

Boegner's final paragraph made the case for the special position the French Protestant Church took in protesting against the government injustices of the war years. The victims of this government injustice were identified as "tens of thousands of Frenchmen" who had been the targets of "abominable treatment during the past four years." "Some of us, in France, have publicly protested against . . . the odious measures inflicted on our compatriots. And our churches have considered it their primary duty to make their criticism known." The Church, he continued, did not accept as a justification for these government excesses, that "insurrections" had to be put down in such times of national crisis: very often this justification was founded simply on having superior force.

However, there is ambiguity in his argument. Since Boegner clearly did not include among the victims of government injustice the tens of thousands of non-French, mostly Jewish refugees who flooded France during the war, did that mean he saw the Church as being selective on whose rights it championed? His public protests and activities during the war displayed a similar ambiguity.

There was no question, though, about his general position on Nazi anti-Semitism. His attacks on it showed up early. In 1933 Boegner visited the pro-Hitler leaders of the German Protestant Church and was quoted in a French newspaper as saying, "Not one Christian outside Germany can understand defrocking a legitimately ordained minister because he has Jewish blood in his veins."[18]

In March 1939 he called together the Carême (Lenten) conference, in Passy, on the theme of the church and racism.[19] Boegner spoke uncompromisingly on racism and targeted anti-Semitism as its most egregious fault: he referred to the distress of Czech Jews in particular and proclaimed, "Between Christianity and racism, between the churches and those states that are, more or less openly, the auxiliaries or champions of racism, there is no possible agreement or compromise." He questioned whether there existed an identifiable Jewish race, referred to the massive emigration and misery suffered by Jews, and denounced the persecutions they had undergone—particularly by the actions of Popes Innocent II and Paul IV, and of Martin Luther.

His exhortation to his audience of pastors suggested no political action by the church, only by individuals: they should be like the Good Samaritan by helping the victims of suffering. He acknowledged there was "a Jewish problem facing Europe and the world . . . particularly the substantial immigration of Jews now facing the French public." He urged that people remain cool-headed: "No satisfactory solution will ever be reached in an atmosphere charged with emotion."

After the quick French defeat and the establishment of the Vichy government in 1940, Boegner welcomed Pétain, as did the large majority of the Protestants and the French in general. Boegner worked to get Pétain's ear and to exert some influence, but reluctantly, over the next year, came to the conclusion that the Vichy government was headless. Despite his initial deference to Pétain, he wasn't blind to the issues. In October 1945 he wrote in his journal (published after the war) that, from his first visit to Vichy in July 1940, one of the persistent themes he had encountered was the "situation of non-Aryans." "That which I would call obsessive anti-

Semitism of several officials was given free rein without any German pressure. 'Those people have done so much evil to the country that they deserve a collective punishment,' a highly placed official declared to me. I foresaw where we were headed and what would be the responsibility of our churches."[20]

In the same entry he wrote that one Vichy minister, to whom he had protested about the Statute for Jews of October 1940, told him, "It is a law of 'defense'; it will bring terrible injustices, but it must be 'absolute,'" while a second official added, "The *maréchal* did not want that [the Statute]." Boegner commented in Pétain's defense, "I am convinced that it was true."

As one French historian, Pierre Bolle, noted, Boegner, despite his eloquence and strength of person, had been reproached by some for his expediency and unnecessary deference to Pétain.[21] He stayed loyal too long, critics say, when it was obvious that oppression, particularly of the Jewish refugees, was increasing apace. Boegner's defense, according to Bolle, was that he trusted Pétain at first because of the number of Protestants in Pétain's entourage and because of Pétain's praise of the moral fiber of Protestantism. In addition, showing loyalty to Pétain gave the church an inside track for influencing Pétain's vaunted policy of political moralism.

A more muscular and activist reaction to anti-Semitism came from another pastor at this time, Jacques Martin, who served in a parish in Toureille's home department of Hérault, in the Cévennes. Martin published *"l'Antisémitisme païen . . . et chrétien"* ("Pagan . . . and Christian Anti-Semitism") in the *Revue du christianisme social* in August 1939, which some historians consider the most lucid and prophetic of Protestant commentary on the role of anti-Semitism in the coming war.[22] Martin first spoke caustically of "the inertia of our Protestant public . . . a reserve and caution from which political motives cannot be excluded." Anti-Semitism was one of the scourges that, in certain periods of human history, rained terror and death on Europe. He foresaw a time soon to come of total desperation for the Jews, a diaspora more cruel and destructive than the one in the first century C.E., when the Romans destroyed the Temple in Jerusalem.

He reported at this early stage about the concentration camps: "Five thousand Polish Jews have been sent by special train to a small Polish village where they must live as best they can, forbidden either to enter Poland or to return to Germany. Other groups of expelled Jews live outside the gates of several countries, in some sort of neutral territory, at the borders of Germany. . . . These refugees keep waiting for some hypothetical visa, many wandering across Europe and the world, others between two frontiers, in this 'no man's land' where thousands of miserable people are stabled together. The only way out is death."

Martin's message to his fellow Protestants was clearly activist, and he clearly considered anti-Semitism to be the poison in the coming conflict:

And Christians—have they not been relying on a convenient interpretation of scripture, too easily choosing the heavens, in the hope of eternal salvation, abandoning the world to its sin and death? That is why they could so easily deal with the world, reconcile themselves to evil, align themselves with the state, that crucified their Master. . . . The response of the Christian must be the return to oneself, to a new consciousness of the message of the Kingdom and its justice, to a messianic hope and its inexorable demands for the immediate present. It must be a new conversion rejecting all the shackles of a world that must be vanquished, beginning with the shackles of anti-Semitism. Because, to speak like Nietzsche for a moment, in order to believe in their Savior, Christians must seem a little more saved.

The year following the publication of Martin's article, on October 17, 1940, the Vichy government issued an explanation of its Statute for Jews, astounding in its blatant anti-Semitism:

In its task of national reconstruction the government has had, from the very first, to study the problem of Jews and of certain other foreigners who, abusing our hospitality, have contributed not a little to our defeat. . . . With certain quite honorable exceptions . . . the dominating influence of the Jews has made itself everywhere felt, especially in public services, leading finally to decay. All observers agree in affirming the evil effect of their activity in recent years. . . .

In its firm dignity of purpose, the government has refused to undertake reprisals: it respects the person and the property of Jews: merely prevents them from assuming certain social functions, of authority, of management, of control over intellectual life. Experience has proven to the government, as to all impartial minds, that Jews in these functions have encouraged individualistic tendencies that have almost pushed the country to anarchy. Our disaster imposes on us the task of regrouping the forces of French society whose characteristics have been established by heredity. This is not a matter of massive vengeance but of establishing a crucially needed security in France.

The government may absolve from certain general restrictions prescribed in the national interest of France, those Jews who deserve well of the fatherland, and this proves in what a humane spirit the government has regulated a problem that is universal, as demonstrated by our present disaster.[23]

On October 25, 1940, Boegner officially opposed the Statute, at a meeting of all Protestant leaders in the southern zone, called together by the Vichy government. This was the first official protest from any church in France, against the anti-Semitic measures of the Vichy government. Boegner had already argued on behalf of the Jews—in his protest against turning over German refugees to the Nazis in June 1940, and in his meeting with the Grand Rabbi of France in July 1940. He protested against the Statute again in a December 23 letter to eight church leaders.

After Vichy's promulgation of the Statute for Jews in October 1940, a meeting of pastors was called in Ganges, in the Cévennes, led by Pastor Elie Gounelle, director of *Revue du Christianisme social*, who had been conducting a series of study groups there for the past two years. Jacques Martin, one of the participants, described a day devoted to the problem of anti-Semitism and the Bible. He commented on the need for intellectual preparation among the Protestants: "Interest in helping the Jews did not emerge spontaneously, nor was it part of the memory of the Camisards! A long preparation, a period of reflection came first, often with the opposition of some Protestant theology or other, that considered the Jews and Judaism a simple preamble to Christianity, no more—when it was actually a large spiritual issue on which was grafted, from 1942 on, the problem of saving human beings."[24]

Religious and National Identity of Refugees

On September 20, 1940, Toureille received a letter from W. A. Visser't Hooft, director of the WCC, saying that they were very happy to have Toureille coordinate aid to refugees in Vichy, and pointing out the double difficulty of dealing with the Vichy government and the WCC's lack of funds. To cope with the latter, they would appeal to the Americans and, if funds are obtained, intend to concentrate them on aid to "Christian refugees."

Visser't Hooft's emphasis on "Christian" and "Protestant" refugees in this letter was probably accurate concerning WCC intentions in the fall of 1940, but the needs of the oppressed Jewish populations in France, both refugee and native, soon overwhelmed this restriction on aid, particularly for the people like Toureille, working at ground level. Immediately after Vichy had promulgated the Statute for Jews, 40,000 Jewish foreigners were interned in the southern zone, at Gurs, Noé, Récébédou, Rivesaltes, Brens, Rieucros, and Les Milles. Although Toureille was put in charge of 12,000 Protestant refugees and camp internees in Vichy France, the vast majority were Jewish refugees who were aided through a Protestant cover.

The question of who Toureille's parishioners were, officially, was further complicated by the fact that so many of the German refugees were of mixed religious orientation—some born Catholic or Protestant but married to Jews, who could also have converted to their spouse's religion as recently as 1940 or after they were put in the camps. Such recent conversions were suspected, reasonably, of being for the convert's own protection. But Toureille, throughout his Chaplaincy, took them all seriously as part of his pastoral charge, fueled by his lifelong, self-imposed duty to build the Church through evangelism.

In his October 16 letter to Toureille, Freudenberg expanded the definition of those whom the WCC should be aiding: Although one of their main working pastors had been concerned only with the "non-Aryan refugees," the organization, from the ecumenical point of view, should also be responsible for the Czech Protestants, refugees of other nationalities, and the "German Aryan refugees," such as the Spanish Civil War veterans being held in camps. He asked Toureille to further refine the categories of refugees who needed help, and to give him approximate numbers.

A great hindrance to their efforts, Toureille wrote to Freudenberg on November 7, was the constant movement of refugees from one camp to another and the frequent establishment of new policies toward refugees and internees by the Vichy and German authorities. He felt it important that their aid be extended not only to German refugees but also to "Czech, Polish and others."

On November 25 Toureille wrote a long report to Freudenberg in which he insisted on a new point that was probably in response to a request from Freudenberg: "Since my appointed work in the camps is to help Protestants and the coordination among us is now effective and cordial, it would be better if you do not ask me to take on Jews or non-Protestants. The Jews have excellent associations, remarkably organized and effective." He also insisted that Freudenberg not quote him, Toureille, as the source of this view, until the Committee of Nîmes had approved his report. He added that his colleagues on the Committee had been respectful of his work and had sent him several times to visit the camps. He found the meeting of the Committee to be positive—"a new stage in our work"—so all the more reason not to interfere with the activities of the Jewish associations.

In these first two years of the war, it must have seemed most efficient to the aid organizations to focus their activities on their own constituencies so as not to overlap funding appeals, emigration requests, and badgering of authorities. Very few of these organizations, if any, guessed, in the winter of 1940, at the virulence of the anti-Semitism among the Nazi authorities and its power to stir the same reaction among Vichy sympathizers. Toureille did know of such views within Germany, from his experience in the World Alliance conferences on minorities and his writing on the subject in the late 1930s. But, like his colleagues-in-aid in 1940, he could not have imagined that a policy of extermination of a people would or could be carried out in France.

On December 5, 1940, Freudenberg replied to Toureille's November 25 letter, treating the issue of whether Jews should be included on their lists. He agreed that the Jewish aid organizations should take care of their own. However, the demand for help was so urgent among the refugees, especially those from Germany, that there was no time to ask particulars of background and religion, which were often complicated by cases of Jews with Christian parents. Toureille, therefore, would continue to get lists with Jews on them. In addition, the Jewish organizations had not been active at the beginning of the war, another reason that Freudenberg stretched his categories of those needing help. But, he noted that he intended to work out a better division of aid according to religious identification, by coordinating more with other aid organizations.

Emigration and Liberation from the Camps

Concerning emigration, Freudenberg advised Toureille, in an October 16 letter, to encourage the camp commandants to issue passes and leaves to the internees so they could contact their consulates. On the difficulty of the refugees' obtaining exit visas, he pointed out that, after visiting Berlin and consulting with authorities in Berne, he was convinced the German authorities had a strong desire to speed up emigration of refugees. He advised Toureille to get this message across to the Vichy authorities. He had been told, in Berlin, that Germany had no interest in taking back masses of refugees from France—"they say they are well rid of these people and want them to stay out." Freudenberg added that the Dominican Republic had been mentioned as a place of settlement for the refugees, and they should prepare for that possibility.

Freudenberg wrote on October 23 that, for one major issue—finding a place to which the refugees could emigrate—appeals were directed particularly to the United States and through the American agencies of the YMCA and the American Quakers, but also to Sweden, the Dominican Republic, and Ecuador. Conditions of payment for emigration were complex and had to be negotiated through layers of bureaucracy. These proposed host countries imposed various conditions. Ecuador, for example, preferred Christians to Jews, and they wanted farmers, industrial specialists with capital, and technicians rather than small businessmen, doctors, and lawyers.

On the subject of liberation from the camps and emigration for the refugees, Toureille's November 25 letter to Freudenberg on Committee of Nîmes activities was bleak: even if one were absolutely ready to emigrate, with all the proper papers, one still could not leave, even with money, because there were no departure boats available to refugees. Passage to Spain was very difficult to obtain and very uncertain. Chances were extraordinarily small of being liberated from the camps by any Vichy authority, since the final authority was the German Commission of Control, the Kundt Commission. In addition, the cost to the internee, if liberation were granted by the German Commission, was 12,000 francs for one year of existence outside the camp.

Finally, when an internee was liberated from a camp, he or she was put into a residence that was scarcely better—because in France, food and supplies were being depleted more and more, and foreigners were very much resented in the little villages where they were forced to lodge. "I don't advise, for the moment, trying to make the emigration arrangements you told me about. . . . Please understand about the situation of those who are not in the camps. *Their* situation is just as tragic, they live the life of hunted beasts, prey to despair and to rejection from everyone around them."

At the end of this November 25 letter, Toureille mentioned an experiment that might offer a way to liberate some of the camp internees. If the prefecture of l'Hérault would permit it, he would sponsor a couple and their three-year-old daughter; he would set them up in a small house on his mother's property where they would raise rabbits. If the experiment worked, he would try to extend this kind of arrangement to get others out of the camps and into farms in "our Protestant Midi." He didn't give Freudenberg the details on why he chose this family's case but "it is truly tragic and worthy of all our efforts."

In a December 5 letter, Freudenberg disagreed with Toureille on the hopelessness of finding a way for refugees to be liberated from the camps and to emigrate from France. He claimed to speak from the point of view of an insider with the German authorities: "I will tell you confidentially: You are mistaken about the tendencies of the particular commission you mentioned [the German Commission of Control, the Kundt Commission]. I have known its director for a long time and recently discussed our problem with him. In principle, his mission concerns only the repatriation of German Aryans, although he has also proposed the closing of certain camps not equipped for cold weather. The rumors you have heard about his commission are clearly inexact. Be very prudent and only accuse those who deserve it—I can't say it any other way." To make a test case, he had encouraged one family to find the funds and then ask for liberation. He would inform Toureille of the outcome.

During the December 10 meeting of the Committee of Nîmes, Toureille took an active part in the discussion of how to liberate the children from the camps, arguing that "scholarly obligation" to educate them be the justification. He also urged that the Committee get the aged out of the camps and place them in aid centers.[25]

Toureille wrote angrily to Henriod on December 15 that he was against trying to liberate the internees: "I would be infinitely grateful to you if you could make M. Freudenberg understand that it is perfectly useless to insist on the liberation of new arrivals to the camps. I have told him again and again, but he seems not to understand. All these overtures agitate our authorities to a supreme degree. If we continue to bother them this way, NOTHING will be obtained from them and they will put all kinds of roadblocks in our path. I speak from full knowledge on this issue. Would you please dot the i's and cross the t's for our excellent colleague Freudenberg, with whom, otherwise, I am very happy to collaborate."

Toureille continued, that, contrary to what Freudenberg had just written in his last letter, his [Toureille's] view on liberations was entirely shared by the members of the Committee of Nîmes, including the Jewish groups.

"I say clearly and categorically: the liberation of the new arrivals does not depend on us. And from the French point of view, it is not desired or desirable." The reasons include availability of food and clothing, and national security, since "some of the new arrivals are too imprinted with their German education and lack tact in dealing with the French."

Freudenberg's response to Toureille's letter was one of his own to Henriod. His tone was warm and diplomatic toward Toureille, but did not veer from his original views on the issues Toureille had raised on liberation. "Tell Toureille I am also very happy to collaborate with him," he begins, "and that I am delighted with his frankness, and would like to respond in the same spirit." Freudenberg found it very difficult to accept a purely negative answer on the question of liberation of new camp internees, because it was an incontestable fact that such liberations had happened. There had been a terrible mortality rate at Gurs, which showed that the lives of the older internees were in danger. He could not give up on this point just because the numbers of liberated were few. He therefore begged "our dear colleague Toureille" not to accept the present state of things but to be more flexible when the occasion arose to do something. No one was pestering the authorities—"we are only trying to help."

Organization and Funding: Camp Conditions

On October 16, 1940, Freudenberg's letter to Toureille launched into a long discussion of how they should be organized and what their goals should be. First, he and Toureille would now have to take on the task of making lists of refugees in need, by getting access to the refugees' dossiers, the majority of which, unfortunately, were not being made available by the Vichy authorities. Freudenberg summarized the refugees' needs into two categories—the great distress of being interned and deprived of the means to live, and the problem of where to emigrate. In the internment camps, he noted, people suffered morally and physically, especially from severe dysentery. "The uncertainty about their future creates crises of nerves and leads to a rapid weakening of morale."

He asked Toureille's opinion on placing their work under the auspices of the American Red Cross or the American Quakers, who had funding and could do the most to facilitate emigration of refugees to the United States. He also asked Toureille to clarify the relationship his church would have to his new position with the WCC, particularly since Boegner was a member of both organizations. He mentioned some detailed matters. His office had a large supply of Bibles in German that they could send to Toureille in any quantity he wanted.

During the fall of 1940 Toureille was hard at work developing his lines of communication: reporting to and setting up his administration with Boegner; writing letters and sending aid to the refugees. He had distributed a total of 3,050 francs to refugees on November 7, for example. He wrote to Freudenberg on that date that he would try to find one responsible liaison person in each camp and obtain lists of the internees who were Protestant. He also planned to contact other organizations helping refugees in France, with the caveat that the Vichy authorities were very suspicious of anything that sounded international, and that he was better off saying he represented the Protestant Federation of France.

Ten days later, on November 17, Toureille insisted to Freudenberg (and had Boegner's agreement) that all their organization's funds, books, and supplies sent to refugees in Vichy France should pass through his office rather than go directly to individuals. He explained that he knew the needs in each camp and could distribute the aid the most economically. He trusted that there would be a steady stream of aid from the outside: "I am persuaded that . . . all true Christians in the world will wish to help their brothers who suffer. And I repeat, their greatest present suffering is hunger."

He had great need of Bibles and asked for a minimum of 150 in German, 50 in Czech, and 50 in Polish. He hinted at censorship of mail, advising Freudenberg to be cautious: "Be very prudent in your letters and advise everyone to be so. We are no longer masters in our own country, particularly on this subject. Please understand me on this." As he did constantly in his correspondence, he pleaded for more funds—"The need is immense and urgent. The internees who have been here for a long time (more than the recent arrivals) are hungry and cold." He had also found some uplift in his work: "I am very encouraged in my work with the refugees and I find among them great joy as their pastor and truly beautiful souls. I am grateful to you for having called me to this work. There is nothing else I would rather be doing now."

Toureille was outraged to learn that the Swiss were demanding 40 francs to send 150 Bibles. "With the present distress the internees are suffering, I find it totally abusive that 40 francs must be paid for sending these Bibles. With this sum, we could very well feed some starving stomachs.

The greatest suffering in the camps is from hunger. We have to alleviate that." Incidentally, he continued, we "free" French no longer eat our fill either, above all, the young. "According to the Maréchal," he continued dryly, "the restrictions on food have been imposed on us by the conquerors. All the more reason, then, for helping the camps."

Parallel to the hunger for daily bread, there was "spiritual hunger." If necessary, he begged Freudenberg, "touch the heart" of the Swiss authorities on this subject. "In such circumstances, we can't resort to splitting hairs on costs—this is a case of suffering men, women and children. (These are neither of my own blood nor language. I can therefore talk more freely and forcefully, right?) Above all, it is about the Word of God."

In his November 25 letter to Freudenberg, Toureille asserted that the situation at the camps was worsening: "People are suffering terribly from hunger. Here is the daily diet, told me in confidence: in the morning, 1/4 liter of light coffee; at noon, 1/3 liter of watery soup and 300 grms. of bread; in the evening, 1/3 liter of so-called soup, containing no vegetables, and 20–30 grms. of meat, bone and fat included." There was one blanket for every three persons. Those with money could buy at the canteen, three figs, twelve chestnuts, or two dry biscuits for one franc.

Toureille rejoiced that the Committee on Aid to the Refugees (CAR), also part of the Committee of Nîmes, had decided to donate 20,000 francs, in 2,000-francs-a-month installments, to establish a new canteen at Gurs, with better provisions. The CAR was a Jewish aid organization which, Toureille said gratefully, gave him 1,000 francs to visit the camps. Toureille's tone in the letter grew bitter again. The camp food was not sustaining the inmates. The mortality among the new arrivals from Germany was very high. Those internees who had relatives in Switzerland were deceived in thinking they would be allowed to receive food and clothing from them.

From November 24 onward (the day preceding Toureille's letter), all the material aid sent to Gurs would no longer be distributed—"a decision imposed by . . . you can imagine whom." Those materials and food sent before November 24 would be distributed sparsely, at the rate of ten packages a day, per section. But each section in a camp contained 1,000–1,200 people. Toureille urged Freudenberg to report this new policy to Vichy and to the Geneva office, and to protest for humanitarian reasons. "I repeat: at Gurs people are dying, literally, of hunger. Tell that to the too-happy Swiss citizens."

Toureille listed the Christmas package he would send to those internees on his camp list: note paper, pencils, soap, toilet paper, tablecloth. He would try to get toothpaste, but probably it could not be obtained without ration cards. He instructed Freudenberg to send the Bibles to the camp addressed to himself, Pastor Toureille, with his title—not to send them directly to the internees. "I will tell you why sometime, orally. Multiply the appeals for our dear refugees and internees," he cried. "In the camps (it is an undeniable fact), people are dying from hunger. Those who are at liberty (!) are all candidates for internment. Try to move our good Swiss co-believers and others. In the face of such distress, it is impossible to be indifferent."

On December 5, Freudenberg wrote to Toureille that constant pleas for administrative assistance had to be met and promised to do so. He added that, like Toureille, the main part of his job was to coordinate resources across and between religious groups, made more difficult by the earlier slowness of the Jewish groups to organize and get information. Another problem was that "the Americans, whether Jews or Christians, are very reserved in their reaction to the misery in Europe."

Freudenberg reiterated the difficulties of shipping aid from Switzerland. No exporting of textiles was permitted and all attempts to obtain exceptions for the clothing already collected had been turned down because of fears of future shortages in Switzerland and the needs of Swiss internees, particularly the Poles there. For sending chocolate, cheese, and other foods, a special authorization was always required. And the maximum amount of goods that could be sent per month, per sender, was two kilograms. However, Freudenberg was able, with much difficulty, to authorize the sending of seventeen Christmas packages for the refugees outside the camps and seventy to eighty for the Camp of Gurs. The matter of delivery of Bibles, hymnals, and religious texts was urgent: Toureille should follow up on this, including whether the necessary duties have been paid on the French side. Freudenberg would check with the YMCA on the sending of Swiss newspapers and illustrated magazines, much in demand at Gurs—with the caveat that one needed to take "political precautions" on this.

"Don't be too hard on our Swiss friends," he said to Toureille. "I have collected around 5,000 Swiss Francs now and people here are being flooded by appeals from all sides. Two parishes alone have given 800 SF each. We are working hard on this."

A new issue was that of the refugees who had enlisted in the French Foreign Legion at the beginning of the war. Most were now being held in forced labor camps in Algeria, in deplorable conditions, while others had returned to France. Freudenberg closed, "I rejoice in our collaboration, that will grow closer and closer, I'm sure of it. And when this work almost overwhelms us, let us think together on 2 Corinthians 4, 1 ['Therefore, seeing we have this ministry, as we have received mercy, we faint not.']."

In the minutes of the December 10 meeting of the Committee of Nîmes (presumably written by Toureille as secretary), the same issues of help to the refugees were discussed.[26] Lowrie proposed sending to the U.S. State Department a report and request for aid to the camps. The letter—and there is no evidence in the minutes that this letter was actually sent—gave a clear picture of the situation as the Committee saw it at that time. It described the camp population, estimated at 60,000 in the Unoccupied Zone, as non-French and "unwanted in France," including some Spanish Civil War refugees, some aliens interned at the outbreak of the war, and some foreigners rounded up by French police after having fled from the Low Countries and Northern France in June 1940.

The letter identifies as Jews only the "approximately 7,000 German Jews recently forced into exile from Baden and the Palatinate," although later historians have identified almost three-quarters of this camp population as Jews, at the end of 1940.[27] "It must be made clear that the majority of these people are of excellent social standing in their own communities and many of outstanding intellectual capacity and achievement," the letter continued. But the camp conditions were so primitive that "unless adequate help can be given soon, thousands of these unfortunates, most of whom are interned only because French authorities are unable to support them in any other manner, will die before the winter is over." Only a government, added the letter, could provide the scale of assistance needed, and the Committee could guarantee that aid to the camps would not filter into the French national economy, now controlled by the enemy.

The prediction of thousands dying turned out to be accurate. Thousands did die during that first winter (in Gurs alone, more than 1,000),[28] when international aid was nonexistent or reluctant, including that from the U.S. government.

In a letter to Toureille on December 12, Freudenberg remarked on the specialness of Christmas celebration for Germans, his compatriots, and asked Toureille to "be patient" with their demands in the camps at this time, "a unique occasion for raising their spirits and maintaining morale. . . . You will see that after Christmas in the camps, everything done for the internees will leave a deep well of gratitude."

Taking into account the importance that Christmas celebration held for Germans, Toureille wrote to Henriod on December 15 that the requests of the camp internees were still unrealistic: "I know many French families who will not have everything that some of the internees would like to have, in this sad Christmas of war." The Christmas wishes of the Gurs internees had, "let us just say simply, amused nearly all the French who hear it."

Toureille went on to explain that this did not mean that he did not like his work. "No, I would not want to be doing anything else now. And one forms such strong attachments to these people. I have gained great pastoral joy from them and consecrate myself entirely to them, with all my heart, and work to ease their days in all things."

Freudenberg commented, in a December 20 letter, that it was good advice from Toureille to spread the aid efforts to other camps, since Toureille had just sent him a brief letter, listing forty-two Czech Protestants interned at the Camp of Le Vernet, Ariège, who needed help. But it was precisely the tragedy of the new arrivals at Gurs that stirred the strongest sympathies in Switzerland. He added, "I am grateful that he [Toureille] recognizes that these misunderstandings and frictions, this lack of tact from the refugees, are largely due to the tragic, even grotesque, situation of the new arrivals."

As Toureille's correspondence and reports throughout the war showed, his focus on those individuals whom he was helping and those with whom he was working gave him the heart and energy to continue. This seemed to be the only way to keep going when, later during the war, despair dominated as the numbers of those who needed to be saved grew astronomically into thousands and then into unfathomable millions.

Toureille's Personal Life

In one of his first letters reporting to the WCC on his activities, dated October 9, 1940, Toureille described setting up his home and office in Cournonterral, Hérault, on his mother's property, since it was impossible for him to find a furnished place in Nîmes that was within his budget of 800–1200 francs a month and large enough for his wife and five children.

He asked pardon for the somewhat surly tone of his letter (he had just claimed adamantly that he was in complete disagreement with the Quakers of Toulouse on an unidentified issue.) He ascribed this mood to political events, since the Statute for Jews had been promulgated by Vichy only six days earlier, and to his own temporary illness with intestinal problems and the ill health of his children.

Toureille's activities were carried on in the midst of family difficulties in Cournonterral. On November 7, he again asked pardon for the depressed tone of his letter but explained that his oldest son, Simon, had had a life-threatening bout with diphtheria. "Excuse the anxiety that I have caused you by my silence, but we, in my family, have just lived through days of anguish for our oldest son. My wife is very fatigued by this illness, after the difficulty of settling us in here in our new home."

Marc Toureille recalled the beginning war years this way:

The winter of 1940–41 was the worst of the war. We were still under the shock of defeat, and Pétain was planting the seeds of a shameful collaboration. We had almost nothing to eat except rutabagas three times day. And it was one of the coldest winters in years. My mother was very sick for months. We tried to raise chickens and ducks but had to get rid of them because we had no grain. We couldn't even get hay for the horses and had to tie them up to the ceiling because they got too weak to stand on their own. They had to be replaced by mules or oxen who were not so particular about their feed. Like many other people, we bought goats, three of them. It was my job to take care of them. One, an Alpine named Turquoise, was as friendly and attached to me as a dog would be. When I was hungry, which was a good part of the time, she would let me suckle her. I am convinced she saved my life.

Toureille's youngest daughter, Anne-Marie, characterized both of her parents during these beginning war years and throughout the German occupation:

Truth be told, during the war years our father was a stranger to his family. He was gone much of the time; we resented him for it and it was very difficult for our mother. We always said he helped strangers and neglected his own children. Later I realized the strangers needed him more than we did. Without him many would have died; he did a lot of good, and I am proud of it.

He always carried a portable typewriter with him and spent his traveling time working with the machine on his lap, using mostly two fingers in each hand, typing rapidly and accurately. His printing by hand was impeccable. He was very organized and knew where everything was. He saved the backs of used envelopes for scratch paper. He spoke many languages.

My mother was a good Christian, kind and generous and at times emotional. She raised us well, read her Bible daily. When food became scarce, she locked the meager rations in a closet to save for meal times. We used ration books, waited in lines for hours just for a piece of bread, a head of lettuce or some fish. One Christmas eve, after the Americans arrived [in 1944], a group of Protestant German prisoners had been escorted to our church. While the guard was looking somewhere else, my mother slipped an American candy bar into one prisoner's hand. (From a letter to the author, August 9, 1996)

6

The War, 1941

Chronology

March and April 1941: Germany invades North Africa, Yugoslavia, and Greece.

March 26, 1941: Marc Boegner writes letters of protest to Prime Minister Admiral Darlan, on behalf of the Jewish refugees in France, and to Grand Rabbi Israel Schwartz, in support of the Jewish community.

March 29, 1941: Vichy creation of the CGQJ (Commissariat général aux questions juives; Bureau for Jewish Affairs).

May 1941: The German book *The Village on the Mountain,* is sold in a bookstore in Le Chambon-sur-Lignon.

June 2, 1941: A new Statute for Jews; beginning of registering of Jews and "Aryanization" of the economy.

June 22, 1941: German army invades the Soviet Union. Mobile killing squads begin mass murders of Jews, Gypsies, and Communist leaders.

July 10, 1941: Deportation of a pastor near Paris, Pastor Loewen, because he is a "defender of Jews."

July 1941: Establishment of MACE (*Maison d'accueil chrétienne pour enfants;* Christian Children's Home) near Nice, for Czechoslovak refugee children, by Toureille and D. Lowrie.

September 16–17, 1941: Sixteen Protestant theologians write the eight theses of Pomeyrol: the seventh condemns anti-Semitism and "all statutes separating out the Jews from the human community."

September 23, 1941: Soviet prisoners of war and Polish prisoners are killed in Nazi test of gas chambers, Auschwitz, in occupied Poland.

September 28–29, 1941: Nearly 34,000 Jews are murdered by mobile killing squads, Babi Yar, near Kiev, Ukraine.

September 28, 1941: Pierre Toureille gives a talk in Zurich on conditions in the French internment camps.

October–November 1941: First group of German and Austrian Jews deported to ghettos in Eastern Europe.

December 7, 1941: Japan attacks Pearl Harbor.
December 8, 1941: Gassing operations begin at Chelmno "extermination" camp, in occupied Poland.
December 11, 1941: Germany declares war on the United States.

Internment Camp Conditions

Conditions in the French internment camps were known to the outside world by the first three months of 1941. The *New York Times* published articles describing conditions as disgraceful; several months earlier the Swiss press had done the same.[1] During January and February, every letter between Freudenberg and Toureille was fraught with the urgency the aid organizations felt in saving lives in the camps. "There is little time ... there is violent suffering ... a typhus epidemic for several months," Freudenberg wrote on January 16.

Meanwhile, food in France continued to get more and more scarce. There were rumors that the prefects could no longer authorize food ration certificates. In such worsening conditions, Freudenberg and Toureille suspected that their aid work might be cut off at any time by the authorities. On January 17 Freudenberg saw some hope: "In any case, the continuation of our work is assured for some time further. The negotiations with our Swedish friends seem to be developing positively."

On April 23 Freudenberg reported to Toureille that he had received letters from internees in France describing the conditions in the camps as improving, particularly at Gurs. He reported that relations with the authorities were "harmonious" and the equipping of the barracks, communication between the barracks, and the installation of sanitary facilities were much better than in the winter before. Some older people had even asked to stay at Gurs instead of being transferred to another camp.

Récébédou and Noé were also installing better facilities, although the camp authorities were thought to be too rigid, particularly at Noé. For example, they had forbidden the importation of bread, meat, sugar, condensed milk, oil, lard, butter, soap, and all other necessities. Nearly all the small packages of aid sent from Portugal or elsewhere had been confiscated there, although they were sent through without a problem at other camps. At Gurs there was no objection to newspapers or Swiss magazines, for example, while at Noé they were forbidden.

Toureille reported to Freudenberg on June 19 that there was

dissatisfaction among the internees with a certain chaplain, because he distributed the supplies from their aid packages "practically by the dropperful," appearing at the camp only once a week, at the most, and using no means of transporting the aid packages to the camp, which was five kilometers from the train station. He was old and walked the distance, so he could not carry many packages at once. Toureille suggested delivering the aid to the camp through the local YMCA agent and camp doctor. The doctor was available at all hours to the internees, who increased constantly in number in spite of some departures from the camp.

In that same letter, Toureille wrote that he was touched by reports from Djelfa, a camp in Algeria, that there were eighteen "faithful Protestants" who had organized themselves without a pastor. "I find that profoundly moving and beautiful—there, in that climate, in that environment, given the recent and earlier history of these men [transferred from internment camps in France]."

Toureille went on to mention that the whole group needed hymnals and brief, incisive meditative readings, which Toureille asked Freudenberg to furnish. "These far-away brothers, so faithful, have the right to our most maternal solicitude. Do the impossible for them—in food, clothing, medicine." In response, Freudenberg sent Toureille several books so that he could perform baptisms, marriages and funeral services in German. Freudenberg also included some prayers for occasions but added, "I insist that we not identify ourselves with the text of these prayers. A careful choice has to be made, according to the circumstances [probably referring to whether the internees were Christian]." He added that Toureille also needed to manage the distribution of Bibles donated by the American Bible Society to the refugees in France and make a report to that organization.

On August 5 and 8 Toureille wrote to Freudenberg that conditions in the camps were worsening. He made the point that "we must support, first of all if not exclusively, our brothers in the faith. At the camp at Noé, TB is spreading very rapidly and we have to support them with appropriate medicine. Do this quickly, very quickly. Believe me. By the end of this month it will already be too late for many. I am sending you, today, for the sake of our brothers with TB at Noé, a real, heart-rending S.O.S. Do the impossible for them. They are our biggest charge." Everywhere, he noted, from the camps and from those refugees outside, he got anguished appeals for shoes and clothing. "I am absolutely powerless to do anything about it."

Toureille added that attempts by Vichy to open new camps had fallen through, possibly because camp populations were diminishing, there were no places to create new ones, and the expenses that new camps would entail could not be paid. The Committee of Nîmes had tried to find a way to lessen the worsening conditions in the camps, including proposing that Récébédou become a medical camp for TB and other illnesses. The elderly people from all the camps could perhaps be housed at Noé, where there were nearly 2,000 spaces with no more than 1,300 people there at the time.

What worried everyone the most, however, was the question of proper heating for the coming winter and warm clothing. "That is, believe me, the most somber question and is the one in which foreign aid can help us the most. Nakedness," Toureille added shockingly, "is supportable in summer, and can be tolerated the first days of fall. It is intolerable in winter. . . . And what can you do, on the outside, to help us with finding clothing? It is no good to say, still, that one can do nothing about problems of foreigners. Here, it is getting worse and worse and worse."

On November 4 Freudenberg sent Toureille a Christmas brochure from the WCC, addressed to the French "prisoners of war." He proposed sending 800 of these to the refugees and internees, because they "love to be considered members of one grand ecumenical family, at the side of the prisoners, who are in a similar situation." Toureille's assistant answered that the brochures would be very welcome because the sermons of Karl Barth and Alfred de Quervain, which the Chaplaincy had distributed, had been received with great enthusiasm.

Emigration, Liberation, Escape

At a Committee of Nîmes meeting on January 10,[2] R.-R. Lambert proposed a resolution that was approved, authorizing the French organizations within the Committee to urge the Vichy Ministry of the Interior or of Defense to liberate from the camps all French war veterans—and their families, Toureille added. Joseph J. Schwartz, of the American Joint Distribution Committee (a Jewish organization), raised a question that cast a pall over the ultimate worth of such a resolution. His statement was recorded in the minutes without comment or evidence of discussion: "M. Schwartz remarked that all the proposals are useful, but that the Committee should observe one principle—the camps must not be accepted as a permanent institution."

In a letter to Freudenberg on January 20, it seemed that Toureille could not let go of his argument with Freudenberg over whether they should be pushing for liberation of the new arrivals at Gurs. He repeated that he had brought up the question to the Committee of Nîmes and received a unanimous "no" answer. No one there knew of any cases of liberation, he continued; if Freudenberg knew of some, he should give Toureille the particulars. The Committee members also told him that the new arrivals were almost never given leaves. All this confirmed what he claims he had already concluded: "There is truly nothing to be done."

But according to other reports, in 1941 there was still a door open for refugees to emigrate to other countries, although the bureaucratic procedure for reaching this door was so cumbersome and changeable that many were unable to pass through.[3] The director, in 1941, of the transit camp at les Milles claimed that about 10,000 refugees had found the means to emigrate, although that number was never verified and may have been inflated.[4] It includes those leaving clandestinely after January 1942, when emigration was officially prohibited, through July 1942, when the camps were sealed and mass deportations began. The director claimed that he granted leaves to internees who could reach the consulates and organizations that could help them emigrate, at the risk of their being arrested by the police and returned to the camp.

Concerning Toureille's skepticism that newly arrived camp internees were being liberated by authorities, Freudenberg wrote on January 22 that he would send him a list and advised, "We beg you, on this issue so vital for the internees, to act with flexibility and to not lose sight of the individual aspects of each case." He added later, on February 13, that the WCC knew about requests for liberation from the camps through refugee aid groups and through Robert Weil, a lawyer in Toulouse, who represented Jewish organizations.

The first indication in Toureille's correspondence with Freudenberg that he was involved in helping refugees emigrate is in his February 1 telegram: "Urgent give me all addresses useful to emigrants Lisbon other than Joy [Dr. Charles Joy, Director of the Unitarian Aid Committee in Lisbon]." Freudenberg answered on February 5 that Dr. Joy, a Quaker group, and several Jewish organizations in Marseille and Toulouse were the only contacts he knew of that would be useful to emigrants to Portugal. He had been trying to form a Protestant center for refugees in Lisbon, but it was far from materializing.

On February 4 Freudenberg pressed Toureille to obtain liberation for one camp internee who needed medical help. This case was an indication of how conditions in the camps in 1941 and the near hopelessness of obtaining proper medical care for those who were seriously ill, made liberation a priority for the aid groups. Freudenberg wrote:

[In the Camp of Gurs, in the infirmary] there is a young man who has been seriously ill for a long time, suffering from septicemia, malaria, and jaundice, and who now suffers from heart disease and has had a fever for two and a half months. His parents in Cologne and the office of aid to non-Aryan Christians have written to me several times about him. M. Goldschmidt has informed me that arrangements are proceeding to obtain emergency treatment at a hospital. The latest news on him indicates there is no time to lose. According to the inquiries I've made, means of supporting him are available. I would be very grateful if you would find the way to obtain his liberation and admission to a hospital or sanatorium. I should also add that his parents hope for his return to Holland, but I don't think that would be feasible. Please keep me informed so that I can inform his parents.

On the first mention in the Freudenberg-Toureille correspondence of rescue work that affected Freudenberg personally, he sent a heartfelt thanks to Toureille on May 12 from himself, his wife, and her family, the Liefmanns. Toureille had been looking after a brother from this family, who died in unexplained circumstances, and his two sisters. Freudenberg sympathetically analyzed their present situation:

After the cruel loss of her brother, it is of course very sad that Dr. L. must also be separated from her sister. We agree that Dr. L. most needs care, needs to be calmed and encouraged. I have the impression that she learned much the last time and I beg you very sincerely to give her, in the future, your help and counsel—she will need it. It is a question now of stabilizing her position there. She is being advised by a lawyer in Pau and I hope he will succeed. Meanwhile, we will continue arrangements for her emigration to the United States. But that is still a long road to take. Please help her as much as possible and forget the trouble she has caused us. She is the one who suffers the most.

Freudenberg added that the Swiss refugee committee invited Toureille to respond with more liberality to requests for help. "A very narrow and parsimonious policy has been imposed [by the camp authorities] these last months," Freudenberg continued; with the present amelioration of conditions his committee proposed that Toureille take more initiative.

Freudenberg wanted Toureille to inform the committee on how he was thinking and what he would like to do. They could, for example, continue without risk to contribute to Czech refugees, if Toureille would give them more information with which they could appeal to Swiss donors.

Christian Home for Children (MACE)

Lowrie reported in his book, *The Hunted Children*, that by spring 1941 the Committee of Nîmes agencies were busy removing children from the camps and putting them into homes or children's colonies, with reluctant consent from Vichy. Toureille and Lowrie set up a school-colony for children of Czechoslovak internees in the village of Vence, in the lower Alps north of Nice. Like Toureille, Lowrie had special past ties to Czechoslovakia. Some of his years of service had been spent in Prague, and he was a friend of Tomáš Masaryk, about whom he wrote a book. Through the YMCA as the founding organization, Lowrie and Toureille rented the buildings of a former private school, called their new school MACE (*Maison d'accueil chrétienne pour enfants;* Christian Home for Children), and set up a Czech refugee historian, Joseph Fišera, as director. The "Christian" in the title was a cover for the large majority of Jewish children in the school. One of the conditions for getting permission to set up the school, from the Vichy authorities in Vence, was that the school staff would abstain from all political activity.

Toureille spoke at the inauguration ceremony for MACE, which was announced in the local newspaper, *L'Éclaireur de Nice et du Sud-Est,* July 22, 1941. One accompanying photograph is of several men in shirt sleeves rebuilding a rough-cut stone building against a hillside; and the other photograph shows ten children in bibs sitting in front of a sunny window, around a table set with large soup bowls, watched over by a woman holding the smallest child in her lap. Toureille, in an article written in 1947, described the environment this way: "On one side, the Mediterranean, always blue, under an azure sky. Flowers bloom there all year, the hills are covered with orange and olive trees. The mountains point their summits to the sky, and the Alps stand on the horizon, covered with eternal snow. It is in such a countryside that the home for children was planted."[5]

In this same year, Toureille sent his two youngest children to MACE, Anne-Marie, age ten, and Jean, age six. Both were supposed to live there for a short time only, but Anne-Marie refused to go home and stayed there for almost two years. Conditions had been and remained difficult at home.

Her mother was recovering from a winter-long illness, and the family was cramped together on her grandmother's third floor in Cournonterral. Her brothers and sister continued their schooling—Marc and Francine through the mail, Jean, when he returned home from MACE, at the local school, and Simon, the oldest, at the Collège Cévenol in Le Chambon-sur-Lignon.

Anne-Marie's vivid memories of her first day at MACE were sent to the author in a letter dated July 21, 1996:

The home was located two kilometers from Vence, in the Alpes Maritimes. It was a former children's home or summer camp. It had two swimming pools, two dormitories, a kitchen in a separate building, a dining room, faculty housing, a garden area. Mr. Fišera introduced me to the 39 children all lined up and staring at me, wondering whether I was friend or foe. I was shown to my bed in the girls' dorm, given a black pen and told to write the number 40 on all my possessions. Since I was a very independent little girl of 10, this did not sit too well with me.

I said goodbye to my father and joined the children in a trip to the river. There I was thrown into the water with my clothes on, then ordered by one of the male chaperons to get out without help. I was furious! I managed to make it ashore, looked up at the man, ready to kick him, as he asked, "What would you have done if a German soldier had thrown you in?" That was my first survival lesson. On the way back to the home, I was told to take off my shoes and walk barefoot like the rest of the group—over rocks and dry grass. I was a mess—and was not too crazy about the food either. My first night was horrible and I couldn't sleep, I was so sore physically and mentally.

These two years at MACE were the best years of her childhood, Anne-Marie remembered. The man who had thrown her in the water became her favorite adult, Uncle Karol (most of the adults were addressed as aunt or uncle). Anne-Marie was the only French child there for a while, and she learned Czech quickly; later a French teacher was included among the Czech faculty. Anne-Marie also learned Yiddish, even though it was dangerous to speak it. Her assigned jobs were to tend to the melon and tomato plants and, in the winter, to help the seamstress in the dress shop. All the children learned traditional Czech songs and dances and performed for the local authorities and for audiences in Vence, in exchange for food. Anne-Marie is still strongly tied to her MACE days: "I really loved my new family and I wish I could find some of the survivors. Some went to Israel such as Tante Ida [a nurse at MACE] and my friend Judith with whom I corresponded for many years until we lost touch. Her three brothers emigrated to Cincinnati years ago. Quite a few came to the States long before I did and I hope to find them some day before it is too late."

She kept many photos of her MACE mates, that show healthy-looking children, well fed and relaxed, alone or in groups against backgrounds of stone farm houses and mountains, swimming in a river and a pool, engaged in pillow fights, babies getting bathed in metal wash tubs. But, she added, "I also recall new shipments of children from the concentration camps. They would go through the garbage cans and fight over discarded cabbage cores or vegetable peelings. They were shaved to get rid of head lice, bathed, and given new clothes. Their old clothes were burned." On the backs of the photographs are certain poignant reminders: "Five years old. He watched the Germans execute his parents." "She was deported. Very kind woman." "British father, Yugoslav mother, who died on train." Photographs of herself show a sturdy girl with animated face and smooth dark hair.

Her brother Jean remembers, in an April 2001 letter to the author:

I was at M.A.C.E. for Christmas 1941, Easter 1942 and the whole summer of 1943. . . . All I remember about Mr. Fišera [the director] is that he was a redhead with freckles, like me, and had his office in a little house located at the edge of a ravine. The children were mostly Czech, but had quite varied backgrounds. Many of them were the children of coal miners, some of whom had worked in Belgium. There were also many Jewish children. We were told that we were all in the same boat and had to be discreet about where we came from.

Although there was some effort to maintain a Czech setting, French was the dominant language. One of the things that impressed me the most was how well these children could sing and dance at the same time. Once we gave a concert in Vence. One of the girls sang a solo in Yiddish, but the audience was told that the song was in Flemish.

By mid-July 1941, Lowrie reported in his memoir, there were 80 children in residence in MACE—23 under the age of six, 49 of elementary school age, and 8 children between the ages of fifteen and eighteen.[6] By autumn there were 130 children, and more than 600 passed through the home over the next two years. Lowrie and Toureille also purchased a nearby farm to provide self-sufficiency in growing food and living quarters for those parents who were not interned in the camps. This independent food planting was part of a larger effort of the Committee of Nîmes to provide Czechoslovak refugees with independent food and work sources, which the refugees carried out with great industry and success to the astonishment of the local French farmers.

By the first autumn harvest, some 500 Czechoslovaks, some of whom the Committee had managed to liberate from the camps, were self-sufficient in providing the food they needed for themselves and the 130 children (by this time) settled in MACE. This harvest produced two carloads of potatoes that were shipped to all the Czechoslovaks in Marseille for the winter. All this was from a province in which the locals had asserted that potatoes could never be grown.

Thirty adults, who had lived comfortably in Belgium before the war, took charge of the cooking, clothing, household management, and gardens. Toureille, in his 1947 article, described them as having never experienced shortages before, or waiting in line.[7] They complained often how poorly their present conditions compared to what they used to have, although they had much more than the other French citizens around them, especially in the agriculturally poor region around Nice. Toureille encouraged Fišera to tell them what he and his fellow students were told in Prague in 1922, when making invidious comparisons between present conditions and what they were accustomed to: "And I have a grandmother in China who owns mines of creamed prunes!" Fišera used this expression so often that potential complainers would interrupt themselves with, "I know, I know, you're going to tell me about your Chinese grandmother and her mines!"[8]

Lowrie described the conditions in this school as excellent in its care and training, and in a healthful Riviera climate of clean running water, rich soil, and bright sun: "I had seen some of these youngsters in the camps, undernourished, without decent shelter or any semblance of family life, and threatened with serious moral deterioration by the promiscuity and complete lack of privacy behind the barbed wire. The difference after a short time at Vence was almost unbelievable: rosy cheeks and clear eyes. . . . Records showed that in six months these children had gained an average of thirteen pounds each in weight. Incipient spinal curvature due to the life in the camps was gone; highly nervous, 'difficult' youngsters had become normal."

The man whom Toureille set up as MACE director, Joseph Fišera, combined several of the qualities that were closest to Toureille's heart. Fišera was an ardent Czech patriot, a member of a small but active Protestant minority—the Evangelical Church of Czech Brothers—and an admirer of the traditional liberty of conscience championed by republican France. He fled his native Prague after the Munich Pact of September 1938—"the betrayal of my native land and of France itself," he wrote in a 1992 article.[9] He tried to join the French army but met with a climate of "pseudo-pacifism," as he calls it, preceding the German occupation of Czechoslovakia in March 1939.

Fišera continued, in his 1992 article, to describe his wartime activities. He associated himself with a small, budding resistance group, which, along with his MACE work, led him from a stage of "non-acceptance, of refusal to submit to evil," to active resistance, including armed combat by the end of the war. "Refusal to submit to evil is not a heresy," he commented. "It has to be understood in the same sense as the martyr John Huss was understood, and the great exile and founder of modern pedagogy, John-Amos Comenius, bishop of the United Czech Brothers." Like Toureille, Fišera received the Medal of the Just from Yad Vashem for his rescue and resistance work. He paid tribute to "all the French Protestants, unforgettable and modest, who never turned away anyone who was oppressed, and who enabled us to open our own places of refuge." Pierre Toureille was one of the first names on his list of tribute, along with another pastor, Bovet, who obtained false baptismal certificates to save Czech Jews and their children, "without ever trying to convert them." MACE, Fišera explained, was a refuge for children of all religions, but more than 60 percent were Jewish.

Fišera remembered, with particular gratitude, two Protestant functionaries: the prefect, M. Freund-Valade, who allowed him and his staff to extract dozens of children from the internment camps, and another official who helped him at a camp near Nice where, in August 1942, he had voluntarily followed a group of Jews being taken there in order to save twelve whom he knew. "How can I ever efface from my memory that day when François de Seynes and I fell to our knees in front of Marc Freund-Valade to liberate our friends from Nazi hands, when they were already in the deportation train." Freund-Valade succeeded in freeing four from the group on the death train, including a pregnant woman near term. When Fišera himself was arrested in October 1943 by the S.S., the same prefect, Freund-Valade, freed him, enabling him to flee to the underground with his wife and daughter.

A month before Fišera's arrest, MACE and all its residents had been reestablished in another safe haven. Fišera remembered that after the

German forces moved into southeastern France in September 1943, MACE was ordered out of its residence. It moved with the help of local officials to a chateau in la Creuse belonging to the daughter and niece of a Czech painter, Brozik. Conditions were rougher there, it was higher in the mountains in a more isolated region but nearer the battlefields. Fišera remarked that the move was also made possible by "the active aid of rail-road workers all along the long climb of 910 km toward la Creuse. This proved that, in these tragic years, not all trains are death trains."

The Committee of Nîmes and the World Council of Churches

In spring 1941, the Committee of Nîmes agencies were engaged in clandestine efforts to give Jews passage into Switzerland, often with forged visas to such remote countries as Mexico or Cambodia. And every agency was trying to find places to hide Jews from the Vichy police. Lowrie, in his memoir, described the Committee's participation in the clandestine passage to Switzerland: "Small groups of refugees were es-corted, almost always by night, from station to station toward the Swiss border. For a time the groups were turned over to professional "passers" for the arduous and dangerous crossing of the frontier line, members of the Nîmes Committee paying the very considerable fee these smugglers charged. Later the task became so dangerous that the professionals re-tired from business and our amateurs had to carry on. As the war went on, the Germans were unable to watch the Swiss frontier as meticulously as formerly (although they now used dogs), which made it easier for the am-ateur passers."[10]

Beginning in the same period, Lowrie remembered, the foreign Jews in the Jewish organizations of the Committee of Nîmes began to disap-pear, one by one. "They had not left their posts voluntarily: they had simply been started on the way to Auschwitz as a result of what sometimes seemed like reckless courage."[11] They would all have been able to escape into Switzerland if they had wanted, but felt duty bound to stay on. This was the story, later in the war, of Toureille's friend and colleague-in-aid, R. R. Lambert. Lowrie added: "One of the veteran Jewish leaders wrote me from the children's home he was managing and said that this letter would probably be the last I would receive from him. It was."[12]

On June 1, 1941, one day before a second Vichy Statute for Jews was promulgated (see figure 1, and registration of all Jews and the "Aryaniza-tion" of the economy began, Toureille sent Freudenberg an editorial. This

RACIAL DECLARATION (in compliance with the Statute for Jews, June 2, 1941)

Name: _____

Answer "Yes" or "No" to the following:

	Paternal	Maternal

Is or was your grandfather of the Jewish race?
Does he, or did he belong to the Jewish religion?
Did he convert to another religion before June 25,
1940? Which?

[Same questions for one's grandmothers, spouses' grandparents, and oneself]

Does your case apply to Articles 3, 7 and 8 of the law of June 2, 1941,
because of one of the following:

(Attach certified copies of required documents in each case)

1. Do you have identification as a combattant as established by Article 101 of the law of December 19, 1926?
2. Did you receive a citation in the 1939–1940 campaign?
3. Does this citation give you the right to wear the Croix de Guerre?
4. Do you hold the Medaille militaire or the Legion d'Honneur for wartime service?
5. Are you a ward of the State or a war orphan?
6. Are you a parent or widow of a combattant who died for France?
7. Are you a prisoner of war on leave?
8. Is your spouse a prisoner of war?
9. Are you a parent or child of a prisoner of war?
10. Have you, or your family (if settled in France for five generations), rendered exceptional services to the French Nation?

Place and date of signature: _____

Signature under oath: _____

Note: The original document is in the possession of Marc Toureille.

editorial was signed PAN, without a date or the name of the newspaper from which it was taken. It demonstrated that the political context in which the rescue groups were working was highly unfavorable for achieving liberations from the internment camps. It showed the ugly public and official mood toward the refugees and toward liberations. The popular view was that those who could produce should be the ones to be liberated, like the farmers, rather than those who would only consume; the French needed more food, not more money.

To illustrate this popular view, the editorial writer included a sample letter from a reader: "We are menaced by the hideous specter of famine and we still have to support in our homes more than a million foreigners, half of whom, at least, do nothing to help us and are satisfied to spend money, which no longer interests us since we are food-poor. Can't the government ask these guests to cut short their visit and go to some other country where the food is easier to get and more abundant? What would one say of the father of a family who has trouble feeding his children but who receives several guests at his table each day?"

France has always had to handle the foreigner problem with extreme delicacy, the editorial continued, and in times of plenty France, the land of Liberty, was the place of refuge for the whole world—"All who have worries in their own lands take the train for France." Many of these guests love France and are willing to suffer for her, as several have already proven. But others, the writer warned, love her as the hunter loves quail. To demonstrate the argument that most of these refugees do no work and therefore live like parasites, the writer ended with a story about a rich banker—adding "Jewish, I am sure"—who was arrested trying to cross over "fraudulently" into Portugal. "Why, after living in France over 20 years, do you suddenly want to leave?" the judge asked him. "Because now in France," the banker answered, "no one can conduct business, so I have to look elsewhere." This was a sign, finished the writer, that such people did not love the French for themselves; they considered France a family boarding house.

Toureille warned Freudenberg that the tendency of the aid organizations to push for liberating those who were able to pay is in disfavor. Vichy, he continued, had been very clear about not wanting to fix a standard sum for supporting those refugees who already had some means. Such a figure depended completely on the local prefect and the cost of living in each area. Presently the sum ranged from 1,000–2,000 francs a month. Those who had more were considered dangerous because they would be tempted to do business in the black market. So, he concluded, the "too rich" would not be liberated. The scandals already occurring in this area had raised "justified complaints" from the French population. "I can say to you, categorically: there is not and will not be fixed regulations on this. . . . Each case is examined on its own. In any case, today the tendency is not for liberations—much the contrary!"

In addition, Toureille continued, certain departments had been closed to foreigners—and they were considered undesirables in the cities. No one liked to see them assemble in groups. The most immediate and diffi-cult question was to find a prefect who was willing to sign a certificate of lodging since the restriction on places of refuge was becoming tighter and tighter.

On June 9, Toureille addressed the problem of emigration for the refugees with a tragic assurance: "In the present circumstances, ALL the experts here on this question agree that the problem has become one of the past. Emigration is completely blocked." Emigration ship *Martinique* had been suspended, and the two other boats that had left in May had been ordered to return to Morocco and their passengers were sent to the Camp of Oued-Zem. Another boat bound for Brazil had been ordered back to Dakar. The Committee of Nîmes was searching for Spanish or Portuguese boats to take émigrés to Morocco and then to the Americas. But there were big problems in meeting the constantly increasing rates being charged for these passages, and risks "of all kinds." British immi-gration control had become more and more severe, and the Americans had become terribly tight on admitting foreigners. "Their latest restric-tions, some think here, rule out completely any immigration to the U.S.A."

The minutes of the June 15 meeting of the Committee of Nîmes ver-ified Toureille's points to Freudenberg on the refugees' chances of emi-gration.[13] A report by one of its members informed the Committee that all emigration to the United States would be cut off after June 18, and no new visas would be granted. Those internees awaiting emigration in the em-barkment centers had been turned back to the camps. Some opted to join the foreign labor groups (*Groupes de travailleurs étrangers*, GTE), which the government had recently replenished with more refugees. The Com-mittee was concerned about the conditions under which these foreign workers were forced to live and asked Toureille to speak to Vichy officials about this—in particular about students being drafted for these groups when they should be allowed to finish their studies.

On June 19, Toureille wrote to Freudenberg about a case that encapsulated the problems of a Jewish refugee family trying to get out of France. Toureille's rendition implied the desperation of their situation and his own pessimism about being able to save all of the family.

Dr. K. has asked me today, through his daughter Mme. H., to give you his new address in a military hospital in the Occupied Zone, because he has not yet been transferred to Germany, as was first believed. K. is racially 100% Jewish. He converted to Protestantism at age 17. His former, and real name, was N. He married his first wife when she was only 17 and he, 18. For the above reasons, the marriage had to be held in England, not Germany. K.'s second, and present wife did not know about his Jewish origin, which he never mentioned to her. His son-in-law, H., also Jewish but not baptized, is a refugee in l'Hérault and has been assigned to the G.T.E. at Agde. H.'s wife, and his daughter, 15 years old, who was born mute, still live in l'Hérault. I have arranged for Mme. H. to be cared for by a local doctor and pastor. She is presently without any means of support. Her father, Dr. K., is, for me, a very doubtful case and one on which the greatest reserve and prudence should be imposed.[14]

A new problem appeared in an August 5 letter from Toureille to Freudenberg concerning the internees' taking sick leaves from the camps. In October 1940, Toureille pointed out, there were 54,450 people in the camps, not including those in North Africa. In July 1941 there were 31,198 internees, including the North African group. "This gives an idea of how many have left the camps, and we can assume that 2/3 of that number were liberated or went on sick leave. Of the remaining 1/3, there were repatriations, escapes, assignment to the forced labor groups (GTE), and deaths." Until recently, the camp authorities had accorded these camp leaves liberally to a great number of internees, especially those who could offer money to speed up the authorization.

Understandably in these conditions, he continued, the sick leave privilege was being abused and complaints were coming from both those internees who did not have the money to pay for a leave and from the local French population who "are not always enchanted with sharing their vital space, and food, with newcomers." Now obtaining a sick leave was more difficult. Request for permission had to pass through the Chief Physician of the camp of origin. "There is nothing abusive or abnormal in this regulation that could justify an intervention by our Committee of Coordination," Toureille added, evidently in response to Freudenberg's asking for his intervention on behalf of Freudenberg's cousin, who had fears about asking for medical help. There were several alternatives still possible to those internees who had finished their medical treatment. They could return to the camp, obtain a leave identified as "means of subsistence considered sufficient," probably serve in the GTE, or, finally, agree to try to produce their own food, which was becoming increasingly more scarce. Toureille then responded to several of the individual cases he was asked to handle, including reassurances to Freudenberg's cousin that she had nothing to fear. He wrote her a long letter and advised her to stay in the prefecture where she was when asking for sick leave.

His last paragraph in his August 5 letter to Freudenberg explained the seriousness of his intent to help, with the same slightly defensive tone that he often used with Freudenberg. "I am always at the disposition of your cousin to give her the advice that I think is the best adapted to her case. She can have full confidence in me: I will always give her sure tips and never advise her in a way that would cause the least worry. I thought her July 26 letter was infinitely more calm than the July 22 one. These two dates tell, better than all argument, with what promptness I have responded to her, in spite of the incessant moving around and the enormous burden of my work."

On August 12 Toureille had to respond again to the case of Freudenberg's cousin, who surprised Toureille by her extreme nervousness about asking for medical leave from the camp. There was no question that she had to be reintegrated in the camp when her leave was finished, but because there had been abuses of the privilege of medical leave, those finishing their leaves had to be permitted back into the camp by the Chief Physician himself, in the interest of the truly sick. Toureille issued an indulgent but warning reprimand to Freudenberg: "Your cousin is writing everywhere [for a place in which to take her medical leave]. I repeat, I understand her in view of the company of émigrés in which she moves—but it surprises me. . . . I advise her, and you, that she should go to Aix-les-Bains for treatment. But she must do it quickly, very quickly. And not lose time consulting with everyone. That ends up discouraging the associations that are concerned about these cases, to know that their advice isn't being followed."

The general situation on sick leaves was becoming more ominous. "In fact, there are no longer real liberations. Soon there will only be medical leaves, for the truly ill, and short term leaves, renewable every three months, for those preparing their emigration." Toureille put the burden of help on the Swiss, who could simplify the situation if they would accept a certain number of the refugees from France. The food situation was becoming daily "more tragic" in France. "We have to find a way for the largest number possible to emigrate, in spite of the always unfavorable circumstances for doing it." He could say more, he added, but knew that Freudenberg would understand his reserve.

On November 20 Freudenberg pressed Toureille to see the urgency with which they must all work now to free as many internees as they could from the camps in France, given the ominous deportation of internees from German camps to eastern Europe—which Freudenberg referred to obliquely as "plans already in the works." He also urged Toureille to be more broad-gauged, implying perhaps that Toureille not always act in a strictly legal way, in how he worked this out: "You must, *before* your departure [for camps in North Africa], devise a policy on the liberation of certain categories of Protestant refugee internees. We have been informed that there are plans already in the works and that we may have to make far-reaching decisions immediately. If it is necessary for us, for example, to guarantee that a good 100 people be taken in by rest homes, what will the cost be? Will the State continue to contribute to this placement and to what extent? We hope that you are *in direct contact* on this, with Lowrie, Guillon, CIMADE, etc. You know that we do not shirk our responsibilities. We cannot allow our coreligionaries to be less well placed than others because they lack money. It is clear that we must examine the question carefully before making a decision and must take into account what we can do and what surpasses our means. We urge you, then, to not leave before furnishing us with the necessary information for making a decision. All efforts must be made to get these people out of the camps."

On December 3, 1941, the Committee of Nîmes opened its afternoon session by discussing the chances of liberating certain foreign workers in the GTE groups, particularly those who had some means of self-support. Toureille, appointed delegate to the Vichy authorities, was asked to submit a list of foreign workers who could be liberated. These workers were of special concern for Toureille, prompting one historian to comment, "Toureille . . . fought with ferocity to safeguard the Protestant refugees assigned to the G.T.E."[15] The Committee also determined that it was time for a big push with the authorities on liberating children from the camps and placing them in homes.

Organization and Funding

As the administrative structure of Toureille's liaison with Freudenberg became more solidified, differences in style and priorities among Toureille and his colleagues-in-aid became more pronounced. On January 20, 1941, Toureille complained to Freudenberg that their organization was not working well because requests and distribution of donations were going directly from Freudenberg to the recipients, over Toureille's head. "This is bad," he asserted, "since I am the one responsible for dealing with the civil, military and church authorities for our work here in France." He continued in the same severe tone: "It is rather painful, now, to have to tell you in the most direct manner, that it is undesirable and has been so from the moment my office began, for you to correspond directly (and principally by circulars) with refugees or internees at Gurs or elsewhere. Others have begged me to tell you to send to me directly, all those seeking help. You can give me instructions but they do not want you to give instructions directly to the refugees."

The reason for Toureille's insistence that all distribution of aid pass through him was not based simply on a personal need for control. It resided more in his care not to offend and, more seriously, endanger the refugees. "Please conform to this request if you do not want our work, so crucial, to be compromised or even rendered impossible," he pleaded. He gave as an example of Freudenberg's "imprudence," the sending of calendars that distressed some of the recipients "because of certain details [unspecified] on the calendars [not further explained]." He was more specific on Freudenberg's request for the names of the refugees and internees in France. "A good number" of the refugees were "categorically opposed to being identified, particularly to the Germans." Some of the new arrivals at Gurs seemed to have had no objection to this, but Toureille had now received orders (assumedly from Boegner) to no longer furnish names to Freudenberg, only numbers and locations.

The refugees and internees themselves obviously sensed the danger in being identified as receiving foreign aid. They still hoped the authorities, both Vichy and German, would liberate them from the camps and allow them to emigrate, so they had to avoid offending their captors. In addition, given their recent past experiences in being registered and then rounded up and exiled, they may have felt there was some safety in anonymity and large numbers. The atmosphere produced relentless anxiety among them with suspicions among the pessimistic that they would never get out. "My work continues without respite," Toureille commented somberly to Freudenberg, "and I now reach nearly 5,000 people."

On January 24 Toureille sent Freudenberg a telegram repeating his usual request for funding in the same impatient tone: "To avoid overlap, always consult with me before assigning any funds for France. Continue to cover my disbursements fully each week for all sums spent by me under your instructions concerning non-parishioners. Waiting impatiently for my salary for January." It is probable that "non-parishioners" referred to the Jewish refugees and internees, who made up the large majority of those who needed help and who, as Freudenberg pointed out in an earlier letter, were in such urgent need that there was no time to distinguish them from Protestants. Toureille was complying with the directive to aid the Jewish refugees but still wanted to make a bookkeeping distinction between Protestant and non-Protestant recipients.

Freudenberg responded to this strongly worded letter and telegram as soon as he received it. "Your letter of January 20 has arrived and it convinces me of the crucial necessity of our exchanging personal views," he began, proposing that they meet in the next month. He continued, somewhat testily: "Like you, I do not act as a private individual but as secretary of a committee, of which MM. Henriod, Visser't Hooft and Prof. Keller are the members. We are undertaking the work of the Ecumenical Church, work for which we all carry responsibility as servants of the church. We have had the advantage of fully discussing this work with President Boegner who explained to us very clearly both the general situation and your position."

He then listed the points on which he and Toureille agreed. First, for all general activities and questions, he needed to work through Toureille. It went without saying that they both had to inform each other on all information that impinged on their aid mission. Second, it was certainly necessary to be prudent in direct correspondence with the internees, which should be as limited as possible. He explained that one of the circulars sent by him to the camps, which Toureille found imprudent, was in response to an urgent situation, and he willingly agreed to send no additional circulars.

He mentioned that since the CIMADE representative Madeleine Barot had set up interior communications from the Gurs camp, the aid situation had become more centralized. Third, although Toureille had "justifiably" asked that Freudenberg not bombard the local pastor with requests coming from inside the camp, Freudenberg argued that he had to still keep in direct contact with this pastor to make sure the aid was being distributed fairly to the internees.

He then set out where he and the committee were in disagreement with Toureille, "responding with the same brotherly frankness that I find in your letter":

The members of my committee have authorized me to tell you that it is impossible for us to renounce all direct contact with the refugees. We cannot mechanize work like ours by centralizing it completely. By its nature, it is of an individual character, and very often, spiritual. Let's take some practical examples. One internee asks us to inform a Swiss family of his situation and to ask them for aid. Do we then have to return this letter to the internee and ask him to address it to you first? Or suppose a Swiss or German asks us for information on an internee at Gurs. Do we have to send this request to you? Isn't it more practical to write directly to this internee if his address is known, or ask whoever is in charge of his section at the camp, or ask the CIMADE agents to give us the information? This procedure saves an enormous amount of work and at least three weeks time.

Freudenberg continued by giving more reasons for direct contact between himself and the refugees. If someone sent them money for aid to an internee, they could set up an aid organization based on this donation, in Geneva. A friendly, consoling word directly from Switzerland made a big difference in camp morale. Finally, if their committee were no longer to receive the floods of letters directly from Gurs, speaking of all the misery and demonstrating the marvelous Christian spirit in certain of the camps, they would never be able to appeal to their Swiss friends for money or "move them spiritually," as Toureille himself put it.

Toureille's telegram to Freudenberg on January 27 was an emotional communication, although it puzzled its recipients because of Toureille's elliptical remark about stopping his activities. The gist of the telegram seemed to have been a response to Freudenberg's brief letter, written January 22, in which Freudenberg mentioned Boegner's suggestion that he, Freudenberg, and Toureille meet in Nîmes "to discuss in tranquility the problems involved in continuing our work, particularly reaching agreement on how to use our funds and receive Boegner's approval of our program." Toureille may have seen this as a criticism from his superior, Boegner, of how he was handling his activities. Freudenberg had also proposed several possible dates for his visit. Toureille telegraphed back: "Date doesn't matter. Let me know a week in advance. Will absolutely accompany you everywhere. Cessation of work impossible because it would be a disgrace."

This telegram caused Freudenberg to consult immediately with Henriod and Visser't Hooft, who issued Toureille an invitation to Geneva. Freudenberg wrote to Toureille on January 28, "We hope very sincerely to see you here soon so that we can establish, by common accord, a solid basis for our future work. As for the last sentence of your telegram, where you very justifiably reject the possibility of quitting the work, I have talked with M. Henriod about this but we don't understand what is on your mind. On our side, there is not the slightest question of stopping. On the contrary, we have only begun and we want to consolidate the work as much as possible."

Toureille accepted the invitation on January 31, explaining a little better what he intended by "cessation of work" in his previous telegram: "Urgent meet Annemasse. Extremely important send me duplicates all your correspondence for foreign brother France [*sic*]. Circulars and printed materials all kinds must pass through me. If not continuation of work impossible. Take careful note. Fraternally, Toureille."

The Committee of Nîmes meeting of January 10, 1941,[16] focused on education for children in the camps "in order to create centers of professional instruction for youth to ease their chances of emigration," and vocational training for adults—both kinds were to be organized by ORT (*Organisation pour la reconstruction et le travail*, a Jewish vocational training agency). On January 27 Lowrie reported to the Committee on two meetings he had with the Vichy authorities in charge of the camps. Toureille had accompanied him for the second meeting. The talks were "amicable" and "frank," Lowrie said, and Vichy accepted the proposals to establish education programs set up by ORT, recreation centers, and more aid.

Due to imminent changes at Gurs, Freudenberg wrote to Toureille on February 5, referring probably to administrative tightening or perhaps moving of internees elsewhere. Toureille was to set up lists of aid recipients with individual addresses on them, since Gurs authorities had now forbidden sending as many as fifty packages to one person, as Toureille had requested be sent to the pastor at Gurs. Freudenberg would be sending a total of 100 packages of food and clothing, at a value of 500 Swiss francs; the packages were limited to shoes, shirts, blouses, vests, and underwear.

Freudenberg wrote a set of notes about talks he had had with Toureille on February 13, 1941, in Annemasse (a border town in Switzerland through which many of the refugees from France passed). Since the notes are not dated, it is not clear whether they were written before or after the February 13 meeting, but they show a just appreciation for Toureille's accomplishments and problems. The notes also ask probing questions invoked by Toureille's individualistic style struggling to work within a bureaucracy, in a time of extraordinary crisis.

Freudenberg had no doubts that Toureille maintained an extended correspondence with the refugees, one that was "well appreciated, according to many witnesses." Freudenberg continued: "I know little of his methods and what I would like to call his policy of charity. How does he make connections with the other chaplains, with Mlle. Barot, etc. Does he give them subsidies? Does he contribute to the collective efforts of the different organizations? Does he follow up on these interesting efforts to stabilize the lives of certain refugees?"

Freudenberg mentioned the case of G., a refugee discussed in chapter 5, whom Toureille had set up breeding rabbits on his mother's property in Cournonterral.[17] "How has he distributed blankets, for example? Who helps him in his correspondence and accounting?" This last question led to the suggestion that Toureille was overloaded with work and needed an assistant, who should be hired for him by the Office of Joint Aid (of the WCC, presumably).

Freudenberg continued: Toureille needed to be assured the Swiss Protestants understood that they had to support the work of the Reformed Church of France. "In our propaganda on this issue, which has otherwise been very quiet, we have always underlined the efforts and courage of the French church and the good will of its authorities, and we never cease speaking of the spiritual fruits that such sacrifices bring." Thus, the great importance of continued direct contact between the Swiss and the camp of Gurs, which, for the Swiss, had become "the symbol of this remarkable movement of Christian brotherhood."

Freudenberg intended to review the finances of their organization, including contacts, sources of contribution, and problems in the distribution of food, clothing, and books. These included such issues as getting aid through the tight mail system, getting them into the actual hands of the refugees past the increasingly severe controls of the camp authorities, and encouraging the recipients—through the local pastors—to share the goods with needier fellow refugees. Freudenberg's office had by now widened its net by sending food and clothing to the refugees who were able to emigrate to Portugal but who had no means of support there.

Despite Toureille's continued request that books destined for the camp internees be sent to him first, Freudenberg wanted to try sending them through the local Red Cross, which required no postage. He also wanted Toureille to inform the Swiss refugee committee on what he had arranged for book distribution through the American Bible Society. Then, on Toureille's working with authorities, Freudenberg noted: "We beg Toureille to inform us frankly of the difficulties and the rules that he has to face. Also, Toureille must insist to whoever is relevant, that our work merits full confidence and that this kind of aid, necessarily spiritual and individual, requires a certain flexibility and cannot survive under too much regimentation."

Freudenberg intended to tell Toureille of his own relations with important agents working on refugee relief and to explain that their close contact with him was legitimate and inevitable, and that he had a "pastoral duty" to keep those contacts. He considered the work of "our French friends" as his top priority and would always inform Toureille fully of his activities, but he found it unreasonable for Toureille to expect him to send copies of all his correspondence with these contacts. In general, he found that the coordination of all the aid groups that had occurred so far, especially concerning Gurs, had improved remarkably.

Freudenberg's and Toureille's actual meeting at Annemasse eased Freudenberg's mind about tensions in their communications with each other. "You can scarcely imagine what relief and satisfaction I gained after our meeting and exchange of views with M. Henriod," he wrote to Toureille on February 17. "It was extremely painful to work in an atmosphere of uncertainty and misunderstanding. Now all is cleared up and I feel very encouraged."

In a February 26 letter, Freudenberg asked Toureille the questions most crucial to carrying out their aid work: "What are we to think of this moving of internees? Will Gurs be closed? Little good is spoken of

Rivesaltes. Have many women and children been sent there? The L. family and Mme. B. have written that they are being sent to Récébédou. What are the conditions at this camp? We need examples illustrating the physical situation and how our funds are being used. I know I ask a lot, but, believe me, the continuation of our work depends on this information."

In the letter Freudenberg wrote to Toureille on March 14, he could barely repress his impatience on several administrative points. First, that Toureille cooperate more fully with Mlle. Barot [of CIMADE] on their joint aid efforts: "It seems necessary to us that she always be ready to fill in the gaps in distributing small gifts to the most needy." Next, on the distribution of Bibles and religious books to the internees, Geneva was still waiting for Toureille's word on arranging this through the French Red Cross. They also awaited his arrangements on the sending of goods to internees through Portugal: "We heard that the Portuguese frontier will soon be closed for such mailing. It depends solely on you whether we can still take advantage of this situation."

Next on his mind was Toureille's return of Freudenberg's letters to two French pastors who were helping to distribute packages to the refugees. Freudenberg chastised Toureille for sending him their names without the addresses, which Freudenberg had tried and failed to find out on his own. "This mess shows clearly how incomplete information hinders our work. It is surely not too much to ask that you give us the exact addresses of your principal collaborators." His final complaint was a repeat of the importance of direct reports from Toureille on their work and the kind of aid they were giving the refugees. "All our Swiss donors ask us, with justification, for more complete information on how their donations are being used. The Swiss Aid to Children Victimized by War knows how to attract public interest because it always distributes direct reports from its collaborators." "Excuse my impatience," was his last line, "but we have the impression that the contact between us leaves something to be desired and that the work suffers as a result."

On May 12 Freudenberg sent Toureille the personal story of a Swiss donor with missionary leanings, who was proposing a way to help refugees outside the camps:

L. is a tailor in a large village of the Canton of Berne. Through his hard work he has made a modest fortune. He devotes himself entirely to work in the Kingdom of God. All his earnings not needed for the support of his nice family of four children, are put at the disposal of Christian works. His guiding principle is to help on the Christian front or where needed most urgently, where seeds of Christianity are planted in fertile soil. He has also subsidized the churches of the Diaspora [of Protestants, from France since the sixteenth century] in Eastern Europe and has sent aid, through Paris, to the missions in east Africa, to the Armenians, and to the soldiers from Madagascar now in France. He does all this service with a great independence of character and with great enthusiasm, but—and this is important to know—also with great prudence and peasant sobriety.

This man was most interested in establishing homeless refugees in the countryside. Freudenberg had spoken to him of several cases he might help, and he had donated spontaneously "a beautiful sum" of 4,000 French francs to be given to two French pastor colleagues for the needy refugees, along with letters and photographs from the donor. In return someone from the group being helped had to correspond directly with L. in French or German. Here was an especially strong case requiring direct contact between donor and recipient: L. wanted to know a little of each of their lives, the kinds of things that occupied their time and thoughts, their plans for the future.

Toureille's reaction to L.'s case was not completely positive. On June 1 Toureille wrote: "I am fully convinced that he is an excellent man and I would even say very congenial with my way of thinking, but his letters are very confused and often incomprehensible, for me and for others." It seemed that L.'s pet project of establishing Protestant farming colonies would be opposed by the authorities. There were individual farmers who established themselves in the countryside with their families, Toureille continued, "but we must absolutely avoid all grouping together of so many foreigners." He then suggested they use L.'s donation in several ways, issuing some warnings on procedure. The warnings showed his uneasiness about the Vichy authorities' attitude toward the aid, and he insisted that he must maintain direct control, and hinted that they were being watched:

1. Give 500 Francs a month, for four months, to the Camp of Argelès, for the Spanish Protestant women there who have been shamefully abandoned by everyone—"Mr. L. would be doing an honorable thing for them."
2. Give 500 Francs a month, for four months, to the Protestant women and children at Rieucros, two or three of whom could correspond with L. "At Rieucros our women have been interned for the longest time of anyone—you understand what that means—since November 1939. Even worse, at Argelès the Spanish women have been there more than three years."

3. Several warnings about L.: He should not propose publicly that he serve as intermediary in correspondence; he can do that without saying so, with tact and prudence. He should limit his comments on personally organizing this aid, to his few correspondents, without generalizing. Toureille wrote with passion, "If he isn't careful about this: Watch out! Trouble! And I won't respond at all." And again, "I insist on being in contact with everyone—direct contact." The list continued that L. should not send too much at any one time, to an individual or a family. "That will do no good," Toureille ended.

4. It would be better if L. himself not determine who the recipients of the funds should be. "Those who write the most, or the best, are not always the ones whom we should be most interested in helping. Since I have personal contact with everyone and the means of surveillance and investigation of each situation, I can best advise in full knowledge of our goals."

Toureille's work in the Committee of Nîmes at this time took place within a tighter organizational structure than his work with Freudenberg.[18] The Committee's Constitution of July 1941 included several clues on how it was organized, how it was balancing information that could be made public with information to be kept confidential, and how it was dealing with the Vichy government. The Constitution stated that the Executive Committee was to receive a monthly written report from each group about the work accomplished in the camps. "To the extent that each group wishes, these written reports will be distributed to the whole Committee. Oral reports will be considered confidential." In addition, the Executive Committee considered it "of the essence to inform all the aid groups of all changes about to take place in the camps or by the Authorities."

The only other mention of the Committee's relations with the Vichy government was: "Regarding exterior relations, . . . the Executive Committee, either its several members or its President, will represent the whole Committee when meeting with the French government, civil, religious and military authorities, or national and international organizations."

On September 28 Toureille was in Switzerland for meetings with Freudenberg. While there, he gave a number of speeches on the camps and refugees in France, which had a powerful appeal to potential Swiss donors. The French Consul General in Zurich wrote the following report to the French ambassador in Berne:

The lecture [was] organized by the Protestant Mission and held in Zurich the evening of September 28, at the temple of the French Evangelical Mission. The subject was: "The Gospel among the refugees and prisoners" and the speakers were the French pastor Toureille, chaplain to the concentration camps in France, and Geneva pastor Freudenberg. This lecture was given as well, I am told, in other cities in Switzerland, including Berne. I heard that Pastor Toureille's talk, very eloquent and of high quality, was, in his description of the conditions of the internees, very objective, devoid of all polemics, and inspired by elevated humane sentiments that made a strong impression on the audience.[19]

On October 4, 1941, Toureille attended a top-level meeting in Geneva to discuss the administrative structure of Protestant aid to refugees in France.[20] Marc Boegner represented the Protestant Federation of France, and Visser't Hooft, H. Henriod, A. Freudenberg, and Charles Guillon, the WCC in Geneva. They agreed on the following measures to solidify their organization: (1) The Protestant Federation would form a special committee on refugees, which would make more efficient its relations with Toureille's organization, including appointing a treasurer to control disbursements; Toureille had to make a report to Boegner and Geneva every three months; (2) Boegner would work on division of labor between CIMADE and Toureille's Chaplaincy and insure cordial collaboration between the two; (3) If necessary, Boegner would also arbitrate any problems between Toureille and the pastors working with him; (4) To avoid past late arrivals of monthly aid and allocations to the pastors, Toureille would send these subsidies a month in advance; (5) The WCC Committee for Refugees would send funds for Toureille's work to the Protestant Federation and directly to Toureille himself. The Protestant Federation should send Toureille, monthly, the sum of 50,000 French francs plus 5,400 francs for Bibles.

Further talks with Toureille covered specific issues. These included funds for Christmas gifts and celebrations in the camps, stocking aid for emergencies, working with the Unitarian Bureau in Marseille for sending aid through Portugal, and individuals who needed assistance. Toureille's reaction to the organizational changes, particularly the tighter control of his actions by Boegner and the implication of dissatisfaction with his work, appeared in a letter to Freudenberg a few days later on October 11.

In this October letter, Toureille revealed how much the pressure of his work was grating on his nerves and affecting his ability to work with his colleagues: "It seems to me, in the course of the talk with President Boegner, Dr. Visser't Hooft and Henriod, that no one has the least idea of what our work is here. At other times, this inquiry would have demoralized me.

But now I have learned to deal better with disappointment. Nonetheless, we must better represent what we are doing here, in these very primitive living conditions." He then proposed a certain young man for the new function of treasurer of the Chaplaincy, adding with annoyance, "After what has been said, I am eager to be discharged of these functions that I never sought in the first place." After addressing questions about distribution of aid and information to individuals, he sent his warm regards and thanks to Mme. Freudenberg for having him as a guest in their home and reiterated his warmth of feeling for Freudenberg as his brother-in-service.

On October 30 Henriod, at Freudenberg's urging, wrote a gracious and placating reply to Toureille's October 11 letter. He expressed his own gratitude to Toureille for coming to Geneva and making such a "profound impression" on those listening to his talks on conditions in southern France. "We are still reaping encouraging and material benefits from this visit." Henriod then explained that he, himself, was not satisfied with all that was said in their meeting, but since Toureille had not reacted more clearly to the criticisms at the time, Henriod had not protested, since he knew little about the details. He added, "For my part, I think I have truly understood the very difficult conditions of your work, which make me admire the results that much more, as I have repeatedly told M. Boegner and all others concerned."

He felt sure that Visser't Hooft, the Director of the WCC, felt the same. He then suggested, in what was probably his key conclusion from Toureille's letter, that the offended tone had been directed at Boegner, and explained that because Boegner was so busy, he did not realize that "certain past difficulties" had been cleared up. "In any case, I am persuaded that whatever was said was only for the sake of making the work more effective and harmonious and to help you."

That led him to urge Toureille to collaborate more closely with CIMADE, an issue on which Toureille had been dragging his feet. Henriod reminded him, "You have publicly praised the work of CIMADE and, once again, your activities under these particular conditions seem to me to be that of a true Christian. But have you perhaps overestimated the repercussions of these past misunderstandings or their causes?"

At the end of 1941, on December 23, Toureille's letter to Freudenberg demonstrated how much his responsibilities had accelerated. He had to postpone his trip to camps in North Africa for two reasons: He hadn't been able to obtain a visa, despite interventions from such highly placed people as Boegner; and because of Lowrie's departure [Germany declared war on the United States ten days earlier], Toureille had to assume permanently the presidency of the Committee of Coordination of Nîmes, "a truly heavy charge." He also had to be available for consultation by Vichy officials, in particular both the Inspector-General of the camps and his chief officer.

That same day Toureille sent Freudenberg a second letter reporting on changes in the organization of the internment camps, according to the Inspector-General of the camps, André Jean-Faure. As Toureille commented skeptically, the information was disturbingly incomplete, lacking precise dates. Eleven hundred old or sick internees would be sent out of Gurs (where there were only 4,750 people at that moment) to three other areas. The 250 tubercular internees taken to Noé and Gurs would be sent to a sanatorium where there were already some 30 tubercular patients from the Gurs area. Other smaller camps would be set up in the Drôme area. Those in the camp of Les Milles would be emigrated on neutral-country boats, if they could still be found. Some internees, nearly always those "judged difficult or dangerous," would be sent to North Africa.

Toureille's conclusions from this report were surprisingly upbeat. Perhaps he wrote the letter under official scrutiny. "It is not at all a question of 'liberations,' but rather of closing the large camps and creating smaller camps better installed, where the discipline will be paternal and the food and lodging better, in spite of the hard times and the difficulties in procuring materials. . . . In sum, a new camp policy is developing. It seems to be having excellent results and to be justifying the hopes placed in it."

Spiritual Resistance

In March 1941, Pastor Jean Cadier was exhorting his Montpellier congregation to remember and emulate their Huguenot history: "We are weak, few in number. But the history of the French Reformed Church is there for us to remember—that hundreds of men, organizing in secret resistance, amidst persecution, were able to hold back the royal troops, brave the persecutors and save freedom of conscience and worship. How many Camisards were there against 80,000 royal troops? A little more than 2,000. But they were organized spiritually in an extraordinary resistance. The hours we are now living in the history of the world match in gravity this heroic time in the Desert."[21]

As a product of this history, Boegner wrote in that same month one of

the most widely known documents of Protestant protest against the oppression of Jews in France: his letter to the Grand Rabbi of France, Israel
Schwartz, on March 26, 1941, on behalf of the Protestant churches. It became the first public move in defense of the Jews among the churches of
France. Boegner, however, had not intended that the letter be made public. He had been pressured for months by some of his church members to
intervene with Vichy authorities on behalf of the Jews, but his preference
was to keep a reserved manner and speak quietly to officials on an individual basis. His letter, however, was disseminated widely and, in an ironic
twist, published by an anti-Semitic journal in the Occupied Zone in an attempt to smear Boegner as a traitor.

Boegner's letter to the Grand Rabbi demonstrated some of the ambi-
guities in the French Protestants' relationship to Jews. Boegner made a
distinction between the native French Jews and the Jewish refugees flooding France from Germany and Eastern Europe, who appeared to be creating resentment and undue burdens with their hurried naturalizations
and need for aid. This distinction sat uncomfortably with the links he drew
between the histories of religious persecution suffered by both Jews and
Protestants, each as a people. Boegner's protest also sat uncomfortably
with his own religious/political ethic on justice for all peoples.

Boegner sent a second letter on the same day to Admiral Darlan,
France's vice premier, who was about to appoint a high commissioner
for Jewish affairs. This letter made the same distinction between refugee
and French Jews, asserting that the "problem" with the refugee group
should be resolved "with respect for persons and . . . justice," and that
the second group be absolved of the requirements of the Vichy Statute
for Jews. Boegner's distinction between the two groups of Jews was not
unusual at this period. French Jews by and large made the same distinction, considering themselves primarily French rather than members of a
peoplehood without national boundaries.

In May 1941, a small book appeared in a bookstore in Le Chambon-
sur-Lignon, which inspired many French Protestants beginning to take
part in what was later called the spiritual resistance. Titled *The Village on
the Mountain: Portrait of the Church Faithful under the Nazi regime, a
True Story*, the book tells of a Protestant village in the mountains of southern Germany, Lindenkopf, whose pastor resisted the Nazis' attempt to
dominate mind and spirit and was arrested by them at the end.[22] The
whole village was moved by his example and vowed to continue his spiritual resistance.

The mountain setting for this story—the mountain as a symbol of spiritual strength and the bonding of the whole village in resistance—hit a special chord with those French Protestants in the predominantly Protestant villages in central and southern France who were still tied strongly to their Huguenot history. In mystical language, in the tone of a religious parable, the townspeople spoke to each other at the end of the story: "We see how big and powerful is the Third Reich and how small and poor is our church, and how it will become still poorer. But we have heard. Our ears have been opened and we have heard. We can no longer forget, and whoever among us does forget, will not find peace, because the word that was heard will haunt him. We pray for our pastor . . . for his wife . . . and for ourselves: 'God, we believe. Come help us in our lack of faith!' Our village of Lindenkopf is on a mountain. Amen."

Originally written in German and published in German and French in Switzerland in 1939, the book had first appeared in a religious journal in Le Chambon in April 1940, before becoming available in a bookstore there the next year. It was also translated into English, Danish, Dutch, Norwegian, and Swedish. Out of the many war stories of how the book affected people, there was one told by a pastor in southern France, in Grasse, who, in November 1943, was confronted by two German soldiers in anguish for the crimes committed by their armies and their destruction of the Jews. The pastor was suddenly reminded of *The Village on the Mountain* as he listened to their manner of speaking, then was joyful at their acknowledgment of their faith in that same church as in the story, the Confessing Church of Germany.[23]

In September 1941, an important meeting of Protestant pastors and lay people was called at Pomeyrol by the Dutch director of the WCC forming in Geneva, Visser't Hooft, with the purpose of preparing the French Protestant Church for spiritual resistance. The outcome was bold and courageous: participants drafted what they called the Eight Theses, dealing with ties between the church and the state, limits to obeying the state, and respect for the individual. The seventh thesis clarified the ambiguous attitude toward Jews that emerged in Boegner's letter to the Grand Rabbi. This thesis raised "a solemn protest against all statutes rejecting Jews from the human community." It was the only public condemnation by Christians of the second Statute for Jews during this period.[24] The eighth thesis, phrased with religious fervor, condemned collaboration: "The church considers it a spiritual necessity to resist all totalitarian and idolatrous influences."

The effects of the Eight Theses were large. The meeting participants distributed them throughout the southern zone, Visser't Hooft published them in Geneva, and the Faculty of Theology at Montpellier helped build a small group of resistants who based their actions on the Theses and who would later make up the "maquis of theologians" in Isère during the summer of 1943. The Theses even made their way, the next year, to theology students in Paris, but there was no public support from Boegner nor any privately written assessment. He was standing by Pétain at this period and, at a meeting of church groups in September 1941, he urged stronger support for the *maréchal* and those who worked with him. As one historian pointed out, with the Theses of Pomeyrol, Boegner could no longer ignore the growing tendency among the church leaders to take a clear position on Vichy, particularly its hostile policies toward foreigners, especially Jews.[25]

Religious and National Identity

In his letters to Freudenberg, Toureille still referred to the internees as "our parishioners" and "Protestants," although camp statistics later showed that by June 1941, almost 80 percent of the internees in the southern camps were Jewish.[26] Toureille was well aware of this but presumably constrained his language to the limitations arranged with the Vichy authorities. He also continued to analyze the camp situations by telling stories about individuals there and how they mixed with others, particularly on issues of religious and national identity. For example, in a June 19 letter Toureille took an active part in the case of a Madame Z., since it involved the whole atmosphere of the Récébédou camp.

In taking up the case of Mme. Z., Toureille pointed out the general situation at Récébédou: since none of the three pastors assigned there knew German, and because there were also Spanish Protestants in the camp, "our Protestant community at Récébédou is divided and that is, I must say, a cause for great worry and distress. Because if 'the children of light' are divided, in what way are they superior to 'the children of the world'?" "For the first time," he added, "I, as Chief Chaplain, did not appoint someone in charge, and the troubles grow from there."

The Protestant community at the Récébédou camp had appointed their own directors, including Mme. Z. Toureille defended her: "Mme. Z. has several advantages for us: she has lived a long time in France, is well known by the authorities and therefore, will be important in this group as long as a camp exists in France. We still want, for a little while, to be masters in our own land."

The pastors in the camp had confidence in Mme. Z., he continued, and it was not exactly true that she liked to dominate. She did have "a sense of order and of how things should be." She was, without doubt, from one of the poorest backgrounds at the camp, so it was understandable that she would want to "redress certain wrongs." Another internee, V., was also appointed as director of Protestant activities and wanted to consider as Protestant only those who actually practiced the religion (presumably leaving out the Jewish internees, who were seeking solace in the one intellectual and spiritual outlet available). V.'s attitude struck Toureille as not surprising, even if the concept behind it was too severe for these circumstances. Yet another internee, Mlle. D., rendered certain services to the camp community, particularly putting on biblical tableaux for their group sessions.

At the camp at Rivesaltes, the chaplain held services every Saturday at 4 PM for forty to fifty people, a dozen of whom were *sympathisants* (which could mean fellow-believers, or more probably non-believers, Jews, who sought out the services for their spiritual tone). Toureille added that there were presently twenty-eight "Protestant" children at Rivesaltes, from the ages of one month to sixteen years, belonging to five nationalities. Their religious instruction was therefore immensely difficult to address, and Toureille intended to adjust to the circumstances on his next visit. Any supplies and aid that the Swiss office could send, in addition to children's books, religious or not, would be very welcome at the camp, particularly dictionaries in German, Spanish, and Polish. Toureille proposed sending Freudenberg a list of children for Swiss sponsorship, for which he would first need an order from the Geneva office, under whatever pretext they might figure out.

He added: "You have absolutely no idea of the enormity of this work and the fatigue I feel. I would need three full-time secretaries to get out quickly a list like the one on the children. So you should understand my delay in getting it to you."

Toureille seemed irate, in an August 5 letter to Freudenberg, at what must have been a comment by someone in Geneva that the Protestant children refugees were not as needy as "the others" (probably meaning the Jewish children). His insistence on not making a special case of the Jews showed up in several ways during this year, including statements in several letters about "taking care of our own." For example, on August 10 he sent a list of seven names to Freudenberg and said, "[These] are not Protestant. I don't see, therefore, any reason that we would have to support them." This remains a puzzle, because plentiful testimony from those he rescued shows that, from the beginning of his rescue efforts, Toureille realized that those who most needed his help were the Jewish refugees. And he certainly realized long before 1941, in his international church work in the 1930s, that Jews would be made a special target for persecution by the Nazis.

One possibility is that, since his letters to Switzerland were consistently opened by Vichy authorities, Toureille was trying to conceal the fact that he was helping Jews by insisting that only the Protestants were his charge. Since he was trying to save Jews by claiming they were Protestants (by recent conversions, with false baptismal certificates, for example), he may have been trying to protect that group of recent converts by insisting they were now Protestants. Another possibility is that, in 1941, he still believed that the Jewish rescue agencies that he worked with on the Committee of Nîmes could handle the needs of the Jewish refugees, and his job was to cover the needs of all groups equitably.

In any case, Freudenberg's more open letters about liberating Jews from the camps and helping them escape the authorities continually made Toureille nervous. He frequently reprimanded Freudenberg to be more discreet and to keep his language more in line with the language Vichy permitted the rescue agencies. And if, in 1941, Toureille thought the Jewish rescue agencies could take care of their own, the winter of 1941–42 soon clarified for all rescue groups how desperate was the situation in the internment camps and how dark was the future of the majority of the internees—because they were Jewish.

By November, Jews still in Germany and Austria had, for the past month, been deported by the Germans to ghettos in Eastern Europe. On November 15 Toureille reported to Freudenberg that, by definition of his role as Protestant chaplain, his hands were legally tied in extending help to seven Austrians at the Camp of Noé. "Only one of them is Protestant," he explained, "and his name appears on the list of those who receive aid from us, at Noé. I don't see what more we can do for him, his situation being that of all our other parishioners there. The other six Austrians are not on the list of our parishioners and I cannot do anything for them.

Those in charge, and the pastors don't consider them to be Protestants. What more can anyone ask of us, then, on this subject?"

Maintaining the same formalistic language, he offered a way around the legalities that strongly implied obtaining false papers: "If [these men] are truly Protestants, they should write to me and give proof. An inquest will follow and the conclusions will be communicated to you." Freudenberg's answer was that Toureille's proposals were too unwieldy for the present crisis.

Toureille's Personal Life

Toureille's first communication with Freudenberg in the new year, on January 2, 1941, four months after they began their collaboration in aiding refugees, was a brief telegram: "My wife very seriously ill." A few weeks later he commented in a letter: "My wife is getting a little better but her state is *very* grave. It is a drama directly related to the work I am doing with the refugees and foreign internees. We have been on the frontier of death. Christmas and the New Year will leave frightful memories. I have rarely lived such sad moments."

On August 5 there was some good news: Toureille had finally succeeded in finding an apartment of six small rooms, in Montpellier, for his family. It would be more economical than living in Cournonterral because he could save the fifteen kilometers he always had to travel by bicycle, day and night. "This traveling had become a hardship for me, because of the increasing difficulty in getting enough nourishment." His new apartment for his family was midway between the Faculty of Theology (where his two assistants would get their meals) and the train station, "which is my real center of operation." Now he would look for office space.

On August 17 Toureille reported bad personal news: "At the last moment, the Military Authority, still all powerful here, has requisitioned the apartment that I had rented, for one year. I have to start all over again. Everything I have written to you on this subject is now null and void. We have to start looking again, and wait. In spite of this setback, we aren't taking it too badly. We hope to have found a new apartment before the beginning of October—for the education of our children. Our oldest will be taking his baccalaureate this year."

On August 26 a short telegram to Freudenberg announced Toureille's one-day visit to Geneva the following day. He was taking his son Marc, suffering from excessive loss of weight, to live with a local family under the auspices of the Red Cross.

On October 11, Toureille mentioned his family again: "We finally have hopes of finding an apartment in Lunel, a small town on the railroad line between Nîmes and Montpellier. The great advantage for me is that I wouldn't have to do the 17 kilometers by bicycle before and after each trip that I do now. Also, there is a school where our children could take regular classes. But since my wife is more and more fatigued and losing weight, we have decided to leave our daughter Anne-Marie in Vence for this winter, and to put our oldest son in Le Chambon to prepare for his baccalaureate. All this imposes financial sacrifices on us, but it has to be done."

He added that his staff had been reduced due to illness and other demands, but "we continue to assume a task that is very much beyond the strength of two men to accomplish."

7

The War, 1942

Chronology

January 20, 1942: Fifteen Nazi leaders meet at Wannsee, Berlin, to discuss the "final solution to the Jewish question."

June 1, 1942: Jews in France and the Netherlands are required to wear identifying stars.

> **May 29, 1942:** All Jews from ages six to eighty, in the Occupied Zone of France, are ordered to wear the yellow Star of David.

> July 1, 1942: The Prefect of la Drôme reports that thousands of Protestants from Lyons and surrounding areas intend to campaign forcefully against obliging Jews in the Occupied Zone to wear the yellow star.

> **July 16–17, 1942:** Thirteen thousand foreign-born Jews rounded up in Paris, confined in *Vél' d'Hiv'* (Winter Stadium).

1942: Nazi camps, in Poland—Auschwitz-Birkenau, Treblinka, Sobibor, Belzec, and Majdanek-Lublin—begin mass murder of Jews in gas chambers.

> **August 6–16, 1942:** Roundup and deportation of refugees from the Camp des Milles, near Aix; Pastor Manen has large role in saving people.

> **August 18, 1942:** Boegner and Cardinal Gerlier meet and agree to each write a letter to Pétain protesting turning over foreign Jews to the Nazis.

> **August 19, 1942:** Donald Lowrie, Committee of Nîmes, informs Boegner: "The situation will get worse—only the intervention of the Christian churches will alleviate it."

> **August 25–26, 1942:** Large roundups of Jews, southern zone.

> **August 27, 1942:** Boegner letter of protest to Pierre Laval.

> **September 6, 1942:** Annual meeting of French Protestants, Musée du Désert, near Mialet, Gard; sixty-two pastors attend; set up system of mountain areas of refuge for Jews.

> **September 16–19, 1942:** Meeting of fifty-two pastors of the southern zone, in Pomeyrol, with head of the World Council of Churches (WCC) in Geneva, W. A. Visser't Hooft.

My brothers, there are times when God says nothing. There are times
when, in the face of the unleashing of evil forces and the unrolling of inevitable events, we find only silence from God. A terrible silence that confronts faith with its most formidable test. A silence before which we must
supplicate and hope without cease.

    —Pastor Jean Cadier to his Montpellier congregation, May 1942

Above all, I beg you, don't makes heroes out of my wife and me. We did
what we did, because we could not have done otherwise! That's all!

    —An unnamed pastor-rescuer

Organization and Funding

In the first Committee of Nîmes meeting of the new year, January 14,
1942, Donald Lowrie was back in France and presiding.[1] Although Toureille's letter to Freudenberg of the month before indicated otherwise,
Lowrie was probably able to reenter Vichy France as a representative of
international aid. This was an important meeting for the Committee. The
guest was Commandant Doussau, Vichy Inspector-General of the GTE,
the foreign workers groups. His presence set the tone of amelioration and
cooperation, which the Committee was trying hard to maintain with the
Vichy authorities. The minutes hint at the tension created by this requirement to be diplomatic, mixed with the Committee's need to push mightily on the issues crucial to its aiding the refugees.

Dealing with Vichy

Toureille reported on his meeting with the Vichy Inspector-General of
the camps and internment centers, André Jean-Faure. Toureille and his
colleague, Father Arnou, were received by Jean-Faure "in the warmest
and most cordial fashion," and all the members of the Committee were invited to pay a visit to the camps. Jean-Faure had visited the camp at les
Milles and was "enthusiastic" about what he saw. At Gurs, he planned to
take down sixty barracks that were not repairable and eliminate the
barbed wire between the camp sections. These grand plans never came to
fruition. The massive roundups and deportations a few months later virtually emptied the camps, as part of the Final Solution planned in secret
by the Nazis at Wannsee in Berlin, a week after this January 14 Committee of Nîmes meeting.

There were, however, a few pieces of good news from Vichy to the

Committee. At Gurs and Noé, 260 tubercular patients had been sent to a sanatorium, and all children liberated from the camps would receive six to seven and one-half francs a day allocation, to be given by Jean-Faure to those taking care of them. Toureille made some pointed remarks on liberating all French army veterans from the camps and the GTE, urging that Doussau bring this up with Pétain's cabinet—and Doussau agreed. Another issue demanding attention, the Committee members urged, was the transfer to North Africa of much of the camp population. A special committee, including Toureille, was formed to present a list of pressing cases for liberation to Vichy. The Committee members continued to raise those issues on the camps that needed the most immediate attention: opening the French Red Cross offices; setting up better medical services; ameliorating the conditions under which internees were to be transferred from one camp to another; more help from Vichy on providing food and clothing; a dire lack of blankets and bedding.

Commandant Doussau gave a grand exhortation at the end, placing the burden of refugee care more squarely than ever on the shoulders of the aid groups. One wonders what the Committee's genuine reaction was to his speech: "You are making colossal efforts of all kinds—money, clothing, food. But you must constantly renew these efforts. Creating centers that can produce their own means of existence—that is the formula to follow. You could buy some property and create centers for the internees or other refugees who, at the moment, are at the mercy of the police because they have no means."

Donald Lowrie opened the February 25 Committee of Nîmes meeting with a report of his visit, accompanied by Toureille and Father Arnou, to Pétain's office. The meeting continued to reveal the urgency in which the Committee was acting, and their growing desperation in the face of the conditions under which the refugees were living. The purpose of Lowrie's delegation to Pétain was to follow through on the proposals they had aired before Commandant Doussau. Vichy officials had not yet responded to them, except for Jean-Faure's promise to give them the daily allocation for children placed in homes and centers. A list of these children, Lowrie promised, would be sent each month directly to Jean-Faure.

On February 23, 1942, Toureille sent Freudenberg a bold proposal that would vastly increase both his responsibilities and the suspicions against him no doubt already building with the Vichy authorities: he proposed that he organize aid in the Occupied Zone, and that he travel there soon. One of his contacts in Paris had told him of the distress among the refugees there and the lack of funds among the organizations trying to help them. All work would be risky and difficult in the Occupied Zone, he realized, but he added that he and the Committee of Nîmes could study the problem and send Freudenberg some propositions. However, there is no evidence that his proposal ever materialized. He added that some of the families were split between the Occupied and the Non-occupied Zones. Postcards were the only permitted means of correspondence across the two zones, he cautioned: "This is very strictly enforced. Great prudence is necessary. You can't insist too much on this point. You understand, I'm sure."

The GTE

Toureille told the Committee, on February 25, that the situation for those in the GTE was worsening. He estimated there were about 55,000 to 60,000 of them now in France. Their wives were in a "tragic" dilemma—only about 2 percent of them received an allocation. One twenty-six-year-old wife with four children, who asked to be repatriated to the Saar, was told by the authorities that they would consider the request only if she divorced her husband. Dr. Joseph Weill, of OSE, agreed with Toureille that the situation for the foreign workers was worse than that of the camp internees. The Committee decided that they all would gather specific cases of abuse among the GTE and present them, as a delegation, to a higher official than Commandant Doussau.

One of the last meetings of the Committee of Nîmes took place on April 15, 1942, a month and a half before the Jews in the Occupied Zone were required to wear the yellow star and two months before the mass roundups that summer and fall. Lowrie continued to talk about his contacts with Vichy authorities and their reassurances. His and Toureille's March 4 meeting with an official concerning the GTE, wrested more promises of improving conditions of health, safety, allocations and family integration, and possibilities of education for the youth. This official described himself as ready to study, with sympathy, all propositions and modifications suggested by the Committee. Lowrie issued one general warning: that it would be dangerous to give out information on conditions in the GTE "because of the chance of reprisals."

The Vichy representative present at this meeting, Colonel Tavernier, gave a long report on the history of the GTE, with statistics: there were

70,000 foreign workers in the Unoccupied Zone in spring 1940; there were now 18,000 actually working, out of a total group of 22,000. His remarks on the foreign Jewish workers were ominous in what they implied about the chances of these workers escaping deportation. He made a specific promise to Toureille that all foreign workers including Jews, who were in place before February 2, 1941, would continue to be members of the GTE. "He does not think," Toureille's minutes continued, "that the occupying power would want to take back to Germany such men who would be hostile." The Jewish workers would not be liberated if their kind of work might take jobs —especially farm work—away from the French. And "a battle without mercy will be waged against those who lie about the kind of work they would do."

Toureille was insistent with this official on a number of points. He urged that those men who were physically disabled be classified into a different category, and that favor be shown to those who had volunteered for French military service. The work regulations and the penal code should be applied equally to the foreign workers and to their managers, he continued. In addition, the lamentable state of the workers' wives must be addressed with "more tact and discretion." Those government social service people visiting the wives must be truly qualified and sensitive to the situation. The Colonel said he was ready to respect all the arguments of the Committee, but "it is impossible to proceed now with massive liberations." This remark was followed by Grand Rabbi Salzer who raised the point that the Jewish groups of workers included men who were unable to do hard labor. "Instructions have been given," answered the Colonel, "for sending them to the group with limited capacities for work."

A letter of April 22 from the Vichy Chief of the Foreign Office informed the Committee of Nîmes about the triage system it had set up for grouping the foreign workers according to their capacities. In response, on April 30, Toureille addressed a letter to Colonel Tavernier, asking that Vichy modify its plans for those foreigners unable to work in the GTE: "We insist that those men with physical restrictions be classified separately and sent to the foreign worker's center created by the Social Service for Foreigners set up in Nébouzat, Puy de Dôme. This is an interesting experiment that has our complete support and that merits being developed."

What must be avoided at all cost, Toureille continued, is that those men who served in the French army as foreign volunteers or in the armies of the "ex-Allies," or who were working voluntarily in the labor groups, "be submitted to the useless humiliation of being sent to an aid center when they are definitively classified as unable to work. . . . We are convinced that it is in the French national interest to not brutalize these men, many of whom have sacrificed their health to serve France."

Toureille mentioned, as of special interest to the Committee of Nîmes, the case of a foreign worker born in 1886 in Estonia, whose wife, a French-woman, had a right to certain care. Toureille continued: it was "delightful" that Vichy confirmed the Committee's request that those Polish and Czech workers classified as unable to work be sent to the special centers set up in les Bains or in St. Loup near Marseille. "Since reclassifying the T.E. [foreign workers] who are unable to work is assuredly one of the central questions in the present situation, we will be infinitely grateful to you for addressing the issue with the greatest possible benevolence."

On September 30, 1942, Toureille wrote a letter to a member of his aid network, Pastor Bourdon, a letter intercepted by Vichy surveillance agents.[2] Toureille was protesting against the director of the GTE camp at Chanac who had designated as "authentic Jews" ten internees claiming to be Christians— all undoubtedly trying to survive through recent conversion, as Toureille indicated in one case. His bitterness and frustration in dealing with Vichy showed up in almost every sentence:

I believe more than ever now, in the light of recent events, that the church should never agree to serve as the go-between. I believe this but I don't think it's a good idea to put it into practice. Do ask the persons concerned to keep us strictly and completely informed about what is going on. We do not have the gift of divination . . . Fully cognizant in these matters and as a specialist who since 1932 has worked in the ecumenical cadre on behalf of Christian refugees, I assert vehemently as false the claim of the Chief of GTE 321 that, besides Fleischner and Sonnenfeld, all ten others were "echte Juden" [authentic Jews].

I know best the exact situation of my parishioners and it is up to the church to determine who belongs to it and who does not. . . . I assert that these claims are false because I knew these T.E. as Protestants not only at the time of their departure for Chanac but from the time of their stay at Albi, before their stay at Agde. I have known some of them since November 1940, as former military chaplain of the 18th Army Corps. There is not much more that can be done for our good F., because his baptism was after June 23, 1940. Please note that what has happened is not due to the Law, but rather to the pressures of the authorities, as verified indisputably in a letter we received from Mar. Pétain. Let us not be seduced by false reasoning. . . . When all the foreign workers from Chanac are deported, the Chief of this Group will no longer have a job or pay. His interests are the same as those of his men. It's silly of him not to realize this.

The Chaplaincy

By the first months of 1942, Toureille had developed a formal administration for his Chaplaincy, which was called the Administrative Committee of the Chaplaincy of Protestant Foreign Refugees or Internees in France. His daughter, Anne-Marie, remembers the extent to which her father had expanded his operations:

My family had moved to Lunel and my father set up an office in our home, had two secretaries that handled the correspondence—letters of encouragement to the people in the camps. When that became too large, he rented an apartment that he converted into office space. Most of the workers were volunteers. We gathered clothing and Bibles and sent them to the camps. We found housing and hiding places for many. We even hid a Jewish man behind the piano. Occasionally Simon and I were sent to take messages to certain people who were helping, nothing in writing in case we were stopped by the Germans. My father also made false ID papers for many Jews.

In January 1942 the Wehrmacht requisitioned my brother Marc's bedroom, located on the third floor, and made it the regimental treasury of an artillery unit in Lunel. The room faced the street and had a beautiful view of the city. The Germans stayed there a few months.[3] (letter to author, July 21, 1996)

The minutes of the March 14 Chaplaincy meeting in Lunel note that seven people attended, including Toureille.[4] One member, reporting on her impressions while visiting the eight *départements* under their jurisdiction, spoke of "the joy among all the Protestant foreigners in being helped and visited, and how much all of them appreciated their care and contact with Pastor Toureille." In response to Toureille's report of the increasing burdens of their work, the Committee sent to Geneva an urgent request for authorization to hire two more assistants. Toureille, as he had done with the Committee of Nîmes, made a special case of the forced laborers, the GTE, who were detached to isolated factories, mines, or farms, and who needed to be visited individually in order to judge each case and distribute aid.

The minutes then recorded the Chaplaincy committee's direct appeal for help and their reprimand to the French churches, which had not matched their Swiss counterparts in interest and generosity: "The

Committee is very impressed by these reports [of aid activity]. The aid given to our Chaplaincy has come, so far, only from the Swiss Protestants—we regret very much that the French Churches have not shown the same interest. We hope that, now in a climate more favorable, our Churches will truly make an effort to do this, to sustain work that honors not only the pastors, the lay Frenchmen and the foreigners who have given their time and their energy, but also the local parishioners who have been the craftsmen and beneficiaries."

On March 30 Toureille launched into the frankest report yet, in his correspondence with Freudenberg on his problems in collaborating with CIMADE in the camps. The problem sounded partly like one of personal dislike on Toureille's side: "Our relations with CIMADE are still bad. Thursday, at Vichy, I saw [a CIMADE representative] briefly, who flooded me with "I . . . I . . . I", without letting me get a word in on what I thought. It may be time to put an end to this negative relationship. For my part, I have, with absolutely no success, made all the overtures. I cannot go any further. I am tired of all these useless humiliations. To write to you about this is deeply painful. Please understand."

At the April 18 meeting of the Chaplaincy committee, there was a representative from CIMADE present, who suggested continuing the attempts to coordinate the two agencies. The president of the Chaplaincy committee, Pastor Boisset, reported on his conversation with Boegner, which concerned a strengthening of the committee. The Protestant Federation of France, headed by Boegner, and the WCC in Geneva had set up a restructuring of the Chaplaincy committee and an increase in its affiliation with two other Protestant organizations, the Fund for Allocations to Families in Toulouse, and the Aid Society for Pastors of France.

The Chaplaincy's financial state was in jeopardy. Tighter coordination and accounting were being set up; a way had to be found for the Chaplaincy to make aid payments without obvious connection to Geneva. "Above all, the committee is extremely moved by the tragic situation of a constantly increasing number of our parishioners and by the need to augment not only the amount but also the costs of our allocations."

Concerning aid "for the Protestant refugees alone," the minutes continued, spending more than the present allocation of 80,000 francs per month seriously endangered the committee's reserves. In addition, Geneva had recently asked that they administer systematic aid to "the orthodox" (members of the Eastern Orthodox Church), requiring an additional 30,000–40,000 francs per month. "The committee, understanding fully the need, cries out with alarm, hoping to be heard." There was some relief in hearing the treasurer announce, from a Freudenberg letter, that Sweden had given them 35,000 Francs, to be disbursed "without distinguishing the religious identity" of the recipients (with the probable intention of helping the Jewish refugees).

This latter phrase prompted the committee to make some fine distinctions: "Since the committee does essentially religious work (for Protestants and Orthodox only), we would think it inappropriate to help people 'without distinguishing the religious identity'. We therefore would like to be told the percentage [of the funding] to which our work can lay claim and we will accept this sum with gratitude." They proposed that the remainder of the funding be distributed through the Quakers, the Unitarians, and other agencies.

Toureille made several comments on how the Chaplaincy was coordinating its activities. He noted that the work of the Chaplaincy reached those in isolated places through a network of communities in liaison with the French Protestant churches. He made several strongly worded proposals for dividing up the tasks more clearly between the Chaplaincy and CIMADE, which show the growing difficulties among the aid groups simply in keeping track of individual internees, plus the problems that Toureille faced in the past in trying to coordinate with CIMADE. He proposed:

a) that CIMADE be in charge of the social aspects of the camps and that all ecclesiastic work be relegated to the Chaplaincy;

b) that in the camps where there were CIMADE agents, they should collaborate directly with the Chaplaincy in giving notice—"methodically, scrupulously and steadily"—of all the changes (arrivals and departures) among the Protestant and Orthodox parishioners; this must be done in a manner that allowed the Church to follow the internees' displacements, which were constantly increasing. No one in their charge should be lost because of not being notified in time;

c) that CIMADE should take full charge of developing Centers of Aid and that places in these Centers should be reserved for persons "at liberty" with whom the Chaplaincy is in correspondence;

d) that aid work among the GTE groups and those refugees who are living in isolated places should be in the sole charge of the Chaplaincy;

e) that the organization of religious meetings and services be exclusively the charge of the Chaplaincy;

f) that CIMADE and the Chaplaincy form a tighter and more consistent relationship.

The CIMADE representative present at the meeting generally agreed that there should be a clearer division of labor between the two organizations, and he assured the Committee that CIMADE agents would be more effective in getting out information on the parishioners.

Toureille raised the question of what role the French Protestant Church could play in the administration of the committee's aid work. Funding from the church was not available because of the heavy burdens already imposed on it by the war, but the churches could contribute in three ways: 1) by formally arranging that the parishioners serving in the GTE be welcomed into the homes of French Protestant families; 2) by sending religious and other books, already collected in the Protestant parishes, to the isolated internees and by organizing circulating libraries; 3) by collecting clothes, underwear, and shoes in the rural parishes. The committee agreed to the first two proposals but found the third undoable. Toureille also proposed that, since Cardinal Gerlier was represented on the Committee of Coordination of Nîmes, the Protestant Federation of France, under Boegner, should also have a representative. Pastor Boisset, President of this Chaplaincy committee, was proposed.

This meeting ended with the reading of letters from internees, which showed "the spiritual thirst of those in the charge of the Chaplaincy." The final discussion focused on how to accommodate the request of a mother of a fifteen-year-old girl from the Saar, who was living in France far from Protestant centers and needed religious instruction.

At a Chaplaincy committee meeting on May 2, 1942, the operation of the Chaplaincy was further bureaucratized. The shrinking of their finances was again a prime worry, alleviated by a promise of support from America and Sweden, to offset the reduction in funding from the Swiss who were undergoing "very heavy burdens of all kinds." A professional typist/stenographer would be hired for Toureille's office in Lunel for 1200 francs a month, to send out about seventy letters a day, put together reports, and answer the telephone.

Other new staff appointments included two assistants to Toureille.

One, when Toureille was away, would take charge of the office, direct the correspondence with the refugees, and visit the parishioners in Montpellier and Sète, Hérault. Another would support and assist Toureille, particularly concerning his trips. Also appointed was a translator for correspondence with Polish-, Russian-, and Czech-speaking refugees, and for keeping the office records and lists. Toureille was granted two months vacation in August and September, with the suggestion that he spend it in Le Chambon at the Committee's expense.

Toureille described, in a May 7 letter to one of the refugee families he had placed in Mende, his activities as Chief Chaplain during this period: "Our work continues without letup, as does the misery of those whom we are helping—they number more than 12,000, plus the 22 families from the foreign Protestant churches in France: British, Armenian, Dutch, Russian, Czechoslovak. We have just been put in charge of the Russian, Balkan and Near Eastern Orthodox churches, which enlarges our field of action."[5] At the next Chaplaincy committee meeting, on May 16, the members established that their monthly expenses came to 100,000 francs, comprised of aid for groups, individuals, and exceptional cases (*Fr* 69,750), salaries (*Fr* 2,750), travel and lodging (*Fr* 16,000), office costs (*Fr* 7,500), and medicine (*Fr* 4,000).

After a number of cases of exceptional need were raised, the Committee decided that individual refugees outside the camps who needed help, including medical aid, should apply to the local village pastor, and that identity cards should always be renewed whether individuals could pay or not. However, an individual's request for disbursement of 400 francs for planting potatoes was rejected as inappropriate to the Committee's mission.

On the subject of applying for aid to the local village pastor, Toureille wrote to Pastor Bourdon of Mende on October 10, 1942, about the local Catholic church's willingness to help. This letter was intercepted by the Vichy surveillance, apparently with no comment from Vichy authorities. Toureille commented on the local Catholic church's position and the Chaplaincy's own responsibility: "The Fishers [a refugee couple the Chaplaincy is helping] have really been Catholics for a long time. But, in Mende, the Clergy do not want to compromise themselves, do not concern themselves with foreigners and above all with Christians of the Jewish race who could be in danger. That is why the Fishers have turned to us.

But 'cuique suum' [to each his own]; we have, I think, enough to do with
our own without taking care of the sheep from another fold. Unless our intervention is truly necessary."[6]

Camp Conditions, Liberation, and Escape

A letter from Toureille to Freudenberg on March 30, 1942, demonstrated the kind of triage Toureille had to deal with in circumstances that
constantly narrowed the opportunities to administer help. He discussed a
certain woman internee who, all on his team agreed, did not need their
particular help. "She exaggerates her condition a bit—it is not as pitiable
as she describes it," he explained. "Although she deserves sympathy, her
state is far from alarming. Like so many others in France (in the camps and
outside), she suffers from a lack of D vitamins, which causes chilblains, in
her case, of the feet, hindering her walking." He quoted a local pastor as
saying that she had also received "important sums" twice from Swiss
friends, besides her quota sent by the World Council aid. This woman, he
concluded, would be best helped by her obtaining the medicine appropriate for her condition.

That same day he wrote to Freudenberg about another internee case,
this time arguing for aid for K., his wife, and three children, "all congenial
people." They had just been transferred from Gurs to Rivesaltes, then
omitted from the list of Protestants at Rivesaltes and put in the Jewish
block, where the parents, at least, remained. The local pastor at Rivesaltes
"does not seem to be as interested in this family as he should, in spite of
our requests and in spite of the fact that one son should continue his catechism." The family wanted to emigrate to the United States, but Toureille
estimated that the chances were nil. Toureille asked Freudenberg if he
could find aid from a Swiss donor, or even obtain liberation for the family,
since they had sufficient means to support themselves. They particularly
needed, as did all the internees, food and clothing. "This case is typical of
the kind of people who were with us at Gurs, and then were lost [in the
system] as soon as they left."

A week later, a case of liberation came up for discussion, concerning a
physician recently at the camp at Noé, who had been liberated through
their agency. As Toureille had said in the past, he was "pained" to learn
that this internee addressed Freudenberg directly for help, without going
through the Chaplaincy first. "This kind of request must be strongly dis-

couraged—it complicates our work unnecessarily, creates extra costs, and implies that you and I are not working in perfect accord." The physician was being given 500 francs every two weeks, for a two-month period, with the understanding that Toureille would be reimbursed so he could help the constantly increasing number of cases on their hands.

Toureille then took up one of his most constant themes, the fragility of the conditions in liberating camp internees:

Dr. Z. was liberated on the basis of having the means for subsistence. It would be catastrophic, in view of how the system of liberations is being carried out, if his funding is not paid and if he does not keep his word [to follow conditions?]. I must call your attention to the fact that, according to the regulations now in effect, our regular allocations and aid do not constitute, according to our Authorities, a sufficient means of subsistence and that those who have no other means must be interned. It is therefore urgent, for Dr. Z. and for us, that his funding come through the French Red Cross or some other official channel. Dr. Z. is a serious man, but very ill and, as a result, it seems, sometimes a little bitter.

On May 7, 1942, Toureille wrote a letter to one of the families he placed in Mende, a letter intercepted by the Vichy surveillance agents.[7] The Vichy agents titled the letter "Rancor of a Chief Chaplain." Toureille reassured this family, "You are not forgotten in your little faraway corner of the world," and told them he had written to Switzerland to procure "the baptismal certificates in question," reminding them that soon they would have to prove that they are Aryan—if not, "one is automatically considered Jewish." They also risked being drafted into the GTE.

He added a note of personal anguish, concerning his role both as a father and as a politicized pastor. The anguish was not remorse that he had made a mistake in choosing as he did, but rather a clear recognition of what he had sacrificed in doing so: "I have renounced EVERYTHING. I no longer know what family life is: my five children no longer know me. . . . I have sacrificed my health and I have compromised (whatever happens, right or left), my reputation. I have drawn upon myself, even among those whom I want to help, much misunderstanding and hatred, even among my own associates."

Then, a hint that he was considering quitting his Chaplaincy direction, in order to change to what he calls a "radical" new course (which he did not further identify). It could possibly have been an increase in clandestine rescue work, or perhaps he considered quitting his Church duties or joining the Resistance: "There is the possibility that in a short time, I leave all this work and make a radical switch in direction. I know that, right now, I am very tempted. May I ask you, as old friends, to pray for me. . . . I need it very much. May God bless you and keep you! May you accomplish what others have begun."

Spiritual Resistance

In 1942, plans for the Final Solution formulated during the Wannsee Conference in January put into motion the mass roundups of Jews the following spring and summer, as well as launching the death trains from the French internment camps to the extermination camps in Poland and Eastern Europe. Boegner and the Protestant churches were active in their protests.

Boegner wrote a personal letter on June 27, 1942, to Pétain. The letter spoke of "the Jewish problem," referring to the influx of refugees, but objected to Jews wearing the yellow star, primarily because of its injustice to Frenchmen. This was "socially and economically inoperable," the letter argued, and it victimized "Frenchmen, many of whom have shed their blood under our flag, an uncalled-for humiliation, supposedly separating them from the rest of the nation. It exposes six-year-old children to the taunting always possible in the troubled atmosphere in which our population lives."[8]

Boegner also objected to labeling as Jewish those who had been baptized, whether Catholic or Protestant. Implied in this statement was the notion that being a Jew was a lower quality of religious identification than being a Christian: "to wear ostensibly before men the title of Jew while they themselves are proud to wear before God the title of Christian." This was "undeserved suffering that touches Frenchmen and sometimes Christians in their dignity as men and as believers." Boegner commented that his meetings with Pétain at this time left him feeling deeply disturbed and completely powerless.[9]

Pastor A.-N. Bertrand, who had a position in the Occupied Zone equivalent to Boegner's, wrote a letter to F. de Brinon, French representative to the occupation forces in Paris, in August 1942.[10] This letter followed the shocking roundup of tens of thousands of Jews in Paris and their three-day incarceration in the *Vélodrome d'Hiver* under atrocious conditions, and the beginning of mass deportations. Bertrand's central message was broader gauged than Boegner's, reaching beyond national boundaries, beyond French Jews, to Jews and Protestants as peoples; he used the phrase "extermination of a race" to describe what was happening. He asserted that many believed that the anti-Jewish persecution had reached its limit when it set Jews apart by forcing them to wear the yellow star, but subsequent events in July, he continued, had escalated the oppressive violence.

Bertrand's letter suggested that the churches protested the suffering and tried to alleviate it. The churches had to speak out against events "that risk compromising for many long years all possibility of normal relations between two great peoples [the French and the Germans]." The French, although they could not make their sentiments known, also could not "remain indifferent to the extermination of a race, to the undeserved martyrdom of its women and its children." The Germans' cruelty would have a lasting effect on the minds of the French people. He pled for "a Christian church" to be faithful to its duty to speak out and warned the French authorities to listen to "a few Christian voices, solely preoccupied in alleviating sufferings and putting out the flames of hate, . . . rather than those wholly profane voices who know no other answer to violence than that of hatred."

When it came the southern zone's turn to witness these same atrocious roundups and shipments by train to the death camps, Boegner tried to intervene with the authorities by teaming up with the Catholic authority, Cardinal Gerlier—they each would write to Pétain. In his August 20, 1942, letter to Pétain, Boegner no longer focused on injustices to French Jews but instead expressed "the unutterable sadness felt by our churches at the news of decisions made by the French government about foreign Jews."[11] He discarded the explanation that the French and German authorities were giving: "No Frenchman can remain unmoved by what has happened since 2 August in the security and internment camps. One knows that the answer will be that France is only returning to Germany the Jews that were sent here in the fall of 1940. The truth is that men and women who came as refugees to France for political or religious reasons have just been delivered to Germany, and they know what terrible fate awaits them."

Boegner focused on the right of sanctuary, which was both a Christian and a French principle. The churches needed to raise "protests of grief at the abandonment of this principle." At a September 6, 1942, meeting of

Protestant leaders in the south, Boegner wrote that "the hearts of all were heavy with shame and anguish," and he was asked to intervene as vigorously as possible with the authorities.[12] He met with Laval three days later. In October 1945, a few hours after Laval was executed, Boegner remembered his 1942 meeting with Laval. He described—and also seemed to justify—the restraint he felt in dealing with Laval. He explained that, with government officials, it was politic to try private contact before public chastisement: "I have always thought that before protesting to our faithful or to the nation against the faults of a government, we should first go to the persons concerned to say what we think and to show our care not to blame publicly anyone without having first tried to have the unjust measures changed."[13]

"But what could I obtain," Boegner asked in his memoir, "from a man whom the Germans had made to believe—or who pretended to believe—that the Jews taken from France were going to southern Poland to cultivate the land of the Jewish state that Germany said it wished to establish? I spoke to him of massacre; he responded with gardening."

When Boegner told Laval that the churches could not keep silent before such facts of brutality, Laval callously rejoined that the churches had done such things in the past themselves—and added that he had said the same to the Vatican representative, Cardinal Gerlier, whom he had just seen. Let the churches do what they like, he ended—"I shall continue to do what I must."

Boegner, in the following days, tried the American chargé d'affaires, who promised to get authorization to tell Laval that the United States would accept the children of deportees. Boegner then tried the general secretary of the police, then a Protestant Vichy official, who reprimanded the churches for betrayal of the Vichy government.

Second Pomeyrol Conference

Another set of declarations came out of a second conference at Pomeyrol (September 16–19, 1942), attended by fifty-five pastors and organized by Pastor André Trocmé of Le Chambon-sur-Lignon and two others. Taking up such subjects as the church during war and as an international body, the group developed nine principles concerning the Jews intended to be a call to action, including respect for rights of the person and rights of asylum, and rejection of racism, religious persecution, and discrimination against Christians of Jewish origin. "Israel is a chosen people and the testament of God's promise. Man cannot take the place of God in relation to Israel." Visser't Hooft participated fully in this conference, but Boegner limited himself to giving information on activities of the past year.

The Protestant churches and their parishioners' efforts to save Jews and other oppressed foreigners grew more intense and desperate. Historians have added Toureille's name to those individuals and groups who deserve credit. Historian Bolle mentioned Toureille's direction of the Chaplaincy for Protestant refugees and internees, and his role as vice president, then president of the Committee of Nîmes beginning in October 1940.[14] "Pierre Toureille, intervened courageously with the occupation authorities at several instances, took part in the fabrication of false papers and arranged for passage into Switzerland of foreigners and the hounded." After some of the most horrific roundups from the camps in August and September 1942, it was evident that protests to the Vichy government would go nowhere. On November 10 Boegner suspended Protestant conferences, for the safety of the members. The next day, the German army occupied the southern zone. The spiritual resistance now became clandestine, its major mission to help the Jews and preach to the faithful.

Swiss Border Issue

During the summer of 1942, the Swiss border was flooded with illegal refugees, prompting the Swiss authorities to close it. But by August 1942, with verified reports of the death camps as the destination for the deportees from France, the law closing the borders was relaxed, although only at certain times, in response to protests and interventions. The Swiss Division of Police had established, by September 1942, an ambiguous system of border control that generally disallowed Jews from crossing to safety since they were not what the Swiss categorized as political refugees.

Boegner tried to pressure Swiss authorities to allow Jewish foreigners to enter Switzerland, rather than being turned back by Swiss border guards, and subsequently being arrested and deported by the German patrols. He argued that this allowance to Jewish refugees would be done under his personal guarantee. "And with what joy I gave it to all those refugees escorted by the men and women team members of CIMADE in the face of great danger, up to and beyond the barbed wire with which Switzerland had had to encircle itself."[15]

From the Swiss side, Freudenberg was also working actively with the

Swiss authorities to keep the borders open to refugees fleeing deportation. A footnote in Freudenberg's memoir commented on the Swiss authorities' rationale for turning the refugees back.[16] According to the Swiss,
French Jews had to be sent back "because they run no danger in their
country"—which made no sense since "Jews were a thousand times more
in danger than many of the 'politiques' [French political refugees who
were assumably not Jewish]." The interventions attempted by aid groups
focused on the lists of "nonrejectables" [those the border police would not
turn back] established by the border police, on whom the aid organizations applied pressure. Freudenberg gave Boegner much credit for personally pressuring the Department of Justice and the security police of the
Confederation in Switzerland to accept as nonrejectables the names submitted by CIMADE, Toureille's Chaplaincy, and other influential French
and Swiss figures.

Freudenberg and others from international refugee agencies managed to reopen the border from time to time, saving some twelve thousand
people by July 1943.[17] The shock of receiving the information that those
deportations of August and September 1942 meant death on a massive
scale for the Jews sent Freudenberg into action for the duration of the
war. After informing members of the WCC on September 25, 1942, about
the Final Solution, he then contacted people who were connected with
Swiss and Allied authorities in January 1943; in March he sent a joint
memorandum on the Final Solution, drafted with the World Jewish Congress, to United States and British government authorities. Freudenberg
commented in his memoir that this joint memorandum was considered
Zionist propaganda in certain circles in Great Britain—within the government, among some Christian leaders, and even within the Intergovernmental Committee for Refugees.

Freudenberg and his colleagues at the WCC and other church and aid
agencies worked against this tide all through the war, sending precise information to the Allies and neutral countries on what was occurring in the
death camps. Freudenberg commented that he had had a difficult time
finding refuge for the perishing Jewish population of Europe. Swiss aid
groups were swamped with the needs of Jewish refugees in Switzerland,
and American colleagues were of little help. He blamed this lack of help
on the incredulity of public opinion, of governments, and even of the
Christian churches concerning what was really happening in the death
camps.

Freudenberg went on to speculate about the reasons for this nonreaction by the world to Nazi crimes. One reason was foreign policy pressures, as demonstrated in the Evian Conference on the refugee problem convened by President Roosevelt in 1938, in which the delegates declared they could not increase their immigrant quotas. Another reason was that the Nazi extermination plan for Jews was so inhumanly planned and executed that it was impossible to believe. No country was ready or willing to take the extraordinary measures that would have been needed to save the Jews, while there was still time. Freudenberg noted more bitterly that anti-Semitism had played a part: at the Evian Conference, he felt that it was an unspoken assumption that although the extermination measures were intolerable, since they involved mainly Jews, it was not necessary to go to extreme measures to save them.

Deportation

The summer and fall of 1942 in France was one of the blackest periods of the war, when massive numbers of refugees were deported to the death camps of Eastern Europe. For the aid organizations, these deportations swept away forever all plans of saving tens of thousands of refugees under their care. A Protestant witness gave a vivid account of that shocking summer:

When the truck stopped, dawn was breaking on the radiant countryside washed with rain. All alone on the sidetrack of a little station, there was a freight car, a common cattle car. Someone pushed us. The doors closed on us and on six armed guards. Inside was an acetylene lamp.

Each woman seemed to have reached the limit of suffering: one had left her child at camp, another the hope of ever seeing again her crippled husband at Camp Djelfa. . . . There was hunger and thirst. Food was to have been provided, but the insulting little packages had been refused. There was the terrible constraint and shame of being treated like animals, to have only a little pile of straw in a corner to satisfy the need of each one under the eyes of the guards. . . . And of course there was the terrible odor that was not long in taking over. . . . To be fair, I must say that the guards were human within the limits possible. They attempted to explain that they did this work reluctantly and in fear of reprisals on their families in Paris. . . .

Night came. The lighted lamp, swinging with the rhythm of the train, projected deceptive shadows on the walls. . . . In the night, in the noise, with the hunger and cold and half-dried clothes, the interior silence of each one was more profound. . . . "I am content," said the friend who had left her child in camp. "I am going to know what it is to suffer with those of my race." She thought she was going for a time into the ghettos of Poland with the Polish Jews.

I remember the good-looking face of a Russian Communist. We were talking about hope. I told her that I could not live without Christian hope. "I am not without hope," she said to me. "I believe in human progress." (Suzanne Loiseau-Chevalley, CIMADE representative living in camp at Brens with internees, accompanying deportation trainload of women being delivered to the Germans, summer 1942)[18]

From the time of those terrible events to the present day, those who were in France during the war and who felt a responsibility to save lives, still ask themselves some painful questions: When did we first know this would happen and could we have prevented it? Could we have saved more people? Did we make the right choices?

An American representative of the American Friends Service Committee and member of the Committee of Nîmes remembered the pain of having to make certain choices:

We learned late in the morning that the first train was to be loaded that evening and depart sometime during the night of August 10 or 11. The selection of the first convoy began late in the afternoon amid a Dantesque scene of heat, confusion and apprehension, with the whole camp population assembled in the courtyard. There was a constant coming and going as people whose names had been called out were moved from one group to another. . . . Piles of suitcases, bags and bundles of the internees' meager possessions were everywhere on the ground. . . .

The stretcher was plying back and forth to the camp infirmary with the limp figures of the weak and old who had fainted in the heat. The guards were even escorting people back and forth in one further act of indignity to the camp latrines. Toward six o'clock the Militia began moving each final group out of the camp gate and toward the line of small French freight cars drawn up on the railroad siding about 300 yards away. As each group left the camp the iron gate clanged shut again. . . .

There came an urgent call that the camp Commandant wanted to see me. When I had elbowed my way through the guards into his office I was confronted by the Intendant de Police from Marseille, in an immaculate linen suit, red ribbon of the Legion of Honor in his lapel. The Protestant pastor from Aix, who had long worked to mitigate the miserable lot of the internees, was also there, along with two representatives of the HICEM [a Jewish emigration association]. The Commandant, face haggard, and with cluttered sheets of the fatal list on the table in front of him, held in his hand one of the old, dark red American passports, dog-eared and worn. What did we wish to do about this man, M. l'Intendant inquired.

This pathetic evidence of at least his past citizenship, proved to have been issued in the twenties and had long, long since expired. It belonged to a Polish internee, who, rapid consultation revealed, was in his late seventies and pretty well senile. Did we want him excluded from the deportation, M. l'Intendant asked. If so, someone else would have to be selected to take his place. What was there to reply but "no, include him," in the vain hope that someone younger, with more of his life ahead of him, might thereby be saved. One had no right to make such a life and death decision, but made it anyway.[19]

French Protestant Community

On May 29, 1942, all Jews from ages six to eighty in the Occupied Zone were ordered to wear the yellow star. The founder of The Little Shepherds of the Cévennes, an organization that placed urban children among farm families during vacations, remembered his reaction: "Before the war, I never had any particular feelings about Jews one way or the other. But what did it for me, what struck me so powerfully, was the simple fact of seeing on the platform of the metro in Paris, a group of children quietly waiting for the arrival of the train. Each one of these children had the yellow star sewn on his chest, a sign of contempt foreshadowing their being sent to a center of regroupment for a destination unknown, but very disquieting. . . . I was overcome by a shock that determined all my future conduct. When . . . someone proposed that I take from each convoy one or several Jewish children, without hesitation and without fear, I agreed."[20]

The French Protestant community took a long look at their own wartime rescue activity during a 1992 conference on Protestants and the war. (This conference produced the book *Les protestants français pendant la seconde guerre mondiale,* Paris, 1994). During one discussion session, several historians pointed out the important role Boegner had played in protesting Vichy's anti-Semitic measures, particularly in 1942, which, with efforts from other religious leaders, actually slowed down deportations for a few months until the Germans occupied the entire country in November. Yet, on the question of knowledge of the Nazis' Final Solution (also called the Holocaust and the Shoah at this conference), there was a clear difference between the reaction of the WCC in 1942 and 1943 (for example, the joint memorandum discussed above, sent out by the WCC and the World Jewish Congress), and Boegner's reaction. He did not seem to take in the enormity of the situation at that time, although, as an officer with the WCC in Geneva, had the same information accessible to him.

In Boegner's journal notes (*Carnets du Pasteur Boegner, 1940–45*, Paris, 1992) referred to by historians at the conference, he seemed to have taken at face value the Vichy official explanation that the Jews were being settled in new homes in Poland and Czechoslovakia. It appears that it was only with his visit to one of the camps in 1945 that Boegner absorbed the meaning of the concentration and death camps. He wrote of his reaction: "We did not know of the horror of these German concentration camps." The historian commenting on this quotation concludes: "People did not discover the incredible reality of the extermination until very late, in the vast majority of cases, . . . even a man like Pastor Boegner."[21]

Several at the 1992 Protestant conference said their knowledge of the Final Solution emerged between December 1942 and fall 1943; others said they didn't know until the Liberation and the return of the deportees. Those who knew the earliest credited their ties with friends and colleagues in Switzerland, such as Charles Guillon or Visser't Hooft, or an underground network. One respondent to a survey on this question gave a not un-common explanation: "I was told in December 1942 or January 1943, but I didn't believe it, because it was so monstrous, I couldn't take it all in."[22]

The historian administering this survey had posed to himself the ques-tion of what knowledge the pastors in France had, in 1942, of the Final So-lution. He sent questionnaires to all those who participated in the second Pomeyrol conference in September 1942, which had focused on the Vichy treatment of Jews. Ten respondents claimed that Visser't Hooft did not speak of the Final Solution in his presentation at the conference.

Yet, in about the same year as the 1992 conference, Pastors Marc Donadille and Jacques Martin took part in a roundtable discussion on the same subject,[23] and clearly remembered that it was through Visser't Hooft's presentation at Pomeyrol and the WCC connection that they heard about the Final Solution. Donadille said: "On the occasion of the second meeting [in Pomeyrol], in September 1942, with some fifty pastors and others, we had "kidnapped" this brave man Visser't Hooft, who came from England via Spain, and listened to him speak. He told us what the fi-nal solution was, which had begun in Germany. We were thus informed. But we had already been informed, and we said so, in our local parish meetings. . . . And we were even, I think, more quickly and more com-pletely informed than the majority of the Germans living in Germany!"

Martin remembered: "I want to add a simple memory of my own. The summer of 1942, we were visited, in Ganges, by a representative of the World Council of Churches [This was probably Adolf Freudenberg]. He was the one who began to inform us about the 'final solution', based on the information the World Council already had."

Donadille explained, with psychological acuity, why he and the other rescuers he worked with reacted as they did to the Final Solution at the time it was happening:

You have to understand our situation. The people who informed us were people we trusted. When Visser't Hooft informed us at Pomeyrol, we had complete confidence in him; we had no doubts that his claims were founded on facts, on verified information. Now, why didn't we talk a lot about it after that? First of all, it is not very wise to say to the Jewish friends we are hiding, who are living in our homes: "Later, they will kill all of you, be careful!" We had other things to do than to analyze "Hitler wants to kill them all."

What haunted us was the fate of these Jewish friends under our roofs. We didn't see beyond that, you must understand, and that was enough to keep us busy! When they were well hidden, when they were secure, when we all ate together, in the Cevenol farms—in these moments we were content, we were happy together and we sang! You have to put yourself in this atmosphere. We didn't spend every day assessing and reflecting theoretically on all these problems, as we now do as the good intellectuals we have become! We were not journalists! We lived from day to day, saying to each other: "In the end, those we save now, will be saved, and one beautiful day, Hitler will fall." So that explains a little why, knowing, we acted as if we had forgotten.

We had not forgotten, but it was urgent to live. And one cannot always live, being haunted by the apocalypse. . . . And we were all young. There were old people among those we were hiding, but most of us were young and needed to feel some happiness. We lived, we didn't reason, we didn't have the time.[24]

The historians reporting the roundtable discussion summed up the issue of knowledge about the Final Solution, this way: "By the end of 1942, the information, notably through Geneva, was passed along of the massacre of Jews deported to the East. What took place after that—the genocide perpetrated by the Nazis, the systematic, "scientific" aspect, what we call the "final solution"—escapes our intelligence, because what was true was not believable. Despite the fact that they were warned, the pastors, like all of us, could not completely believe in a crime that passed human understanding."[25]

A participant at the 1992 Protestant conference on the question of "when did we know," also raised another issue important to a pastor rescuer—what the role of the Church itself should have been in the spiritual resistance. This man was one of those Frenchmen with Swiss contacts during the war and, in searching his own memory of when he first knew, gave a different version than Donadille's of the emotional climate among rescuers and Church representatives:

I went to Switzerland several times during this period. I saw Visser't Hooft there and I also met several Allied agents like, in particular, Allan Dulles, at Berne. But I never heard about the final solution until my last trip, in November 1943. I was very disturbed because there were, in our Dutch-Paris resistance group, a certain number of very active Jews whom I encouraged to stay in Switzerland, because I feared for their lives. But I was told: "No, no, they can continue to work in France."

I want to add that I realize there is a certain absolutism among the younger generation today, who cannot recapture the climate that reigned at that time. It was a climate of terror of the mind, that affected all attitudes and moral positions. We were led to be very prudent in our declarations. I am a little dismayed by this judgment about intentions that is being applied here to the Church and to Marc Boegner because he did not make a decision exactly at the right moment in expressing his disagreement with Pétain and his government. I think it is necessary to differentiate between the Church and its representatives on the one hand, and the individual parishioners on the other, who receive the teaching from the Church and must then take a personal position.[26]

The Church itself could not be taken hostage, this same speaker was told by a pastor during the war. "Each individual Protestant," the speaker continued, "even if engaged personally in the Resistance because of the teaching he had received in the Church . . . , could not involve the Church itself, collectively, could not endanger either its security or that of its parishioners." The speaker felt the same about involving the Church in political resistance during the war as he did about involving his friends— none of whom were ever put in danger, he claimed—and he was glad he had always taken strong precautions to make sure his friends were out of harm's way before accepting their help, "because it put their whole household in danger. . . . I was very concerned about that, and I think that Boegner must have been also, for the Church."[27]

Another historian taking part in this same roundtable discussion, Asher Cohen, pointed out that in August 1942, Grand Rabbi Kaplan went to Cardinal Gerlier to beg him to intervene on behalf of the Jews, "because," the rabbi reported himself as saying, "the Jews were not sent to Germany to work, they were sent to be exterminated." He told Cohen that he was "one hundred percent sure" that he used the word "exterminated," and that he had received the information on the planned extermination from Switzerland. Cohen feels sure that this information came from Jewish sources, as well as from the clandestine movements—which is verified in Visser't Hooft's memo-report on the issue.

The World Council of Churches (WCC)

There is no question that the genocide in operation, in 1942, was foremost on the minds of the WCC directors, and that they were among the earliest to be informed. The head, Visser't Hooft, wrote a memo-report in March 1965, titled "W.C.C. action at the time of the extermination of Jewish people" that laid out how and when he was informed of the Final Solution.[28] His memo had, as attachments, the following reports sent to the WCC by the World Jewish Congress in September 1942:

From a reliable German source with close relations to certain military and industrial circles in Germany, the following information was received:

During the past months a great number of trains arrived in Germany from Belgium, Holland and France. The trains were loaded with Jewish deportees. At the beginning of August the carriages were partly filled with dead bodies, partly with deportees alive. It is reported that since the beginning of August the trains arrived to German frontiers only with corpses.

The corpses are used in special factories. These factories are crowded.

The informer knew personally two of such factories in which corpses are used for the manufacture of soap, glue and train oil.

As to the method of killing, the informer stated that the Nazis began to apply a new procedure. The killing in special gas rooms has been replaced by another method which consists in injecting of air by physicians into the veins of the human body. This procedure is much less expensive than the other one applied formerly. The injection of air into the human body leads to a general poisoning and at last after a few hours the person becomes unconscious. The procedure is applied even before the German frontier is reached so that only corpses arrive in Germany. It is stated that one physician is capable of making 100 such injections an hour.

It is further reported that since the end of 1932 the Nazis had already ordered their physicians to study scientific methods of extermination and the utilization of corpses. In that time the physicians thought that the proceeding was to apply only to biologically and genetically abnormal people. Further, it is stated that as a result of scientific studies the utility value of a corpse is estimated to be 50 Reich Marks.

[A second attachment was a letter from a Swiss Jew living in Warsaw, dated September 4, 1942. He wrote in German code; the words were explained at the bottom of the letter by the World Council recipient:]

I spoke to Mr. Jager. He told me that he will invite all relatives of the Achenu family, with the exception of Miss Eisenzweig, from Warsaw, to Kewer, his countryside home. I am alone here; I feel lonely. . . . As to the citrus fruit I hope I shall receive it in time but I don't know whether I shall have any acquaintances left by then. I feel very weak. A week ago I spoke to Mr. Orlean. Mrs. Gefen telephones very often. Uncle Gerusch works also in Warsaw. He is a very capable worker. His friend Miso works with him. Please pray for me.

Code:
Jager—German
Achenu—our brothers; the Jews
Eisenzweig—those working in the iron industry
Kewer—tomb
citrus fruit—used in Jewish feast of Sukkoth, near end of September
Orlean—probably non-Jew
Gefen—wine tree
Gerusch—deportation
Miso—death

The World Council commentary on the letter concludes that extermination was being applied on a large scale to the 600,000 Jews of Warsaw, that the Germans were driving Jews into the countryside to exterminate them, exempting those working in heavy industry, and that there would not be many Jews left in Warsaw by the end of September. The reference to *Gefen*, the decoder guessed, referred to pogroms at the end of August, usually by drunkards.

Visser't Hooft stated that these September 1942 reports were the first definite ones the World Council received, "that deportation meant extermination." He added that it was in this same period (end of August-beginning of September) that Kurt Gerstein, a Confessing Churchman who had joined the S.S. to seek out the truth, reported about the gas chambers to a Swedish diplomat. Simultaneously, the World Jewish Congress had informed American contacts.

Months went by and more reports were turned into the World Council of Churches. The delay in reaction may have been due, Visser't Hooft explained, to the following: "the impression, not only in Geneva but in many other well informed circles, seems to have been that only a certain number of Jews were being killed, but that many others were put to work." Someone had inserted a marginal note, at this point, that Freudenberg had written a letter on the subject in December and the Red Cross had been approached in that same month.

Le Chambon-sur-Lignon, a More Radical View

André Trocmé, the pastor of Le Chambon-sur-Lignon, had the opposite view of whether the Church collectively, as a body, should risk its existence and that of its community in acts of political resistance to deportation. His Church body and community seem to have been of a different nature from Boegner's. In August 1942, during the massive roundups of foreign Jews, Trocmé and his parishioners made something good happen in Le Chambon. This event reached the level of an exemplum in the history of the French Protestant community's reaction to the Holocaust—a remarkable fusion of communal religious belief and communal action.[29]

On August 10 the Vichy Minister for Youth, George Lamirand, paid a formal visit to Le Chambon, an obvious test of the village's loyalty to Pétain and his program of forming the young minds of the country into a fascist model, including, as Trocmé wrote in his journal, "fascist salute to the flag, bugles, . . . work camps, worship of the native land and of the maréchal." Like many of the other Protestant villages in this central mountain region, Le Chambon and its pastors and elders had always maintained an independence from the state and had been, for centuries, a place of refuge for homeless and oppressed people, as it was now for the hunted foreign refugees. The visit from Lamirand, this Vichy incursion on its youth, was dangerous for the community whichever way they reacted, whether bending to Vichy and betraying their own religious ethics, or resisting it and endangering their lives.

Lamirand was greeted according to plan, with a banquet at a YMCA camp, a youth march to the sports arena, a reception at the Protestant temple, and final religious services. But—the streets were empty of people, there were no flags on the houses, Trocmé's daughter spilled soup on Lamirand's bright blue uniform during the banquet, and he was rudely pushed against by hundreds of children trying to shake his hand at the sports arena. A visiting Swiss pastor gave a sermon in the temple on obedience to the state except when it enforced laws that violated God's law,

"You shall love your neighbor as yourself." Trocmé passed a hymnal to Lamirand, who joined half-heartedly in the singing.

Then, as the group exited the temple, they were met by twelve students from the local Protestant school, Collège Cévenol, including student theologians, who walked up to Lamirand and gave him this manifesto, asking for his answer:

Mister Minister:
We have learned of the frightening scenes which took place three weeks ago in Paris, where the French police, on orders of the occupying power, arrested in their homes all the Jewish families in Paris to hold them in the Vel d'Hiv. Fathers were torn from their families and sent to Germany, children torn from their mothers, who underwent the same fate as their husbands. Knowing by experience that the decrees of the occupying power are, with brief delay, imposed on Unoccupied France, where they are presented as spontaneous decisions by the head of the French government, we are afraid that the measures of deportation of the Jews will soon be applied in the Southern Zone.

We feel obliged to tell you that there are among us a certain number of Jews. But we make no distinction between Jews and non-Jews. It is contrary to the Gospel teaching. If our comrades, whose only fault is to be born in another religion, should receive the order to give themselves up for deportation, or even for registration, they will disobey those orders and we will strive to the utmost to hide them.

Lamirand paled, passed on the duty of responding to the local prefect, and hurried away in his car. The prefect angrily accused Trocmé of endangering "national harmony" and gave the Vichy line that the foreign Jews in France did not belong there and were being sent to a new homeland in Eastern Europe. Trocmé wrote in his journal that he and the Chambonnais were not deceived by this. They understood enough about Nazism to see that the Jews were in danger as a people; the villagers were committing their lives to rescuing them. The prefect asserted that he would be back in a few days to register the Jews living in Le Chambon. "We don't identify people as Jews. Only as human beings," Trocmé answered. "You had better watch out," the prefect threatened. "If you aren't prudent, you are the one I will have to deport. Be warned."

Trocmé—whom one biographer called "a violent man conquered by

God"[30]—gave a sermon a week later on August 16, 1942. One witness reported his saying of the massive roundups of foreign Jews then taking place: "This is a humiliation for Europe, that such things can still happen here and that we, the French, cannot react against these barbarous proceedings from an era that we believed completely past. The Christian church should go to its knees and ask pardon of God for its present weakness and cowardice. Pray to God to inspire our leaders—who authorize such excesses in our land—to be counseled by those more moderate, more benevolent, more humane. I tell you this because I can no longer be quiet. I do not speak in a spirit of hatred, but of sadness and humiliation for the human race and for our country."[31]

Two weeks after the Lamirand visit, the Vichy police came to Le Chambon to round up its Jews. The chief demanded of Trocmé that he hand over a list of the Jews hiding there. Trocmé refused. He then put into operation a plan to warn those hiding in the village to flee to places designated earlier as hideouts. The police stationed themselves in the village for three weeks but found no one. Later, as the Vichy police periodically reappeared for roundups, they ended up empty handed, probably because of the reluctance of a growing number of their members to continue the chase, especially in those communities with their iron commitments to saving innocent lives. After the German occupation of the south of France, Trocmé was on the Gestapo suspect list and eventually had to go into hiding. Before he fled, he and two of his colleagues in Le Chambon had been arrested and sent to an internment camp in 1943, where they conducted religious services for the inmates. They were released in twenty-eight days, perhaps because of the intervention of someone of Boegner's stature. Upon their release they refused to sign an oath swearing fidelity to Pétain. A few days later all the five hundred inmates of that camp were deported to Poland and Silesia. There were no survivors.[32]

Trocmé made his courageous choices in a community culturally steeped in a commitment to God's law, independence from the state, and giving refuge to people being hunted down. Historians have argued about the numbers of refugees saved by the Protestant village communities of the central plateau region, including Le Chambon. But one figure often cited is that, for Le Chambon alone, this one village of three thousand people saved several thousand refugees passing through the region, of whom two-thirds were Jewish.[33] And it was the whole village that received the Award for the Righteous from Yad Vashem. This was therefore not a story of an individual rescuer but a story of collective action, involving the Church in its full collectivity, with Trocmé as one of its spokesmen.

Trocmé and Boegner apparently had an actual confrontation on the question of involving the institution of the Church in resistance to authorities.[34] Jacques Trocmé, who was ten years old in 1943, told of overhearing an argument between his father and "one of the top leaders of the Reformed Church of France . . . the equivalent of the pope . . . the man had a large mustache that swept down on either side of his mouth"—a colorful and fitting description of Boegner. In the dialog the boy imagined Boegner looking like Vercingétorix, the Gaul who tried to defend his country against Julius Caesar

VERCINGÉTORIX: What I want to say is this: you must stop helping refugees.
TROCMÉ: Do you realize what you are asking? These people, especially the Jews, are in very great danger. If we do not shelter them or take them across the mountains to Switzerland, they may well die.
VERCINGÉTORIX: What you are doing is endangering the very existence not only of this village but of the Protestant church of France! You must stop helping them.
TROCMÉ: If we stop, many of them will starve to death, or die of exposure, or be deported and killed. We cannot stop.
VERCINGÉTORIX: You must stop. The Maréchal will take care of them. He will see to it that they are not hurt.
TROCMÉ: No.

Jacques Trocmé was so anguished by this conversation, he lost his trust in the Church as an organization and cut himself off from it. His impassioned reaction was matched by his father's. André Trocmé soon afterward submitted his resignation to the presbyterial council of Le Chambon, but they refused, insisting that he continue helping refugees, against the orders of authorities—including his own church.

The fundamental question of how to weigh risks against moral imperatives for action burdened the minds of all those who were, like Toureille, involved in aiding and then rescuing the refugees in France. However, the environment in which he was acting was broader and more diffuse than Trocmé's. Both had to weigh the security of their church and its parishioners against the security of the refugees they were helping, but Toureille had the additional responsibility of keeping an aid network afloat, across hundreds of miles, which could be effective only with the tolerance of the authority in power. He and his colleagues worked at this as long as possible; finally, in 1942, they came to the realization that the Vichy authority had not only lost whatever power it once had but also had betrayed them into paralysis. During the fall of 1942 and long afterward, maybe for the rest of their lives, they asked themselves if they had made the right choices.

The Committee of Nîmes

In an August 10 memorandum to Tracy Strong, who was General Secretary of the International YMCA, Donald Lowrie was trying to set the record straight on the Committee of Nîmes' reactions to the deportations.[35] Toureille, as vice president, probably read and perhaps had a hand in writing the memorandum. Lowrie related how he and his colleagues on the Committee of Nîmes first knew of the deportations and how they tried to prevent them. Lowrie obviously thought it crucial to get the time frame accurate—what they knew, when—in explaining their performance. This memorandum was admirably detailed on the kinds and numbers of people affected and the actions of individuals, all of which gave it an authenticity that made its content all the more shocking. Lowrie clearly felt he was documenting something momentous for the future and wanted to do so responsibly and directly.

He began, "In spite of attempted complete secrecy on the part of the police and as against a mass of rumors, here are the facts ascertainable up to August 8th." Ten thousand foreign Jews were going to be deported from Vichy France in August, destined for "the Jewish reservation" set up in southeastern Poland by the Germans. Like many others at that time and since, Lowrie considered it important to identify when he and his colleagues first knew the Germans were putting in motion a policy of exterminating the Jews.

He identified his first knowledge of the policy in a July 1942 conversation between Laval and the German director for Jewish affairs, reported to Lowrie by a member of the Vichy National Council. "The German asked Laval, 'When are you going to apply to your Jews in the non-occupied zone the measures we are using in occupied France?' Laval replied, 'The only Jews we have are your Jews. We will send them back to you any time you say.'" At the end of July the Vichy officials in charge of the camps began feverishly to prepare lists, apparently, Lowrie added, not knowing what these lists were for.

Upon hearing of the ten thousand foreign Jews to be deported, the Executive Committee of the Committee of Nîmes sent Lowrie and Toureille to Vichy on August 4 to make an appeal. They saw Pétain's personal secretary who assured them such a thing would not be possible in France. Lowrie wondered—in his own history of this period, *The Hunted Children*—whether this was the first time that Pétain's office had heard of the atrocities. Pétain finally received Lowrie and Toureille on August 6, with his General Secretary, Jardel, sitting between them and the Maréchal, repeating their questions in a loud voice to Pétain and hinting what his reply should be. Pétain said the affair was regrettable but that nothing could be done. Jardel filled Pétain in on the situation: "You know, Monsieur le Maréchal, that the Germans asked to have 10,000 French Jews and that to save them we have been obliged to give up an equal number of foreign Jews. They are to be transported to a sort of 'Jewish state' the Germans have set up near Lublin. There, it appears, they will enjoy a certain liberty."

Lowrie replied, "We cannot believe, Monsieur le Maréchal, that this had been done with your knowledge or that it is inevitable." Pétain opened his hands and shrugged his shoulders: "You know our situation with regard to the Germans." When Lowrie and Toureille appealed for allowing some exemptions to emigrate, especially the children, Pétain told them to telephone Jardel the next day. Lowrie's last remark to Pétain was: "We cannot conceal from you, Monsieur le Maréchal, the unfortunate impression this action will have on public opinion abroad and the serious repercussions it may have on the work of our organizations in France." Pétain waved his hand at them and stood up. Lowrie added that the American Quakers were trying also to appeal to Laval and Pétain, particularly on saving children, but got nowhere.

In that same August 10 memorandum, Lowrie provided the statistical and logistic information on the roundups and the deportation of the first 3,600 people, beginning with the first train that left Gurs at midnight August 6, carrying 1,000 people. He listed the exceptions, for the time being: Rumanian, Hungarian, and Bulgarian citizens, plus army veterans and their families, pregnant women, and parents of children under five, children between five and eighteen who wished to separate from their parents, and husbands or wives of Aryans. Jews of the following nationalities had been taken in the first train: Austrian, Czechoslovak, Danish, Estonian, Latvian, Lithuanian, Polish, Russian, Saarois.

Lowrie then wrote a separate paragraph on who knew about these events ahead of time and were, therefore, responsible for heading them off. He apparently agreed with his informants that the deportation plans were kept almost completely secret: "Incidentally, numerous people, camp directors and officials in Vichy supposedly responsible for the camps, are terrified lest when (as they say) accounts are settled in the future, they may be held responsible. This is evidently not their fault for the whole matter was kept secret and revealed only by accident. Most people in France know nothing about it, even now. No visits to camps are permitted. At one time even pastors and rabbis were excluded, but this order has now been revoked. None of our social workers in the camps may accompany the convoys and our request to set up a service at the frontier station was refused."

Lowrie was remarkably restrained on the justification authorities gave for these deportations. "An explanation of these deportations is not easy to discover," he continued. "To a certain extent it may be due to Germany's urgent need for workers." Laval had promised 350,000 French workmen to the Germans, but since this number could not include Jews, the "workers" explanation for the deportation of Jews didn't make sense. Lowrie concluded with the same explanation that all responsible minds had come to by this time:

Since children, the aged and ill (we know of some cases of epileptics, palsied, insane and even bedridden put into the corral for deportation) are taken and since their destination is uniformly reported (by Laval, Pétain, the police) as the Jewish reservation in Poland, the need for labor does not totally explain this action. In view of the present transport difficulties in Germany it is hard to understand a German *desire* to have these unfortunates. . . . The best explanation we have been able to imagine is this: the general German plan for a new Europe includes 'purification' of undesirable elements. Whereas other parts of the plan are behind the original time-schedule, for example the campaign in Russia, this portion is in the hands of fanatics, and is being relentlessly pushed as originally planned.

Again, Lowrie commented that the remaining Jews in France, including refugees from Germany in 1940, "have few illusions as to the fate awaiting them in Poland." The "few French" who knew about this were "profoundly shocked" and "ashamed of being French."

On August 28, 1942, Lowrie sent a report to the American and British consuls in Geneva.[36] The subject was a worrisome issue for Toureille particularly—Vichy's deportation of foreigners who were formerly soldiers in the French or Allied armies. He took up their case in several sessions of the Committee of Nîmes and may have contributed some of the information in Lowrie's report. Lowrie pointed out that the age limits and the total numbers promised to the Germans for deportation were constantly being widened by the Laval government. Even those at the top of the exemption-from-deportation lists—former soldiers in the Allied armies—were now being taken.

Lowrie's reported that when he inquired about the deportation of veterans, particularly about Czechoslovak or Polish Jews in this category, the Vichy intelligence service answered: "Well, of course, a Jew who simply served in the quartermaster department or spent a few months in training at Agde, is not a combattant. Any man who actually fought at the front, was wounded or is an escaped prisoner, will, of course, be exempt." Lowrie commented, "Against this new interpretation of the rights of ex-soldiers we raise a vehement protest."

The Czechoslovaks and Poles in this group were not evacuated with their compatriots at the defeat of France, because they were too near the front in 1940. Most of them were in the forced labor battalions "under conditions of virtual slavery." Since the Nazis were likely to consider these former soldiers traitors, and since most were Jews who "have no illusion about the fate that awaits them," Lowrie considered the only recourse to be an immediate protest to all French military authorities who would listen. "That anyone with a shred of honor left could acquiesce in this delivery into Nazi hands of veterans who happen to be Jewish, is inconceivable. Marshal Pétain has frequently spoken about having saved the honor of France. The present deportations are a caustic commentary on a new conception of honor."

Lowrie added that he and his Committee members had telegraphed a protest to all military leaders in France and arranged to do the same to various national groups. He proposed that the American consul cable military authorities and veterans' organizations in the United States. They had to hurry. The entire twenty thousand veterans were to be deported before September 20. Pastor Boegner and Cardinal Gerlier would be each making a final protest to Marshal Pétain.

On September 19, 1942, Lowrie wrote another memorandum to Geneva, praising the aid work of the Christian organizations and the "almost unique relationship" that developed between Christians and Jews.[37] Those hearing Grand Rabbi Hirschler's declaration at a Committee of

Nîmes meeting that same month, quoted by Lowrie in this memo, must have found his gratitude almost unbearable, causing both grieving and remorse for what else they might have done:

As Jews, we weep with our martyred brethren. As Frenchmen, we are humiliated. For our country, because we still love her, we despair of the judgment she made of her own civilized peoples, her own children. Nonetheless, in our suffering we have encountered so much active sympathy that we do not despair, either for humanity or for the real France. In the name of the rabbinate, in the name of the Jewish welfare organizations, in the name of martyred Judaism, I am authorized to express to you, to the organizations you represent, and to all your colleagues our profound gratitude. . . . In the hours of anguish through which we are living, overwhelmed by this vast injustice, we face the conscience of the world together with you in this union of men of faith, of good heart and of duty, regardless of their difference of thought, origin, or confession. We render thanks to God who inspires and blesses them.

Lowrie then pronounced a kind of benediction on the departure scene, but it seemed more true to the emotional atmosphere to imagine the agony of the aid workers who were there "before the train pulled out": "Their tireless devotion is something never to be forgotten, and thousands of witnesses have testified, often in the last words they spoke before the train pulled out, taking them into Nazi territory, to the vast comfort and spiritual assurance left with them by our workers' kindness and service."

Saving Jewish Children

On October 6, the separate organizations of the Committee of Nîmes, according to Lowrie's report,[38] were trying to save the approximately 5,000 Jewish children left behind when their parents were deported. Part of the effort was devoted to obtaining visas abroad, to the United States, Mexico, and some South American countries.[39] On September 28, U.S. Secretary of State Cordell Hull offered 1,000 entry visas for the Jewish children, with a possible additional 5,000. On October 16 the American Friends Service Committee went to Laval for cooperation in this emigration effort, working through the U.S. chargé d'affaires H. Pinkney Tuck. Laval's major concern, parroting the Germans' concern, was that these emigrating children not be used to stir up anti-Vichy (and anti-German) publicity. The children should therefore be emigrated in small groups.

On October 16 Vichy agreed to issue 500 visas only, and they had to be limited to orphans—a too-severe limitation, the AFSC representatives pointed out, since not as many as 500 orphans could be verified, because the fate of most of the deported parents was unknown. Vichy further complained that "certain religious groups had evaded the administrative measures by hiding children," and if Vichy now permitted these children to emigrate to the U.S., it might justify these acts and encourage more hiding. Throughout October 1942, the Vichy authorities kept stalling on the emigration plan, imposing new requirements that the American Friends worked feverishly to comply with. Then a new course to the war shut off all chances: the Allies had landed in North Africa and on November 11, the Germans occupied the southern zone in France. Lowrie mentioned that 350 children succeeded later in clandestinely reaching the United States.[40]

Vichy's record on the Jewish children within its borders and the aid groups' attempts to save them, were reported immediately after the war, October 26, 1944, by the Jewish organization OSE (*Oeuvre de secours aux enfants,* or Agency for Aid to Children).[41] Of the 15,000 Jewish children killed or deported (half of the total French population of Jewish children), 2,000 were from Vichy France, many deported with their families in August 1942. The OSE cared for 6,000 children during the occupation, 5,000 of those living in Vichy. The organization lost 80 children to the Gestapo but also 28 OSE workers who were either shot or deported. The same organization also sent 1,500 children to Switzerland.

As a result of denunciations of the deportation of children, particularly by Cardinal Gerlier, Archbishop Salièges of Toulouse, and Pastor Boegner, about 1,400 children were saved in 1942: about 600 children at Rivesaltes camp, 400 at Gurs, and 400 at Les Milles were released while their parents were deported. Cardinal Gerlier and Father Chaillet also saved 40 Jewish children in Lyon, refusing to turn them over to the Gestapo and undergoing arrest, before being released through the intervention of the Cardinal.

Toureille and Lowrie mention two cases of benevolence toward the children of MACE during the year of mass deportations. In a postwar article, Toureille described the few local Vichy functionaries who did not threaten the children of MACE. Toureille paid tribute to the police chief for the Nice region, Marc Freund, an Alsatian Protestant whom he had won over to the Czech cause when the official visited the Czech Republic in 1922.[42] There were other friends, too, among the police administration whom he characterizes as devoted to the Church and from old Protestant families. In another example of benevolence toward MACE, Lowrie wrote in his memoir that when the Germans occupied all of France in November 1942, they assigned the Italian troops to the southeast corner, including the Vence area where MACE was located. According to Lowrie, the Italians showed no animus toward the Czechs and visited MACE only to see the children without interfering with operations there.[43]

During this same period of deportations in 1942, the Center for Czech Aid suffered a blow. Dr. Dubina, its director, his wife, and five administrators were arrested and deported, Dubina to Buchenwald and his wife to Ravensbruck. The Center was reorganized, but its functions diminished under the pressure of harassment from the Vichy authorities and dwindling resources. The new administrator of the Center, a French Protestant former officer of the cavalry, had to go to Switzerland illegally to gather and distribute aid; he was arrested by the Gestapo. He said not one word to his interrogators, was deported to Buchenwald, and died a few days before the liberation of the camp by the Americans.[44]

Toureille later characterized the attitude of the Vichy police toward Czech aid during 1942 and afterward: "From the beginning, the Vichy police were hostile toward us. It did not feel sympathetic toward 'the republic of the Free-Mason Dr. Bénès' [president of the Czechoslovak Republic], who, they said, had adopted, between the two wars, a policy hostile to France. But as time went on, the coming collapse of the Axis powers became more and more a possibility, and the second level administrators first, followed by the top-level bureaucrats and even the Vichy administration itself, became increasingly sympathetic toward us."[45]

Toureille's Rescue Activities: Three Families in Trouble

In July 1942, Pierre Toureille made a phone call to Anna and Ferdinand Sperber that saved their lives.[46] The couple were Viennese Jewish refugees, who had lived comfortably, even elegantly, among a large family—until Hitler's entrance into Vienna in March 1938, provoking their frantic attempts to leave the country. They spent most of their money on precious furs, jewels, and equipment, filled nine trunks, and fled to Belgium where their extended family soon joined them. After three months there, where Anna and her sisters-in-law worked at home as dressmakers, the German bombs started falling, May 1940, at 4 A.M., and, as Anna Sperber described it in her memoir, "The whole population began to walk across the country—destination: the frontier of France."

That same day Ferdinand Sperber was put in a French concentration camp, as a German national, where he remained for more than a year. Anna and the rest of the family fled the city and the bombing, getting the nine large trunks to the train station bound for the French frontier and carrying one bag for daily use. They all went by foot—her mother, two brothers, two sisters-in-law, and two small children, walking twenty miles a day. It was a nightmare vista they passed:

This was the saddest walk we had ever made. Our way led us all along the battlefield, the bombs and the machine guns were our companions, and on the streets lay hundreds of dead soldiers, most of them English. I saw a man looking for something in the pockets of a dead soldier, perhaps for money, but he found only a photo of his wife and baby. Angry, he threw it away. This picture lay like an accusation on the soldier's chest.

On our way we saw dead cows and horses in many gardens, and almost every house was destroyed by the bombs. We spent the nights in these ruins. I remember a woman who ran like crazy, pushing a carriage and crying all the way. I asked her why she was crying. She answered that she was looking for a cemetery—her two children in the carriage were dead.

After seventeen days the family reached the French frontier and waited to cross along with several thousand others. After waiting there five days, lying most of the time on the ground in fear of the bombs, they heard that the Nazis had already entered Paris, so they turned back to Belgium. They returned to Antwerp, amid even worse bombardments, including those from the English and the Americans, and the ever-present fear of Nazi persecutions. Anna learned that all their trunks had disappeared because the trains had been bombed and plundered; they had lost everything. After several months she received a letter from her husband that he would be liberated from the camp in southern France because of illness.

After standing in line for almost two weeks with 100 others, from 6 A.M. to 3 P.M., Anna obtained her visa and started her trip to her husband, 350 kilometers to the south. On the extremely cold train, a French railroad worker insisted she wear his coat during those four days and brought her hot coffee. A German officer gave her a cigarette, told her about his wife and children, and complained that the war was too long and unnecessary. Two French women, returning from visiting their husbands who were prisoners in Germany, were sitting in the same compartment. They looked at Anna hatefully and moved away. A Gestapo control officer shouted at her for fleeing her fatherland: "I didn't tell him that every day I saw so many inhuman things happen that I often thought, if a perfect man existed in a world such as ours, he would die of horror and compassion."

In the Vichy zone, she reached her husband, who collapsed upon seeing her. They settled, as refugees, in a small town that treated them warmly, until the mayor took her aside and said, "Madam, if one day you should need something important from me, I'll be glad to do it." He took her downstairs to the chief of police and told him, "Remember this lady and her husband. You should protect them in any situation." The chief wrote their names in red on his calendar.

A few days later, a young girl who worked at the police station warned them and a few other refugees that at 4 A.M. the next day, the secret police would pick them all up and put them in a concentration camp. The Sperbers, instead of running like the others, felt secure in the promise of safety from the mayor and stayed put. At exactly 4 A.M. that next day, their doorbell rang and two policemen told them to be ready in ten minutes. A large truck with seventy-five people already in it waited in front of their house. The neighbors came in and protested that even a murderer in France could not be arrested between sunset and sunrise. When the Sperbers mentioned their letter from the mayor, the policemen said that this was a direct order from Hitler and that they must obey.

At that moment Ferdinand Sperber had a kidney stone attack and Anna a heart attack. The police doctor pronounced them unfit to be moved and ordered a wait of at least five days. He also told the couple, quietly, that they could escape arrest only if she should be pregnant. Even though this was the worst time to have a child, they set their hopes on her becoming pregnant. On the fourth day, Anna was called to a drugstore three blocks away to receive a long distance call.

Very scared, I heard a man's voice. It was Pastor Pierre Toureille, from a city a few hundred miles away from us. We had never heard of him and I became suspicious, but it was a very kind voice that asked me how he could help us. At this very moment, I knew intuitively that now would come a little sunshine into our distress. From this moment, it was like a godmother's hands, watching over us. He helped us directly and indirectly. He gave us advice about how and where to flee. He sent us money wherever we were and he helped our friends, whom we recommended to him. . . . He sent us certificates, stating we were Protestants and under the protection of his church, and he sent us a little money regularly. . . . I'm certain that if the Nazis would have discovered his activities, he would have been deported.

Toureille contacted several pastors in his Chaplaincy network, who helped the Sperbers flee from place to place for the next four years. Their German accents gave them away, and many local people refused to chance giving them help. They had a number of close calls, including two Vichy policemen who tried to pick them up at their front door at 5 A.M. knocking for an hour, hoping to get a reward from their Nazi commander for delivery of Jews. The Sperbers refused to answer the door, and fortunately (probably because the policemen were acting without the knowledge of their Vichy supervisor) they went away. For four years the Sperbers fled, watching every night, listening for the footsteps.

They reached Lyon on January 1, 1943, where Toureille sent them to a clandestine organization, which permitted them to sleep in the office of the Red Cross, but otherwise they had to find their own shelter. Then Anna Sperber discovered she was four months pregnant, a tragic time for a new child, when they had no roof or money and at a time when the Nazis were deporting newborns along with their parents. Toureille passed them along the pastoral network to Mens, Isère, a small town and center of the growing resistance movement, where the local pastor, Pierre Gothie, protected them—"a modern saint, a big soul," Anna Sperber called him, "a continuation of Pastor Toureille!" Here they stayed for the rest of the war and it was here that their son was born.

After the war the Sperbers heard that Anna's two brothers and one sister-in-law had been deported in July 1943, that the other sister-in-law had escaped and her nine-year-old daughter hidden by nuns, while a 14-month-old niece was hidden by strangers. Anna's mother lost her mind and was placed in a mental hospital. All were eventually reunited with their extended family and reached the United States in 1951. It was only after that, in upper New York State, that they met Pierre Toureille for the first time in person.

The annual meeting of French Protestants on September 6, 1942, at Mialet, brought together sixty-seven pastors and nearly five thousand participants. In the birthplace of the Camisard chief Roland, the assembly renewed their ties to their own Huguenot history, forging their communal "places of memory"—a favorite phrase of French historians—and a solidarity with the persecuted Jews.

That same month, Toureille gave refuge to Robert and Thérèse Papet, a couple who then worked in his Chaplaincy until the end of the war.[47] The WCC in Geneva had alerted Toureille about two German emigrés, a Jew (Robert) and a Protestant "Aryan,"who had married in France in May 1940 after the Nuremberg racial laws in Germany forbid such unions. This meant certain death for the couple if they were caught in German-occupied France.

Toureille's first step was to send Robert Papet the Chaplaincy questionnaire, designed to produce the background and needs of the respondent. Robert Papet replied that he was born Robert Papst in Berlin in 1909, of parents who were naturalized German citizens originally from Poland; he was trained as a mechanical engineer and emigrated to Paris in August 1933. He was put in an internment camp in France in 1939, then joined a regiment of foreign volunteers in the French army, from 1939 to 1940.

To the questions on his abilities, his state of health and means of existence, and his future desires, Papet answered that he spoke and wrote German, French, and English; he was suffering from heart disease; he wanted to emigrate but had no passport or visa; and he needed no material support at the present because he had 4,000 French francs. He had been working as a carpenter in Issoire, Auvergne up to the time of filling out the questionnaire. On the question of whether he possessed a Bible, he answered "no," although his wife did have a New Testament. At the end of the form, Toureille asked, "Could you do something for those less fortunate than you?" Papet's reply was eminently practical: he could donate used clothing, medium size.

Toureille asked the couple to come to Lunel to live in the Toureille home, and he provided them with new identity papers through the cooperation of the Prefecture of Montpellier. Their names were changed to Robert Parlier, born in Metz, and Thérèse Dembert, born in Forbach, in the same area. While awaiting these new papers, the newly named Robert Parlier hid with a pastor in a nearby town. One of the men at the prefecture who was helping him get the papers was later deported.

Papet/Parlier went to pick up his wife with his new identity card in hand, which eased his anxiety when he had to pass through security police rounding up refugees for deportation. In March 1943, Toureille proposed to the couple that they come to work for him in Lunel, for the Chaplaincy. They accepted with gratitude and soon realized that Toureille was endangering himself by taking on people with false papers. In addition, Toureille was exposed to criticism from the local population and his colleagues because the couple was living together without a proper marriage certificate.

They worked for Toureille and the Chaplaincy for the next three years and observed its operations from the inside. Later Robert Papet summed up its rescue activities this way:

The Chaplaincy was conceived and organized by Pastor Toureille. It focused on the Jewish refugees but in order to obtain subsidies from the World Council of Churches in Geneva, it also had to maintain ties with those of Protestant or Orthodox religions, on principle. In a number of cases, the Jewish spouse (known to the Pastor) stayed hidden and the "Aryan" spouse received the allocations and identity papers necessary for survival. Several mysterious persons passed through the private home of Pastor Toureille, just as I did before obtaining my French identity card. The expression "mysterious" is appropriate because some of the Pastor's neighbors suspected him of spying for the Germans, and he was unable to tell the truth and thus defend himself.

On his own debt of gratitude toward Toureille, Papet reflected, "Pastor Toureille not only saved me from deportation as a Jew, but also from certain condemnation because I had fought as a 'foreign volunteer' against Hitler's Germany. His action came at the right moment, because in March 1943, when I was already in Lunel, a Wehrmacht officer came at dawn to look for me in Issoire, but we had already left."

At the end of the war, Toureille wrote a letter of recommendation for Robert Papet/Parlier.[48] Papet's position in the Chaplaincy was office manager, and his abilities, Toureille continued, were thoroughly suited to taking charge, sometimes for more than a month at a time, while Toureille was on the road. Papet had the heavy responsibilities of correspondence in several languages, written and personal interventions with the authorities on behalf of the refugees, receiving visitors, running a staff of twelve people, editing reports, and handling the finances of the Lunel office. Both husband and wife, Toureille continued, collaborated actively in the spiritual resistance of the French Protestant churches, "contributing to saving persons hunted down for religious, racial and political reasons, hiding them, and passing them into Switzerland. . . . The Papets have given proof of personal courage and serenity."

In October 1942, in Lunel, Toureille and his wife crossed paths with Jacob and Sonia Barosin and helped save their lives.[49] Jacob was born in Riga, Latvia, Sonia in Odessa, and the couple had emigrated to Paris through Berlin in 1932; he was an artist and she a concert violinist. He joined the French army and, after its defeat in 1940, was sent to a forced labor camp under Vichy. Liberated in 1941, Jacob and his wife settled in Lunel after finding some work in a nearby town. In October of the following year he received a letter from the prefect that he was to report to the internment camp at Agde in two days, as part of Vichy's mass roundup of foreign Jews for deportation. The Barosins were in a panic—there wasn't enough time to prepare a hiding place.

They went for a walk in the narrow backstreets of the town, Sonia in tears. Suddenly they came upon a woman whom Sonia introduced as Mrs. Toureille, with whom she had shared the last two eels in a rations line a few days before. Mrs. Toureille suggested they see her husband, who had a contact in the office of the Agde camp. In his memoir of this important encounter (*A Remnant*), Barosin inserted his own drawing of the three of them standing in a plain white space, the Barosins leaning anxiously together, Sonia with her hands clasped nervously across her waist and leaning toward the shorter Mrs. Toureille, who is saying something to them in a quiet, restrained way.

Later that afternoon, the Barosins were in Pastor Toureille's office. Barosin remembers his first impression of Toureille clearly: "He was a man of about 5 feet 8 inches like me, middle aged, friendly, with a quick grasp in his eyes." [50] Toureille told Barosin he had been successful twice in keeping men out of Agde, and would try again by writing his contact in the office a letter, adding "You take him this letter from me, and we will pray and see," then smiling when Barosin asked to add his own prayers to Toureille's.

"The day arrived in sorrow and deep anxiety," Barosin continued. "I put socks, a shirt, an aluminum pot and other concentration camp prerequisites into my shoulder bag—the old music all over again—and rushed to the railroad station. Sonia could not hold back her tears. . . . I was desperate. Were we already in the tentacles of the monster? Drancy, Poland? I broke out in a cold sweat. My God, why are You torturing us and abandoning us?" Using Toureille's name when he arrived at the Agde camp office, Barosin reached the proper official, a German Jew, who luckily had been a business acquaintance of Barosin's father (who had emigrated a few years earlier to the United States). Barosin spent several excruciating hours in this office, going through the procedures and physical examination arranged by this official, so that he could be discharged and detached to farm work back in Lunel.

He had to catch a 5 PM train back, the station was a half-hour walk from the camp, and the heavy paperwork that had to be done gave him only fifteen minutes to make it. "Until the big gate I walked normally, wasting precious time . . . but then I started to run as I have never run before, and I ran and ran all the way to the station. I arrived at 4:59, the train was standing there and waiting for me, and the moment I jumped on it, it started to move. . . . This is the stuff miracles are made of . . . based on actions of decency and goodness."

Sonia rushed to meet him when he turned the key of their apartment door in Lunel. The next day they went to thank the Toureilles. "Pastor Toureille, with an increasingly serious expression on his face, listened to my story. The more I spoke, the wider his eyes opened. 'God has hidden you in the shadow of his Hand.'"

Jacob and Sonia Barosin survived the war. After Jacob was again interned, this time at Gurs awaiting deportation, he managed to get a leave to see his wife, and they both went into hiding in several Cévenol villages that were part of the clandestine rescue network.

Throughout that traumatic summer and fall of 1942, Toureille's letters to the Geneva office of the WCC made no broad references to the cataclysmic events occurring under Vichy. The letters were abrupt and focused on details of a few individual cases. On August 27 Toureille listed three of "our parishioners" who were requesting baptismal certificates from Germany. On September 30 he reported that a refugee and his wife and daughter, to whom Toureille had given his own breeding rabbits to set up a business, had sold all the rabbits and the hutch, without permission, and left for Switzerland. Toureille considered this act a betrayal of trust and found the liquidation of a valuable, irreplaceable hutch at a quarter of its real value particularly galling. "This parishioner is not trustworthy and, although he indisputably has talents for writing and chatting, has shown himself to be a very bad worker with a very questionable conscience." "How can we get back the goods or the money?" he asked Freudenberg.

On December 11, Toureille wrote to Freudenberg about a refugee who was asking to change his place of lodging because, Toureille explained sourly, "he is in a home where he isn't allowed to fall back on his old bad habits [including drugs]. What bothers him is precisely this discipline." The refugee had also lied by saying that his aid funding had ended in November. Those Swiss interested in supporting him, Toureille continued, should be warned that "the state of his health, and of his soul, alas, remains the same and will not be changed by any therapy. He is incurably a weak character." Toureille proposed firmness and severity, and a skeptical reading of any tragedy this man may have reported in his letters.

Toureille's Personal Life

On September 27, 1942, Toureille suffered a personal tragedy: his nephew, Jacques Saussine, died of peritonitis in the camp at Récébédou, because he was not given medical help in time. He was a young theology student, the son of a pastor, who was living in the camp and giving aid as a representative of CIMADE. It must have been a hard blow for Toureille, who assumed of his nephew, as he did of himself, a strong impulse to serve, and a severe sense of responsibility. Two months earlier, Saussine felt it necessary to write a letter to Rabbi Kapel, asking him to testify to Toureille that he, Saussine, was indeed present at the deportation of Jews from the Récébédou camp on August 8 and 10. He explained, apologetically, that his uncle did not see his nephew's name in the rabbi's report, "was very surprised," assumed it was an oversight, and supposed that "I [Saussine] would like to correct the omission."

Saussine explained his relationship to his uncle: "I can understand very well how you might have forgotten to mention me after the second deportation. It doesn't matter to me, but Pastor Toureille, being my uncle, was very upset at the thought that I was not doing my work, that I was not accompanying our unhappy friends to the station. Please excuse, Rabbi Kapel, my bothering you about this, but you can see, given my relationship to Pastor Toureille, that it was necessary that I ask this favor of you. I hope to see you again soon at Récébédou, in circumstances less tragic than those when we last met, and I will always be happy to see you and, when possible, be of service to you."[51]

On October 26, 1942, the regional agent of the Vichy Bureau of Inquests and Security in Montpellier sent the following report on Toureille to the Prefect and the head of Vichy police, with copies to the central and local offices of the Bureau for Jewish Affairs (CGQJ, *Commissariat général aux question juives*). This report demonstrated the nature of the Vichy authorities' suspicions about Toureille, the clandestine elements of his work, and the resulting danger he was living under throughout the war:

Pastor Toureille has been reported several times acting on behalf of Jews and foreigners. In October 1941, he helped a foreigner of Jewish origin named R., born in Vienna but baptized in the Protestant religion, who was trying to avoid deportation.

Pastor Toureille, after obtaining an authorized visa to Switzerland, gave a public lecture in Geneva on evangelical activities in the refugee camps in France. He was ill advised to be calling the attention of Swiss public opinion to the refugee camps.

On the other hand, during the current year, 1942, the Resident General of Morocco has refused entrance to Toureille because the latter had no official mission there.

Pastor Toureille has been suspected of organizing passage for foreigners into Spain, a clandestine network in collaboration with the Quakers. This traffic now seems to be suspended, after the arrest of a Belgian and several American officials. Information not verified.

Pastor Toureille's tendencies are Gaullist and anti-government, and he is very sympathetic to Jews and without doubt, helps them obtain the papers they need.

A very strict surveillance must be maintained.

CONCLUSION: From the preceding report, the conclusion is:

1. The so-named TOUREILLE, Pierre, French, is a Protestant pastor working in the concentration camps.
2. He has been active in supporting Jews (source of information is indisputable), in spreading propaganda contrary to the orders of the government.
3. He is suspected of organizing the passage of foreigners to Spain (no formal proof).
4. He is very clearly a Gaullist sympathizer, an Anglophile, and anti-government.

In consequence:

1. I respectfully request that the Chief of the Regional Police order an active surveillance of the activities of Pastor Toureille.
2. I respectfully request that the Prefect of Montpellier order a surveillance of the mail of the party concerned, and that he communicate excerpts to the Regional Director of the Bureau of Inquests and Security [S.E.C., *Section d'enquête et de contrôle*] of Montpellier.[52]

At the end of 1942, the Germans occupied southern France, an event that the Toureille family remembers clearly. Toureille's youngest daughter, Anne-Marie, remembered when the Germans marched into Lunel (in a letter to the author, August 9, 1996). She was about ten years old at the time: "I will never forget that day. It was late afternoon. We could hear rumbling in the distance, a strange dull noise getting louder and louder. Then they appeared in their ugly dark green uniforms, black helmets, black boots. The smell was sickening. Terror spread through my body—a feeling of defeat, loss of freedom, like a mouse being trapped by a cat. I knew this was it, my France, my town, my home were no longer mine. The Boches invaded our homeland, imposed curfews limiting our activities."

Marc Toureille was twelve and remembered this event with the same passion:

November 11, 1942, was the twenty-fourth anniversary of the Allied victory over Germany in World War I. The Americans had landed in North Africa three days earlier. It was about 7:30 PM, pitch dark outside, and, for once, my father was home. We had just sat down to dinner. Suddenly we hear a strange sound, muffled at first, getting louder, the sound of heavy steps. My father gets up, listens a second, and exclaims, "These are not the steps of French soldiers. They are Germans."

We turn off the light and rush to the windows over the street, half hiding behind the slotted blinds. They come, boots hitting the pavement. The shame, the anger, the hate. And the smell of the Wehrmacht—boots, rancid butter, sauerkraut. And hate, hate, not only theirs but mine. I wanted to see them all killed.

Before they round the corner, an officer barks out an order and they all start singing one of those army marching songs that would become much too familiar. I do not remember how long we stood there. But when it was over and the windows were closed, one of us asked my father how we should act toward them. "Just ignore them, pretend not to see them," he said. This was what we did for the rest of the Occupation.

8

The War, 1943–1945 and After

Chronology

January 23, 1943: First inquest, at CGQJ (*Commissariat général aux questions juives*), on "a network for saving Jews," from France to Switzerland, naming as the leaders Charles Guillon and Pastor Trocmé, of Le Chambon-sur-Lignon.

April 19–May 16, 1943: Warsaw Ghetto uprising.

May 19, 1943: Joint report sent out by the World Council of Churches (WCC) and the World Jewish Congress (WJC) on the catastrophic situation for the Jews and ways to help them.

July 1943: First allusion by Vichy officials in Lozère, to the camp in Auschwitz.

August 2, 1943: Inmates revolt at Treblinka.

September 8, 1943: Germans occupy the Italian Zone in France; Jews flee toward Switzerland.

Fall 1943: Danes use boats to smuggle most of their Jews to Sweden.

October 14, 1943: Inmates at Sobibor begin armed revolt.

November 1943: First resistance group of Jewish Boy Scouts of France created in La Malquière, near Vabre.

End of the year, 1943: Creation of Jewish and Jewish-Protestant Resistance groups in the Haute-Loire.

January 1944: President Roosevelt sets up War Refugee Board at urging of Treasury Secretary Henry Morganthau, Jr.

March 19, 1944: Germany occupies Hungary.

May 15–July 9, 1944: Over 430,000 Hungarian Jews are deported to Auschwitz-Birkenau, where most are gassed.

June 6, 1944: Allied powers invade western Europe on D-Day.

July 2, 1944: The Germans set fire to the Kovno ghetto in Lithuania, with the Soviets only miles away; 6,100 men and women are transferred to Dachau and Stutthof concentration camps.

July 20, 1944: German officers fail in attempt to assassinate Hitler.

July 23, 1944: Soviet troops arrive at Majdanek camp.

August 2, 1944: Nazis destroy the Gypsy camp at Auschwitz-Birkenau; around 3,000 Gypsies are gassed.

September 1, 1944: Liberation of southern France; detachment of French forces arrives in Le Chambon-sur-Lignon.

October 7, 1944: Prisoners at Auschwitz-Birkenau revolt and blow up one crematorium.

January 17, 1945: Nazis evacuate Auschwitz; prisoners begin "death marches" toward Germany.

January 27, 1945: Soviet troops enter Auschwitz.

April 1945: U.S. troops liberate survivors at Buchenwald and Dachau camps.

April 30, 1945: Hitler commits suicide in bunker in Berlin.

May 5, 1945: U.S. troops liberate Mauthausen camp.

May 7, 1945: Germany surrenders, and the war ends in Europe.

Because Herod can appoint his functionaries, because he can make his work force build the city of Tiberias, he thinks he can also hire and control minds and souls. It was on this same principle that Sedecias imprisoned Jeremiah, that Joachim killed Uriah, that Joas assassinated Zachariah, that Louis XIV sent the Huguenots to the galleys and to the stake. . . . You know enough history to know that, in the battle between human power and the champions of God, it was the cause of the Jeremiahs, the Uriahs, the John the Baptists, the Huguenots, that triumphed, . . . it was the Spirit that won.

—Pastor Noël Poivre, *Le plateau vivarais*

I can verify that in that period when individual transport was practically nonexistent, the trains were the principal and sometimes only choice for a traveler, except in the places inaccessible to trains, sometimes available by bus, like the one that climbed laboriously from Le Chambon to Fay-sur-Lignon. We, my mother and I, went to La Voulte, from Avignon along the right bank of the Rhône, in this already ancient train built by the C.F.D. Company, those initials that would be taken later as the title of the bulletin of the College Cévenol, standing for "Ça File Doucement" ("That runs slowly"). So, this winding, puffing old train climbed—at very reduced speed and for a very long pause in the station of Cheylard—the whole valley of l'Eyrieux, finally reaching Dunières on the plateau at St.Agrève.

—Bernard Joessel, 1943

Rescue Networks

Because it was through his Chaplaincy office in Lunel that Toureille directed his clandestine rescue activities, this office was under surveillance by the Vichy and Gestapo security police. It was somewhat protected by its status as a Protestant church organization rather than a Vichy-directed one. Marc Toureille recalled his own role in these secret rescue activities: "I knew what my father was doing during the war, but I didn't know the details. Sometimes he would send me on errands. He would say, 'Go to the railroad station and take two bikes. You'll meet someone there, dressed in a long coat, with a newspaper in his hand. Just give him the bike and don't talk to him too much, especially if he has an accent.' I'd take him to a minister in another town, just drop him there; that was it. And I worked in my father's office, stamping mail and taking care of the library. Most of the people working there were given new names because they were Jews in hiding."

Herbert Stein-Schneider, an Austrian refugee who became a Protestant pastor, was a student at the Faculty of Theology in Montpellier in 1943 and 1944 when he was drafted by Toureille to help in the rescue activities set up within the Chaplaincy network. Toureille had heard of him through Dean Henri Leenhardt of the Faculty of Theology (who was also Toureille's brother-in-law). The dean was at that time overseeing a group producing fake documents for those threatened by the authorities. Toureille and Stein-Schneider crossed paths after the war, when Stein-Schneider replaced Toureille as pastor at the French Protestant church in Washington, D.C.

In 1988 Stein-Schneider gathered together what he could remember of his rescue work with the Chaplaincy (in a letter to Marc Toureille). It was not an organization with files and minutes, he pointed out; any files falling in the hands of the Gestapo would have meant death for the names on it. They all existed "only in Pastor Toureille's head," and he "possessed a prodigious memory, knew his flock and handled the files individually and on a personal basis." He was constantly on the move, from one group to another, from city to city, inquiring about the parishioners' needs and organizing border crossings for those most threatened.

Stein-Schneider's task was to visit these groups, contacting only the person in charge, with verbal messages only. He had to memorize the messages given him and report back to Toureille's office in Lunel. He never

Chaplaincy staff in Toureille's office, Lunel, 1944. *Standing, from left:* Mr. Rotkirsh, Marc Toureille, Irène Pouget (from Lunel; married name, Dauthéville), Mr. Pou, Thérèse Parlier (German; Protestant), Robert Parlier (German; Jewish; office manager; name was originally Pabst). *Seated, from left:* Mrs. David (German; Jewish), next two people unidentified, Miss Stricker (friend of Mrs. David); Mrs. Pou; Mr. Stricker (father of Miss Stricker); and Mr. Goldschmidt (Belgian; Jewish).

knew the composition of the groups or how many of their members were actually Christian, whether they had been baptized before being banished by Hitler, how many had a counterfeit certificate of baptism, or how many had, in fact, never been baptized. "We did not differentiate among any of them. They were all threatened by the racial laws and that was enough to be admitted into the Chaplaincy."

He knew best the groups of refugees in Lyon, Grenoble, and Valence, but the names and faces were changing constantly. He estimated that from 30 to 50 percent of them were sent across the Swiss border. "So this was the nature of this Chaplaincy: No document, no danger. . . . What extraordinary things we could have learned if Pastor Toureille had been interviewed during his lifetime. . . . But, as a matter of fact, he did not like to talk about it. I never, in any of his frequent lectures after the war, heard him broach the subject."

On April 14, 1943, the French Protestant church was heard from

Chaplaincy staff in the Lunel municipal park, 1944. *From left:* Ella Ilbak (Estonian; dancer), Mrs. David, Henriette Monier (French), Mr. and Mrs. Schweitzer, Robert Parlier, Délie Toureille, and Pastor Toureille.

again, in a published protest by the Council of the Protestant Federation of France against the February 16 law that instituted the forced labor groups to be sent to Germany (the *Service du travail obligatoire,* STO). The Council stated: "There is unremitting opposition between the Gospel . . . and any conception of man or society that considers labor as merchandise that one has the right to buy or requisition at will."[1] The establishment of the STO sent the majority of young Frenchmen, including Protestant youth, into hiding where, in many cases, they joined armed resistance groups.

The World Council of Churches (WCC)

In February 1943, Visser't Hooft noted in his 1965 memo, the World Council of Churches sent a report on the extermination of the Jews to the High Commissioner for Refugees of the League of Nations.[2] On March 19 and 22, 1943, the WCC and the WJC sent their joint report to the American ambassador in Berne and to the British ambassador. They requested that it be transmitted to the U.S. and British governments, to the U.S. National Council of Churches, to the Archbishop of Canterbury, and to the branches of the WJC in the two countries. The report urged that the governments immediately propose an exchange of German civilians and Jews and a procedure for admitting Jewish refugees to neutral countries.

The only immediate reaction was a "strong speech" in support of these proposals by the Archbishop of Canterbury on March 24. The next document from Geneva on this subject, according to this report, was a letter more than a year later, in June 1944, from the Ecumenical Commission for Refugees. It issued "a solemn and public protest" against the deportation of 400,000 Hungarian Jews to Auschwitz, "where many hundreds of thousands of Jews have been systematically put to death." The next month, July 4, 1944, another letter of protest and report on the Hungarian Jews was sent from Geneva, this one signed by Karl Barth, Emil Brunner, Visser't Hooft, and Paul Vogt, with no clear indication, as Visser't Hooft reported, of where this information was sent.

In a January 1943 letter to a colleague, Freudenberg offered this interpretation of what rescuers at the WCC, particularly German-born ones like himself, were facing:

For three years it has been my duty to deal with a particular example of aggravated guilt incurred by our people and, as the servant of the church, to assist those who were the victims of it. I feel the gigantic burden of it every day. . . . Our preaching must speak quite harshly and unequivocally of the shattering verdict of the cross on the real sins of our people, the Germans. . . . We have to spell out the Ten Commandments. . . . The question of guilt should be taken out of the international political arena. But this can only happen if we ourselves settle our own accounts, and do so radically. The church is called to carry out this reckoning in the light of God's word through prophetic words and action. . . . After we have drunk the heady cup of irresponsible "national" imperialism to the lees, we must turn our strength freely and faithfully to the building of the European peace alliance and at the same time lay the foundations of trust, law and order.[3]

The last letter from Toureille in the Freudenberg-Toureille correspondence in the WCC archives, was dated August [no day given] 1943. Like those at the end of 1942, it focused on small details. This time it was the case of a parishioner requesting, through Freudenberg, to be lodged in a Protestant aid center. He was 68 years old and could pay a small rent of 1,000 francs a month. Toureille's local representative (in the parish where this man was staying) wrote that he was not a very dedicated parishioner: "We almost never see him at the Temple and his manner toward us is not above criticism. I am telling you this because Pastor Freudenberg told me that this request must be examined well." Toureille added his longtime complaint about authorization of aid: "Those who address their requests directly to you, over and above us, are generally less interesting—this is the general opinion of our Committee, and our friends and collaborators."

MACE and Center for Czech Aid (CCA)

On September 8, 1943, the Germans took over the Italian Zone in southeastern France, causing among the Jewish refugees more frantic escape attempts into Switzerland and elsewhere. A few weeks later, two German officers turned up at the MACE colony to inspect the grounds, apparently for its potential as a German military residence.[4] A few days later Director Fišera received the German military order to evacuate the school. The whole establishment—children, parents, staff, animals, farm and school equipment—had to be moved 300 miles away to a chateau in la Creuse, northwest of Vence. The Germans even cooperated in providing the hard-to-obtain railroad cars to do the transporting. It was a completely successful move—no children or animals were lost. The colony remained there for the rest of the war, after which most of the children, unlike the others in hiding, rejoined their parents.

On March 19, 1944, at five o'clock in the morning, the agricultural project in Corrèze that Toureille had helped found as the Center for Czech Aid (CCA) was surrounded and ransacked by the Gestapo, the regular German troops, and Vlassov's Army.[5] Luckily they found no weapons. The younger residents joined the partisans in Corrèze, founding a Czechoslovak group that eventually lost seven men. Another detachment of Czech partisans fighting in Garonne near Toulouse lost some of its men, including the former instructor at MACE, Karol Pajer, a Slovak, Protestant, and gifted teacher who was the favorite of Toureille's youngest daughter, Anne-Marie. Toureille commented later, probably thinking specifically of his daughter, "All who knew him and loved him, missed him and cried."[6]

After the Liberation of June 1944, Toureille had to move MACE from its mountain chateau and find a new home in healthier conditions for the children. He and his staff found another chateau, with a large park area near the ocean on the Spanish frontier, near Bayonne. (He pointed out, in an article written after the war, that here, in 1914, the first Czechoslovak military unit, a company called "Nazdar," had been formed.[7]) The local residents welcomed the children and found the Czech songs and dances they brought with them charming.

Anne-Marie Toureille focused her mourning of those lost in the war on her MACE connections. She mentions the paradox of those memories, which were both anguishing and cherished: "Many of the M.A.C.E. people perished on the infamous trains. Uncle Karol, who was a young Slovak teacher, went underground and was later executed by the Germans as he was trying to return home. I cried for days when my father told me. After 56 years, I still cry when I think of all the friends I will never see again. I learned a great deal very early about life, and I am glad I lived during those times. And in spite of it all, the war years were by far the best years of my young life. Those who never lived through one, do not understand."[8]

Toureille's Personal Life

From May to August 1943, Toureille was watched, summoned, and interrogated by the Vichy police and the Gestapo of Montpellier, and his home was searched. Two of those summons (in the possession of Marc Toureille) from the German Security Police (Gestapo) "request" Toureille to appear at headquarters with all his documents and identity papers, adding "If you do not appear, you will be arrested by the Police." Toureille commented later, "I should say that I was lucky to have been interrogated by a Gestapo official who maintained, in his behavior, some of the Protestant education he had received as a child."[9]

Robert Papet, a German-born Jewish refugee working in the Chaplaincy with his wife, both under false names, described one of these police searches:

The Gestapo from Montpellier, a chief officer and two assistants, burst into the office of the Chaplaincy, 3 rue de l'Isle, in Lunel. Since the Pastor was absent the first day, we personnel were interrogated. The second day Pastor Toureille, returned from his trip, was interrogated in his home, at his office, and then at general Gestapo headquarters in Montpellier. Thanks to his skill and ingenuity, the Pastor persuaded the Gestapo that our work was purely religious, which saved all of our lives.

During the Gestapo's search of our office, we hid some identity papers prepared for a Jewish refugee woman, in the hollowed out wooden toilet seat. I wanted to destroy them but I was constantly watched. Fortunately, these papers remained hidden and were eventually sent on.[10]

Marc Toureille remembered, with amusement:

When the Gestapo came to our house to question my father, they stole books, the most surprising ones! Before the war, my father brought back from Germany, propaganda books that the German kids learned to read from, anti-Semitic books. There was always the classical story about a fat German farmer who got into financial trouble. And into town comes this little skinny Jew, the character with the big nose. He's in rags and leering at the farmer's daughter, a beautiful, blue-eyed blond. He loans money to the German farmer, who then can't repay him. So the Jew becomes fat, with a cigar in his mouth, he's got his arm around the farmer's daughter, and the farmer is in rags—and this was what they were teaching little kids! The Gestapo took all those books. My father wondered whether some Nazi was putting them proudly in his personal collection.

One more example of the Gestapo's surveillance was their harassment of Toureille's wife. Marc told this story of his mother:

In the first months of 1944, my mother, whose maiden name was Lichtenstein, was required by the Vichy authorities to fill out a Racial Declaration, to determine whether she was Jewish. The Lichtenstein family was descended from a long line of rabbis by the name of Mayer. One of them converted to Christianity in the eighteenth century and took the name of Lichtenstein. We assumed this issue was raised with our family because my father's activities were under suspicion, which could mean the arrest and deportation of us all. Fortunately, the Allied bombing of Hamburg had destroyed the family records, delaying any action by Vichy. Then, in August 1944, Lunel was liberated by the first Free French division and that was the end of the matter.

One night, probably in 1943, the doorbell rang. My mother answered the door, then came back up, pale and agitated, saying she might have gotten us into big trouble. The caller was a German officer who clicked his heels and gave the Nazi salute, saying "Heil Hitler. I am your cousin from Hamburg." My mother answered, "No cousin of mine says 'Heil Hitler,'" and she slammed the door in his face. Luckily we never heard from this "cousin" again, although we did hear that he tried the same thing, with the same result, in a visit to my aunt in Montpellier.

The German Retreat

Beginning on August 13, 1944, in Lunel, the long awaited event: the Germans were finally retreating in the south. A time for jubilation and a time for holding one's breath because the retreating army was desperate and dangerous. Marc Toureille remembered: "In August 1944 the Boches were retreating in haste and stole anything with wheels, with or without tires. People hid things on their roofs. Since we could see many roofs from my bedroom window, we went to warn our neighbors, in case German soldiers would search our house for vehicles or beasts of burden."

Pierre Toureille took notes in diary form, reporting with an eye for drama and symbol, providing a small-town microcosm of those weeks of retreat and liberation. Day and night the German troops filed past under the windows, toward Arles and Nîmes. The Allies were near, between Toulon and Nice. On Sunday, August 20, the German railroad officials evacuated the Lunel station. "The Gestapo of Toulouse stop a moment under our windows—their car broke down. They are accompanied by the French Militia of Toulouse. One lieutenant, near the Pont de Vesse, shoots and kills a Gypsy from Lunel who had picked up a revolver from the road; the lieutenant steals the Gypsy's wallet with 40,000 francs."[11]

Toureille described the circus spectacle of the Germans filing past in any manner of vehicle they could confiscate—military trucks, civilian automobiles, horse carts, hearses, garbage trucks, hand carts, children's strollers, baby carriages, motor scooters, stolen bicycles, some without tires. Among these convoys, there were some French Militia families. At 4 P.M. on August 23, the last big German convoy left. The Germans were no longer singing "Die beste Kompagnie"[12]—"Their retreat is worse than ours was in May and June of 1940," he remarked. "I feel well avenged."

The next day five German officers in an automobile were arrested by the Free French forces, at the Pont de Lunel. The town administration was taken over by a Liberation committee, headed by one of the town bakers, Ernest Perrier. On August 25, a remarkable grand calm reigned for a while, followed by Allied bombing that added more flames to the buildings that had been burning for days. The bombs even hit civilians: five were killed and several wounded at the Pont de Lunel.[13] A terrific explosion from the sabotage of a German ammunition train broke seven windows of the Toureille household. More German prisoners were taken by the Free French forces. On August 26, the population of Lunel was urged to deck their homes with flags, and a wild variety appeared: French flags, English, American, Belgian, Czechoslovak, Yugoslav, Polish, Dutch, and Russian. The first newspapers of the Fourth Republic appeared.

Detachments of the French Army of Africa filed past toward Montpellier, on August 29. Toureille's oldest son Simon rode in from Nîmes on a bicycle the very next day. He had been with the underground and had taken part in three battles; he was wearing German boots. On September 2 General de Lattre de Tassigny passed through Lunel, to a wildly cheering crowd. On September 3, the next day, the traditional local festival with the running of the bulls celebrated the Liberation. Collaborators and Militia members were arrested, and more food became available. The curfew was moved back from 9:30 P.M. to 11 P.M.. Toureille ended his diary account with: "We can breathe. France is free. Joy is everywhere. Vive la France!"

"A Train Story"

On August 25, during the heaviest of the Allied bombing, Toureille's diary referred briefly to an explosion that shattered the windows of his house—a local event, a train story from a railroad town that assumed the level of legend in Lunel. It involved the plain and, at the time, anonymous act of individual courage that Toureille admired. Marc Toureille's sister-in-law, his wife Micheline's sister (who still lives in Lunel) narrated in this way:

The Germans were fleeing on an ammunition train, pulled by an old engine they found in an engine graveyard. This engine died in the railroad station of Lunel on August 22, 1944. The Germans gave the order to blow up the train right in the middle of the station, which would have also blown up the town.

Two railroad men from Lunel, Monsieur Marignan, an engineer, and Monsieur Couronne, a conductor, decided they could do something about that. In broad daylight, taking advantage of the confusion from the bombing and the burning buildings, they cut the telephone wires and climbed aboard the engine. They patched it up as best they could, using parts from other old steam engines sitting in the roundhouse. They fired it, got up a head of steam, and pulled out of the station, heading east toward Nîmes.

After a few kilometers, they reached the Mas de Viala, a property owned by the Bruneton family. Fortunately no one was at the Mas at the time. The two men knew that the engine couldn't make it any farther. They jumped off the train and fled through the orchards and bushy trees, into hiding. They were chased by the Germans, but not found. The Germans blew up the train. It made a terrific explosion that heavily damaged the Mas and burned for days afterward. Many windows in Lunel were broken by that explosion.

Monsieur Marignan died long ago. Monsieur Couronne was not from Lunel originally and we have no idea what happened to him.[14]

Toureille's Writings

Anne-Marie Toureille said that, during the war, she remembered her father as always sitting with a typewriter on his lap.[15] This was quite likely, given the enormous amount of correspondence the Chaplaincy required in order to maintain the bodies and spirits of the hundreds of refugees in its care and the scores of people working in its aid network. It was also Toureille's responsibility to compose his letters subtly, with the assumption that the Vichy authorities would be reading them. This meant he was under great pressure to store the most sensitive and dangerous information in his memory only, which, luckily, his colleagues remarked repeatedly, was extraordinary.

But by 1945, Toureille was writing prodigiously because he was following another imperative. He was like Avraham Tory, secretary of the Jewish Council of the Kovno ghetto, Lithuania, who hid five crates of documents in the ghetto in December 1942. In his will, which he packed in the crates, Tory said: "Driven by a force within me, and out of fear that no remnant of the Jewish community of Kovno will survive to tell of its final death agony under Nazi rule, I have continued, while in the Ghetto, to record my diary, which I began on the first day of the outbreak of the war. . . . With awe and reverence, I am hiding in this crate what I have written, noted, and collected, with thrill and anxiety, so that it may serve as material evidence . . . when the Day of Judgment comes."[16]

Like Tory, "with awe and reverence," Toureille was preparing evidence for the Day of Judgment. He was finally able to follow his natural impulse to record in writing the personal crises his parishioners and colleagues had lived through, always with an eye for the moral, spiritual significance in these others' stories that were interlocked with his own. This sudden, voluminous production of manuscripts appeared in a variety of genres. None of the pieces was self-reflective in the way a personal diary or journal would have been, nor were they productions of a scholar/historian. They read like long editorials to his broad public—his parishioners, the refugees, his French compatriots, the international church, and foreign governments.

In these writings, Toureille also reflected, sometimes only obliquely, on the dilemmas he faced as a rescuer—the problem of how much to involve his church while fighting against state injustice; how to be the evangelist while providing spiritual sustenance to the mostly non-Christian refugees; whether, in cooperating with Vichy, the aid organizations were not perpetuating the existence of the internment camps; and, whether he had made the right choices for saving the most people he could and abandoning the fewest. Most accessible to an active solution was the church-state dilemma, for which Toureille could propose new policies for the postwar period. It seemed not to be in his nature to feel remorse or guilt for his choices as an individual; he seemed able to maintain his conviction that he was the vessel of God's Will. But the despair that fell upon him by 1946 is likely to have had some roots in all of these issues.

Certainly, in these postwar writings, he felt it important to write down in detail the stories of the people he had helped, including the ones who eventually perished. The underlying goal of this kind of writing was that of a spiritual historian: to make order out of the turmoil of events, and to determine what roles individuals had played in the scheme of things. Given the broad seriousness of intent and social activism in these papers, Toureille, at the end of the war, still believed firmly that his own role was a large one.

Political Action through the Church

On May 28, 1944, Pastor Jean Cadier gave a sermon in Montpellier on the power of the spirit: "Faced with the power of the Holy Spirit, can one speak of the power of man? Yes, but only of the power of bondage. . . . Twenty men armed with machine guns can round up hundreds of young people for forced labor. . . . But a Christian deported to a concentration camp is more empowered by the Holy Spirit than the brutish army that imprisons him, as the Huguenot forced to sit in the galleys was greater than the guards who beat him with a stick. Before death, only one power lives; before suffering, only one power intervenes; before hatred, only one power shines, the power of the Holy Spirit."[17]

Pierre Toureille also believed in the power of the Spirit in the face of war and oppression, but sought to give it full body at the end of the war by starting a new political/religious action movement, The Christian World Conference on a Just and Durable Peace. In the pamphlet advertising his new proposal, which may have been one of his last attempts to shape French politics and world order in the large, he addressed one of the traditional dilemmas confronting the French Protestant church, especially during the war: the proper role of the church in relation to injustices within the State.[18]

His proposal made the central point that it was not the church itself, as a constituted body, that should be the prime actor, but individuals within it, representing themselves while being inspired by church beliefs. His main reason was not that the church as an institution should avoid putting itself in danger by defying the State, but rather, from a pragmatic point of view, that engaging the church in social action would be paralyzing to those trying to act. This argument was no doubt his conclusion from his own wartime frustrations with rescuing refugees through the church bureaucracy. And such an argument must have been offensive to those church authorities who considered the official church pronouncements and legal activities as effective in saving lives.

In 1944, probably near D-day in June, Toureille mailed out his proposal, titled "Appeal to All French Protestants," with the typed message at the top, "To join, write to Pastor Toureille, 3, rue Rouget de l'Isle, Lunel, Hérault." He began, characteristically, with a combination of descriptive eloquence and a call to action: "The war is not over, but the dawn of victory already lights up the sky; peace, majestic peace will soon come. We must not let ourselves be surprised by her appearance because if we do not prepare her path now, she could be compromised the moment she sets her feet on our land soaked in blood. Christians, most of all, should not allow themselves to be taken unaware. It is their duty to put themselves immediately to work for peace."

The old beaten paths of action wouldn't do, he went on, here including his former organization, the World Alliance for International Friendship through the Churches. The war set new conditions and demanded new methods. And "international friendship" had become too soft a term. In their present world of chaos, a term more precise and powerful, even harsh was needed—the phrase "justice, inflexible justice, brazen justice for all." Toureille continued that peace itself was a fragile concept that could not be established instantaneously. It needed preparation and a concrete, visible foundation.

He then took on the issue of the church itself, in a statement that would be interpreted by some French Protestant church authorities as an attack on them:

You will notice immediately that the word "church" does not appear in the title of this Appeal. That is by design. Not, needless to say, because of ignorance of the immense influence the churches could have; not because of disdain for the assistance the churches could contribute. In fact, if they could do so, the churches would give peace to the world. But, perhaps, all the same, they cannot see it through.

In any case, in proposing that the churches not intervene directly, we rely simply on the lesson of fact. In our country, at least, experience has clearly demonstrated that to introduce the churches as constituted bodies in the French Committee of the Alliance, has been an error—their presence in the heart of this Committee has paralyzed it. Without going into the causes, we limit ourselves to stating the facts. We propose avoiding this error by turning to the adherence of individual Protestants who by engaging only themselves have a much greater liberty of action. This does not hinder them from drawing upon themselves as sources of inspiration.

These words must have amounted, in some minds, to a declaration of independence from the French Protestant Church.

However, Toureille was not talking about complete divorce from the Protestant Church. It had diminished in its effectiveness but, for him, was still the inspirational source for social action. In the coming physical and moral reconstruction of the world, there would be work for everyone—governments, parliaments, ethnic peoples, all Christian elements—"if we take seriously the vocation of a Christian. . . . And let us remember that we do not fight alone. Battling with us is the living God who has a horror of war and infinite pity that extends to the fields of battle, God whose love will disarm all hatred."

The program of action in this Appeal proposed the creation of local groups of individuals, within such organizations as Social Christianity. These small groups would study the problem of international justice, the organization of a "society of nations," the question of race, guarantees to non-white races, work to abolish hatred and prejudice, "to put into practice, in the life of nations, the fundamental unity of the disciples of Jesus Christ and to enrich, by these studies and this action, our Christian faith, to make us more effective members of our church."

Toureille's proposals for putting such an organization into practice included a French Protestant Committee made up of delegates from various organizations considered to be of a similar spirit of action—"even, in some special cases, giving its support to an electoral campaign."

This particular copy of the Appeal was addressed to a pastor in Ariège and is now stored in the archives of the Protestant library in Paris. There has been no indication of whether Toureille succeeded in finding support, but the direction for individual social action described in this circular was one that he himself followed for the rest of his life, beginning the very next year, in 1946.

A second piece of writing by Toureille, in March 1945, also urged the international community of churches to political action, this time in behalf of the vast numbers of refugees and displaced persons after the war. A positive reaction to the guidelines for aiding refugees published earlier by the Swiss Committee of Protestant Churches, Toureille's piece attempted to extend these principles to a kind of international law on refugees.

Many of his points demonstrated his political experience and savvy. He urged, for example, that legislation dealing with refugees within each country be preceded by a mobilizing of public opinion (a job appropriate for the churches, among others), and that the resulting legislation be based in a well-thought-out, effectively administered policy. France learned this lesson at its peril, he noted, arguing that the initial setting up of the internment camps was a mistake, a mistake, he indicated, for reasons of practicality and effectiveness. Beginning in 1928 and throughout the 1930s, France's policies toward refugees had taken the weak form of piecemeal "recommendations," which the targeted refugees could defy with impunity.

Further, this ill–thought-out policy encouraged France's neighbors, like Switzerland and Belgium, to push its undesirable refugees into France. "So what happened in France," he continued, "is that the numbers depending on State care increased enormously and because the State could not legally expel those who were undesirable, they had to imprison them in camps." What was therefore urgently needed, he argued, was agreement and coordination on an international level.

The church role in pushing for such coordination should be significant. Taking the word "church" from the Swiss document he was referring to, Toureille said with passion, "It is important to define this term 'church' . . . This can only be a church that engages itself in daily life, a church that understands its social mission, a church inspirational and magnanimous, a church with a moral authority that is incontestable, a church that is infinitely more than a representative of one religion."

Another point dealt with the Jewish refugees in post-Holocaust France. They should not be singled out as a separate problem, he argued, because to define a group of refugees by race risked a revival of anti-Semitism. He continued that they were no longer facing discrimination on the basis of race, but rather on the basis of people who were displaced and who belonged nowhere. "The new legislation must protect not only those who were forced to emigrate because they were Jewish, but also those who were forced out of their countries for political or ideological reasons, or because they were wise enough not to prostrate themselves before the Baal of their people."

He added that church aid to Jewish refugees was not a first priority since the Jewish aid organizations were much better funded and equipped than were the Christian ones, and that American Jews, for example, had been more generous toward their refugee coreligionaries than American Christians had been toward theirs. And since the liberation, French Jewish organizations had well in hand their aid to those refugees who had hidden in Christian homes. "Judaism is, today, more active than ever . . . so it isn't necessary to carry our one litre of water to the ocean," he concluded.

He reviewed the complex problems involved in allowing the refugees to emigrate to "the country of their choice," or, on the other hand, forcing emigration according to some policy of equal distribution of emigrating peoples or implementing a scheme of general repatriation. Some refugees had little idea where they wanted to go, some were too ill or young or old to move from where they now found themselves, a burdensomely large number wanted to stay in France, some wanted to visit their families and then return to France, and the German Jewish and political refugees wanted to avoid at all costs returning to Germany. Naturalization would not resolve the question—"One can be legally naturalized without being morally and spiritually assimilated. . . . And naturalization is not a right; it is a favor, a gift."

Toureille's antidote for the plight of refugees in France was, unsurprisingly, evangelical—a reviving of the Protestant Church. What was needed, he argued, was a long process of assimilation for those who wanted to stay in France, with the Church playing a major role: "To speak the language, to know the history, to live the same life as all other citizens, is good but not sufficient. It is only when one lives bonded with others by the spirit and the soul, that one is truly assimilated. . . . The French Protestant Church has a magnificent role to play in this assimilation. The Church has therefore every interest in the government's not summarily expelling the refugees living in France during the war."

Describing the situation of people without a country as "morally intolerable and odious," Toureille acknowledged that it was not a problem that would soon be resolved. He urged that a strong international organization be formed to defend the interests of these people, with statutes that clearly maintained their rights—"and diminish in no way their contribution to creating a world more just and more fraternal." He added a plea that the international church organizations should then inform the French churches better, since they had been so isolated during the war: "Isolation continues to weigh too heavily on us. Come to our aid! We count on you to do it. We have suffered too much from our 'encirclement' since November 1942."

His final paragraph reminded his readers of their religious duty to offer refuge to foreigners: "The problem of 'the stranger' has existed at all times and all countries. But it does not always seem that humanity has progressed in this regard. Religious law, as given in Leviticus (Lev. 19:33–34), should be the guide for the church, nationally as well as locally: 'If a stranger lives in your land, you must not do him wrong. The stranger who lives among you will be as one born among you, and you will love him as yourselves, because you were strangers in the land of Egypt. I am the Eternal your God.' 'You are all brothers!' said Jesus. (Matt. 23:8)."

Whether these postwar exhortations to the church were distributed or published is unknown. But Toureille's postwar severance from the French Protestant Church and abrupt departure for Czechoslovakia and the United States in the following years demonstrated his pessimism concerning the Church in France as a vehicle for his spiritual activism.

Role of the Evangelist

The summer and fall months of 1944 were especially traumatic for the refugees in France because the Germans were speeding up their deportations as they retreated, pushing the French rescuers to even more illegal, clandestine, and dangerous measures to save them. By October 1944 the threat of extermination seemed to be over for the refugees, as did the desperate need for flight to the Swiss frontier. But now they had reached the end of their physical and spiritual strength and the means to continue their lives. The rescue agencies still had lifesaving work to do.

In 1945 Toureille made typed copies of letters of tribute he had received during and after the war from the refugees and internees he had helped. Not only are these writers witnesses to his keeping them alive but also, in the religious sense, witnesses to a change in their own spiritual awareness. All were thankful for the simple fact that Toureille cared about them when the world around them did not, and they were renewed by the intensity and depth of his commitment to them.

There was an additional poignancy to these letters, and what must have been an additional agony for Toureille; he wondered how many of these parishioners had survived their internment and he considered how minuscule was the total number of survivors compared with the tens of thousands who were deported and perished. The refugees and internees acknowledged the comfort they had found in reading the religious and historical books Toureille had sent them. In fact, the bulk of the refugees' concerns, in their letters to Toureille, were questions of religious belief and adherence that became crucial to whether they were feeling hope or despair. In addition, their tributes to the letters, readings, and sermons Toureille provided them, showed that his evangelical abilities were effective. Some of the refugees even claimed to be genuine converts to Christianity.

It is obvious in all of Toureille's wartime writing that he felt he was rescuing people's souls by rescuing their lives. But he seemed gratified more by the fact that he had helped refugees maintain a general religious faith than by the number of converts to the Protestant Church. He, of course, realized that these "non-Aryan Christians," meaning Jews recently converted, were mainly trying to save themselves from deportation and death.

Toureille, in his favorite style of narrating individuals' stories to make his point, reported on some of the fortunate and unfortunate cases among his parishioners during this time, and the intertwining of religious affiliations that the war forced on them. His narratives were published in 1944 in a brochure of the Ecumenical Commission for Aid to Refugees in Geneva, and a year later in a book that was published in Geneva.[19]

For example, there was the fortunate case of one German Christian "non-Aryan" who came to France with his wife, daughters, and two sons in 1934 and joined the Foreign Legion in Morocco. In 1943 the Gestapo put him in prison for eight months; there he triumphed over them, according to Toureille, because he renewed his faith. His two sons survived in the Resistance while his wife and daughters lived at subsistence level. In another case, Herbert Stein-Schneider, a Viennese refugee and theology student who worked in Toureille's clandestine Chaplaincy network and later replaced him as pastor at the French Protestant Church in Washington, D.C., saved a small group of parishioners from being shot by SS troops by identifying himself, in German, as a pastor. "We don't shoot pastors," the troops shouted to their commander, who had to relent.

Then, Toureille continued, there were the hopeless, poignant cases. One German "Aryan," a widower whose wife was a Jewish Alsatian and whose daughter was planning to be a missionary doctor, had to serve in the GTE and from there was taken by the Germans upon their retreat from Toulouse. There was no further news of him. A thirteen-year-old Protestant girl, whose mother was "Aryan" Protestant and father was Jewish, volunteered for the Foreign Legion. Arrested with her mother by the Gestapo in 1943, she watched her mother die in prison "under atrocious circumstances," and she herself was then interned in a camp in Dordogne.

A Rumanian Jewish physician working in a government sanatorium in France, served from 1939 to 1940 in the French army and was taken as a prisoner of war to Germany, where he became a Protestant. Repatriated, he received the Croix de Guerre but because of the Statute for Jews, he could no longer work. With the Chaplaincy's help he dedicated himself to studying theology and wanted to do evangelical work among Jewish intellectuals and doctors. Toureille felt close to this man: "A very beautiful and rich character," he called him, and he kept in his personal papers the physician's manuscript, "Jewish Because Christian," written during the war. Engaged in the FFI in the summer of 1944, the man was killed at the age of thirty-eight.

A German Protestant "non-Aryan" businessman and specialist in soldering methods, a world traveler who spoke many languages, broke his leg while working in a forced labor group. The healing progressed slowly. At the point of being deported in September 1942, he escaped and was hidden, with false papers, by a pastor in Lyon. There he did roadwork, then helped out for three months at Toureille's Chaplaincy before joining the Resistance in Lyon. Arrested by the Gestapo in February 1944, he wrote to Toureille from prison, "When you receive this, I will be in Eternity, because I have been condemned to death by a German court martial."

The surviving parishioners were in a great crisis, Toureille concluded, and they needed the help of the Chaplaincy now more than ever. There were a number of persons who were alone, notably women whose husbands had been deported and about whom they had had no news. Toureille reported that these women were in the greatest need for moral and spiritual support—and the Chaplaincy was the only contact they had, to which they could open up. All this necessary aid to these parishioners would take time, and the help of a central Christian organization, a role which the present Chaplaincy had to fill.

In most of these writings, Toureille avoided direct references to his evangelical role with one exception: a twenty-seven-page report, "Some of the children in our charge," dated April 5, 1945. In his conclusion to this report, he stated directly that an urgent concern in saving these children was to save them for the Protestant Church: "We must find sufficient means for enabling the gifted children of our parishioners to study in Protestant schools, as many as possible. We are ready to contact the secondary teaching institutions connected with The Protestant Free School. . . . If we do not act, we will lose one after another of our children to Catholic or Jewish institutions."

The Chaplaincy's present funds allowed only for funding the children's registration in correspondence courses with the Ministry of Education and for purchasing books. These children needed more "to learn from a master teacher and from the presence of comrades doing similar studies." And the state schools would not welcome them, he added, in a sour paragraph on French attitudes toward foreigners: "We will have many sad stories to tell on this subject. In many regions of France, the native population has adapted poorly to foreigners in their area and the French children too easily adopt the prejudices and narrowness of their parents. In the rural schools, the French children are often unconsciously cruel toward their foreign classmates, who are considered 'uncivilized' if they are Spanish, Polish, Russian or Czechoslovak, and 'dirty Boches' if they are German. We know cases in which our charges have been beaten and hurt (one even was hospitalized), while the parents had no way of protesting or reporting the incident." The parents of these refugee children added to the children's feeling of alienation by discouraging them from speaking their native languages, for fear of betraying their origins, particularly the children from Germany.

He ended with a list of necessities to keep the children in a Protestant educational system: a living place for those children who were homeless; vacation programs; scholarships for the children to continue their studies; arrangements with the Protestant secondary and technical schools. "If not, little by little, we will lose all our children."

The stories he related in this April 5 report all involved children from families of mixed religious affiliation, and almost all included at least one

Jewish parent who converted to Christianity, or whose parents were converts. In the telling of the stories, Toureille balanced the two elements of
his passion to rescue: one, his determination to prevent a life from being
snuffed out by an unjust world, and the other, the chance to bring a life
into the church.

Toureille's evangelism was a central impulse throughout his whole life.
In his personal papers, he kept a copy of a talk he gave fifteen years after
the war on the importance of being a religious missionary in the contemporary world. He and his wife had just returned from such an experience
themselves when, from December 1954 to July 1960, he was assigned by
the Board of World Missions of the American Presbyterian Church, to
teach theology in the Belgian Congo. The revolution there in 1960 prevented his return, much to his regret.

This postwar talk demonstrated Toureille's lifelong belief that the
church must be active in its evangelism, his tone as urgent, even as agitat-
ing, as ever. He cited the contemporary problems of development and
their accompanying statistics—conservation, overpopulation, economic
inequity. He surveyed the status of the world's great religions and each
one's number of adherents, and then assigned the church the role he saw
as proper to it:

There is a Buddhist saying, adopted by the Quakers as a motto for their aid to the
needy: "It is better to light a candle than to curse the darkness." It is in passing the
light to others that one disperses the shadows. . . . I often see boxing matches on
television where the boxers lose because they only defend themselves without
ever attacking. The same is true today for the Christian church. It is by going on
the offensive that the Mission will save the world.

Please understand me: it is not uniquely the church's mission to save men socially, economically, politically. But above all else, it is the church that must save
men's souls. If the church does not accomplish this task, nothing else will. A
church that does not evangelize is useless on earth. If the Church does not go to
the front, with zeal and faith, the world will die, however it might be magnificently
equipped technologically, monstrously rich and developed, endowed with superior social legislation and possessed of the best possible material conditions for living comfortably—this world will die because it has no soul. Unless the world has
this peace of the soul that authentic conversion and the assurance of eternal life
can give, all is useless and in vain. The night comes, when no one can work. Let us
work, then, without cease.

Purge Trials

Toureille brought his political/spiritual concerns to another document, a nine-page report, "Some difficult cases," on the postwar purge trials in France. Several of these involved the refugees in his charge accused of being collaborationists and traitors, particularly those of German Jewish background or family connections. After reviewing their cases, he wrote the following as a conclusion—first the political analysis, then the spiritual:

These cases are surely sad and troubling. They are not surprising, however, in the present conditions. It was clear that after the liberation, we had to have a purge period; we could not erase what had happened. But we would have wished, all the same, that the purges had been done with more discernment, justice, charity. But can one really expect that, in a revolutionary epoch like ours? One government official said during a trial: "We must listen when the voice of the people speaks!" That probably explains why it is absolutely impossible to do something effective in these cases.

It is also difficult to have an objective view on each of the accused who is asking us for help. One would wish never to have to judge one's neighbor. Whatever the case may be, even if these brothers and sisters in the faith remain guilty before the law of the day, they are no less our brothers and our sisters in the faith. It is for them that Christ died. The arms of Christ stretched on the Cross, entrusted them to us. We cannot abandon them, even if we can do only very little for them.

Toureille launched into a general defense of these cases, arguing that more than 95 percent of the Chaplaincy's German refugee parishioners had refused to collaborate with the German occupying forces. This was despite threats and pressures, and that those who did so out of necessity, did no worse than French collaborators, and yet were being sentenced more harshly because of their foreign birth. One case report in particular demonstrated the complexities of national and religious identity and the unjust treatment that these refugees underwent.

A German Jewish merchant, R., married a Protestant from Frankfurt and moved with her to Brussels. In 1940 Toureille met them in the internment camp at Gurs, where Mme. R. was an officer of one of the barrack sections and assisted the Chaplaincy in its aid work. Liberated from the camp in 1942, R. became secretary of the local GTE, where he also served as the Chaplaincy's intermediary with the Protestants in that group—"always reliable in all the services he did for us," Toureille commented. In 1943 R. and his wife had a daughter, who was baptized right after her birth; her father commented to Toureille in a letter: "I deeply regret that, because of all that has happened over these last few years, I still have not become a member of my wife's church."

R. had ceased working at the GTE by January 1944 since nearly all his comrades had been deported. In September 1944, he wrote to Toureille: "You cannot imagine how happy my wife and I are to be out of the hands of the Gestapo, who constantly menaced us. They threatened us for eleven years. We hope that now we can live in peace, in France." But R.'s wife was accused of working as a spy at the Gurs camp, although, Toureille explained, her being a barracks section officer was something completely different. R. himself was arrested in October 1944 and imprisoned in Mende, accused of having too much rapport with the Germans, serving as their interpreter, and suspiciously avoiding deportation from the GTE. His wife gave valuable evidence in his favor, including that his director in the GTE could attest to his innocence.

But Toureille found out from the local pastor in Mende that those testifying against R. offered "overwhelming proof" and that R. was considered "a sinister individual who has sold himself to the Gestapo." A local newspaper accused him of being a Gestapo agent and of turning over his compatriots to the Germans; it demanded the death penalty, thus, Toureille added, "effectively condemning him to death." An appeal was refused, because of the incompetence of R.'s lawyer.

R.'s father asked Toureille to intervene, sending him a small painting done by his son in prison. The father visited Toureille in Lunel and brought with him R.'s director in the GTE, who was then a functionary in the social service agency for emigrants and persuaded of R.'s innocence. The father also reported that R. had been brutally beaten in prison to make him confess, and that the judge had refused to take note that at the trial, no witnesses for the prosecution appeared. R. was not given an interpreter, and the cases were being rushed through—a dozen had been judged in one day. "All this could happen only in the revolutionary atmosphere after the liberation," Toureille added.

In January 1945, R.'s father went to Paris to try to get, from certain authorities recommended by the Chaplaincy, a reprieve for his son. At the beginning of February, R. was transferred to another prison in Montpellier where he wrote to Toureille: "Every day, I read the Bible and pray from Matt. 6:9–13 [The Lord's Prayer]." The reprieve was finally granted, and R.'s father wrote a letter of gratitude to Toureille. R. was then transferred to a central prison in Nîmes, from where he asked the Chaplaincy to send him the catechism and religious readings and tried to keep up a steady correspondence, although he was allowed to write only two messages a month, of twenty lines maximum. The case report ended there.

One particular case involving a maverick German refugee offered a different angle on Toureille's personal involvement with those he helped. It piques one's curiosity about what perspective on the war and what personality traits this refugee and Toureille had in common.[20] Ernst Friedrich was a Berliner, "Aryan" and Protestant, an actor, editor of an anarchist journal, photographer, and founder of a pacifist Berlin museum called the *Anti-Krieg Museum.* He fled to France with his son (who had the same name) in 1934; his wife and other children stayed in Brussels or went to England. In the summer of 1940 Toureille made contact with him and his son in the internment camp at St. Cyprien, then at Gurs a few months later. Toureille wrote: "He is not well liked. He is a sour man. I feel affection for him, all the same."

In November 1941, both father and son were liberated from the camp and settled in Lozère, on an abandoned farm. Friedrich "had big ideas," Toureille commented, "he wanted to establish the farm as a haven for refugee children." He funded this enterprise with money sent from Switzerland and 4,000 Francs that he borrowed from Toureille's Chaplaincy and never paid back. In the summer of 1942 the Germans appeared at the farm to arrest the father, who managed to escape into hiding. They picked up the son and turned him over to the Gestapo in Montpellier. He was then put in a military prison, where he spent several months in the same cell as the mayor of Lunel.

Surprisingly, the son was soon freed and returned to the farm, creating mistrust among those who had helped him. Toureille recalled that when he himself was interrogated by the Gestapo in May 1943, there were a lot of questions asked about the Freidrichs; the Gestapo also had in their files all the letters Toureille had written to both the father and son, some fifty in all. In October 1943 the Germans returned to arrest the son, took his livestock, and pressured him to work for them as an interpreter in Mende. The mayor of Lunel advised the son to accept the job and make contact with the Resistance at the same time.

At the Liberation in June 1944, the son was again put in prison, accused of being a spy and betraying French patriots. When reproached for waiting until the German defeat to escape, he responded that he feared reprisals against his friends if he had escaped earlier. The Mende tribunal condemned him to death. His father appealed to Toureille to reverse the decision. At the time Toureille wrote this report in 1945, he could not say for sure what the son's chances were.

Perhaps, in another move to free his son, Friedrich joined the German anti-Nazi maquis late in the war, in September 1944. One historian reporting this story described the others' reaction to Friedrich: "The former members of the International Brigade relate their astonishment at the arrival of this strange person in shorts, with long hair falling to his shoulders and a long beard down to his waist. Ernst Friedrich was dismissed by his communist compatriots who reproached him for having brought up his son so badly."[21]

Where Should the Refugees Go?

In the Toureille report, mentioned above, that was published in Geneva in 1944 by the Ecumenical Commission for Aid to Refugees, he summarized problems facing the survivors among his parishioners, sizing up a confused and traumatic situation with competence and large sympathies:

1) Contrary to expectations, it is difficult if not impossible for these parishioners to find work now, especially when one is a foreigner;
2) All competent authorities insist that no one attempt to return home or move anywhere yet, which confronts these people with great problems and makes them suspect;
3) The local prefects have great latitude in making decisions about foreigners, and first priority is being given to measures taken against German soldiers hiding as civilians and other suspects still on French territory;
4) Some refugee parishioners living clandestinely have not yet regularized their situation, although, in most of the departments, the prefects are understanding and indulgent toward them;
5) The political situation of those parishioners who served in the F.F.I. is presently very favorable, but the material situation of their families and of their own future, is far from reassuring;
6) A difficult spiritual isolation results from the fact that almost all these parishioners are without news of their parents and friends. Only the Chaplaincy corresponds with them;
7) Those who find themselves, again, in camps or aid centers, are in general

people who, because of their age and state of health, cannot do manual work and have no one to care for them.

8) In the great majority of cases, when given their liberty, the internees don't know where to go. Just having to leave the camp is of grave concern among them, and to be liberated without being able to leave France is even more stressful for these unhappy people who, for more than four years, have waited for *their* liberation. Those who can follow an occupation ask fervently that they be given work to do.

In several of his other written pieces in 1945, Toureille repeated that the refugees' hopes for their own future included the desire to not return to their home countries. Many of working age wanted to stay in France. The older people, particularly those who had been deported from Germany in 1940, wanted to rejoin their families in England and America, and only a few longed to return home. Many wanted to move to the large cities in France, especially Paris, in order to find work in business or other occupations. These wishes were understandable, he agreed, since a foreigner in Paris would be the least noticed. However, such a move might further complicate their legal position in France.

On this last issue, Toureille, by January 1945, had become short-tempered with his refugee parishioners who were pressing upon his Chaplaincy their plans to settle in Paris. He sent out a new circular, combining severe reprimands with his continuing role of pastoral caretaking:

Dear parishioners and friends,

It is extremely disagreeable to me that a number of you, despite the precise instructions we gave you in our preceding printed circulars and letters, are going to Paris or the Parisian region to look for work or to find your prewar apartments. We say to you again, today, in the most categorical manner, that it is absolutely undesirable for foreigners to go at present to Paris. All French and international authorities have asked us to inform you of this and make sure you understand it.

It is perfectly useless to think you can find work now in the Parisian region, where there are considerable difficulties of all kinds (lodging, heat, electricity, food) and where the cost of living is high. We ask you, then, in the most formal and urgent manner, to give up going to the Parisian region until the end of hostilities. . . .

In order to be clearly understood, we declare, in the most formal manner, that, except for some rare cases, we will stop all allocations, regular

and exceptional, to those who do not follow this advice. We are convinced,
in acting thus, to be treating you as true friends would, and to be coming
to your defense. You do not know, unfortunately, what we know.

We would be grateful if you would acknowledge receiving this circular
and understanding our intentions, which are, more than ever, devoted to
charity in the name of Christ.

To this letter was attached a lively, nine-page essay, "The Attraction of
Paris," written after the letter as a final report on the issue. In this essay/
report, Toureille elaborated on his argument and attested to its effectiveness in dissuading the parishioners' exodus to Paris. The essay also gave a
journalistic view of Paris in its first winter after the Liberation. His introductory remarks were sympathetic to the impulse to go to Paris: for a great
number of the refugees to France before the war, Paris *was* France, and
the liberation had awakened their nostalgia to return. Like "moths attracted to the light," some of his parishioners had already obtained false
identity cards and, believing themselves secure, flew to Paris where some
were probably apprehended. He cited the case of the son of a German
pastor, formerly in the Foreign Legion, who went to Paris with his wife,
where both were arrested.

Besides the motive of nostalgia, he listed the political, intellectual, and
artistic attractions of the city, and the general wish to return to lodgings
and "all the luxuries and abundance that existed there before the war. Why
wouldn't anyone want to return quickly, after having to live, for more than
four years, in dirty villages, uncomfortable and lost in provincial France?"
In Paris, "one can find friends, one can 'pull through'—there's the key
word for most of our foreign refugees! 'In Paris,' you hear them say to each
other, 'we can always pull through!'"

His reasons against their making such a move were in two categories,
physical and political, with statistics and one-line personal stories and quotations that demonstrated his points. First, the high cost and difficulty of
the journey, the lack of food, fuel, and electrical power during a rough winter, and an insurmountable problem of finding lodging upon arrival: "In
Neuilly, I found our apartment completely ransacked by the Germans and
the apartment itself rented to someone else I would have had to expel";
"Our apartment was occupied by the Germans. Now the Americans are installed there. I have to live in a hotel, and can't send for my wife." Next, the
problem of finding work: The American army had taken in office workers

and interpreters but preferred hiring French to foreigners. A work permit for foreigners had to be obtained, which was still difficult for most professions, since unemployment was rampant: "I walk the street all day looking for work. Nothing, nothing, nothing!"; "An engineer in the Coty perfume industry, today earns only 30 percent more than he earned in 1939, and that is clearly not enough to cover the cost of living."

Toureille made the following sarcastic point on the French bureaucracy as being a large part of the problem for the refugees:

We have to face it: the bureaucratic chicaneries have certainly not disappeared. The bureaucracy is as fumbling and stupid as it was in the past. Didn't it ask (somewhere in France) a prisoner of war escaped from Germany to furnish proof of his escape with a certificate from the German authorities? And under the Vichy regime, foreigners with an identity card could circulate freely. But since the ordinance of December 12, 1944, the movement of foreigners is restrained. . . .

To be able to stay in Paris, the foreigners originating from countries now reputed to be enemies, must report every day to the police headquarters in their area. Only those who were in the Resistance or can give irrefutable proof of their loyalty, are exempt.

Finally, there were the important questions of the effect on the French political scene of a mass refugee exodus to Paris. Toureille's underlying assumption was that a large majority of these refugees would be seeking positions in large business or intellectual enterprises, which would perhaps stir resentment against them for a number of reasons in the postwar reconstruction of Paris at the time. Before the war, the large number of foreigners in Paris had already created resentment; re-creating such a colony at this time might exacerbate the emotional climate and provoke "a kind of anti-Semitism always latent in certain quarters." The "Germans and the German non-Aryans even more, have too strong a tendency to stay together as a group . . . which is considered strongly undesirable by the French authorities as well as by a variety among the French population."

France's need, above all, was for finding agricultural and industrial workers; a large number of foreigners taking over business and intellectual positions was to be avoided. Also, during the war (and still today) the agricultural regions of France sent a large part of its produce to Paris, creating a justifiable jealousy among the other large cities. More foreigners in Paris would aggravate this problem; the natural resources in the provinces would be more easily available to them if they stayed in those rural areas. Finally, it was commonly known that those foreigners who settled in Paris, did not leave, while one of the most serious problems now in France is finding a way to make the demographics more equitable across the country.

Toureille argued that his advice would protect his parishioners from their adversaries in the French population. His final paragraphs returned the focus to his own region—the Protestant rural villages of the south—and the Church as the best haven for strangers, and, in the process, he also expressed a traditional French assurance that certain aspects of French culture and way of life offered something invaluable to the rest of the world:

> The life in provincial France is certainly very austere. The comforts of life are not elaborate. The intellectual level of the populace does not seem very high. But there is a goodness and simplicity, a "sweetness of life" which are specifically French.
>
> Foreigners will be welcomed and accepted only if they submerge themselves in French life and plant themselves in its soil. The experience of the last fifty years has proven abundantly that one can only do that in the provinces.
>
> Finally—last but not least [This phrase is written in English]—the Parisian Protestant churches, which have already so many problems in assimilating the Protestants coming in from the provinces, do not welcome and incorporate foreign Protestants very easily. Parisian Protestants are, too often, meeting in lecture halls where they scarcely know each other. In the provinces, the stranger is more quickly adopted by the local church.
>
> French Protestantism is, above all, provincial and rural. It is in our old French Protestant regions that we wish to see our foreign parishioners settled, because "we will save ourselves together, or we will die separately!"

One other safeguard Toureille offered to his refugee parishioners was a "certificate of loyalty." These certificates were invented by the Chaplaincy, in reaction to the French postwar government's demand that refugees from "enemy" countries (Germany, Hungary, Rumania, Bulgaria, Finland) needed such affidavits from eminent personalities or local authorities, in order to leave the internment camps. In "The reason for our certificates of loyalty," a six-page essay dated April 1945 Toureille explained the origin of the certificates and listed testimonials from the parishioners on their effectiveness in providing freedom of movement. The refugees used these to liberate themselves from the camps and the forced labor groups, to re-enter Paris, to file for naturalization papers, to establish dossiers with the local authorities, to carry with them as an important piece of identification.

Toureille summarized: "It is clear that our certificates of loyalty were an effective aid to a great number of our charges. We are happy to extend to our parishioners the benevolent protection of the church of Jesus Christ. This action obliges us, certainly, to keep abreast of the legislation and rules being issued concerning foreigners. Those who count on us to inform and counsel them are innumerable."

The Psychology of the Internee

One other of Toureille's written documents of 1945 was a long, 140-item questionnaire addressed to former camp internees. Its purpose, Toureille wrote in a covering letter, was to launch an inquiry into "the psychology of the internee." It appeared highly impractical in its unwieldiness and in the scope of human consciousness it was trying to cover. The questions were long and addressed philosophical issues too complex to be handled by a questionnaire. No available evidence survives about the fate of this document, whether it was ever distributed and, if so, what the results were. But, despite Toureille's statement of purpose, the document itself appeared to be much less a survey of others than a self-examination.

Toureille partially explained which of his own emotions propelled his survey by saying that he wanted "to help those who have suffered . . . and to be a testament of gratitude to all those who have given me so much in these sad, crisis-ridden years, even when they wanted to make me believe, sometimes, that it was I who was doing the giving." It seems that finding the answers to his questions was important, not only as probes into the distressed mind of the internees he had helped but also to better understand and alleviate his own mental distress and probable deflation of spirits at the end of the war.

On captivity itself, he posed: "Is it true, in your experience, that at the beginning, the material deprivations intruded on your consciousness, while by the end, it was your consciousness that was the intruder?" or "What do you think of this aphorism: 'Captivity instructs man about the pleasure derived from nourishing one's sadness'?" Other questions assumed a high level of education among the respondents, particularly in using psychological terminology and theory: "Did you experience 'the barbed wire psychosis'?" and "Do you think that the importance of sex is exaggerated in the evolution of human consciousness?" and "Schopenhauer thinks that the sexual impulse relates to notions of death, that it is a manifestation of the will to live. Freud thinks that the power of the sexual impulse emanates from instinct that forces itself upon us. Does your experience confirm either one of these theses?"

Love, of several kinds, became a central topic. On love within the family: "Your comrades' faithfulness to their fiancés or spouses: Was it really steadfast, or just made inevitable by the circumstances?" On love in absence: "It is often said that to love someone absent is to find him again, but also to find him in oneself. What do you think?" On the emotional dynamics of a whole community, including self-concern versus altruism: "Does the fact that each person has his own interests fully explain all the social relations that are created in the camps?" and "What social sentiments have you noticed in the camp? (egoism, altruism, greed, charity, ambition, lack of interest, individualism, group spirit). Give precise examples."

On hope: "Do you think that being completely cut off from normal human life is tragic? Why?" "Can the human being think about the present independently of the past and the future?" "Did you suffer from the fact that you were unable to find out or predict the date of your liberation?" Finally, his questions on his central concern— religious belief—phrased in his characteristic combination of self-questioning and active evangelism: "Have you been struck by the serenity with which the internees bear their fate when they have faith?" "Must one erase the weight of earthly events in order to raise one's eyes to the sky?" "Did you pray more during your stay in the camp? Why?" "In the light of your experiences, what should be the role of the Christian church in the world of tomorrow?" And the final question, one Toureille must have asked himself throughout his life: "How do you think Protestantism can better shed its light?"

Seeking New Missions in Czechoslovakia

Immediately after the intense and traumatic war years, Toureille showed signs of depression, conflicts within himself about his personal life and spiritual beliefs, and threatening nervous collapse. Marc Toureille tried to summarize what the war experience must have cost his father:

It is very hard for me to describe my father's wartime relationship with his family. My understanding of it has obviously gone through many transformations from when I was a child, then a teenager, and now an aging adult. I grew up loving and admiring my father for what he stood for, and for what he did. It is also true that at times I hated him for failing me, for his absence and his infrequent but harsh discipline—as if by this strictness he could make up for lost time.

I am now older and hopefully wiser. I can try to imagine the life he had to lead in order to save so many lives. If we suffered from it, so be it. It was well worth it. For many years I have reproached him for his lack of interest in our education. He wanted us to follow the same path he did, step by step, not understanding our particular interests or ambitions, or the importance of the special circumstances we were living through.

I think later in life, he realized he had failed us in this way, but by that time it no longer mattered. The die was already cast. He had to work at giving us time, maybe during vacations. Sometimes we'd take a bicycle trip, and once in a while I could tell he missed us. But he was not a family man. Circumstances made it that way. But when you're a kid, you don't realize what your father might be going through. Had I been in his place, I don't know what would have been my relationship with my family.

When my father was old and retired to a home in Anduze in 1973, we got talking for the first time in my life. He asked me for forgiveness.

Toureille resigned his position in the French Protestant Church in 1945, perhaps due in part to the rocky wartime relationship with the church's political approach to Vichy. Toureille sought desperately to find another religious mission for himself, preferably outside of France. After trying in vain to find a place for himself in France, he was appointed to the service of the French-speaking community of Czechoslovakia..

On January 10, 1946, as part of his search for a new mission, he wrote the following letter to Josef Fišera, the Czech director of MACE:

My dear friend,

I am waiting, with a certain impatience, for the offer you referred to in your letter preceding the last one. My paid leave is over at the end of February and I absolutely must find a position before then. Because if I don't, I would not be able to take care of my family and would be driven to certain alternatives out of profound despair: accepting a pastoral post, with death in the soul, in order to earn a paltry 5,000 francs a month—or even (I am very serious)—suicide.

It seems impossible to me that, after spending years helping so many people, 24 hours a day (especially the Czechoslovaks!), I can't find, since October, a place that welcomes me, a charitable hand that really helps me.

I am ready to work at anything and would work intensely if engaged in a cause. If you have children who need to be taken across France and into Czechoslovakia, wouldn't that be a good job for me? I want so much to see Czechoslovakia again soon, very soon! Couldn't you arrange, through your authorities, for my being invited for a stay of 15 days to a month, for example, as a beginning?

I would also like to be involved in the projects of Dubina, in whom I have the greatest confidence. He was interested in my participating in his exchange student project, for students and intellectuals. I have much experience in these matters, as you know; I speak eight languages besides French and I have visited forty-some countries in the world.

This is a real SOS I am sending you. I was hesitant to do it, but now I feel that I must, seeing the end of February approaching.

If you can't find anything for me in your work (I am giving you, again, first priority here), could you spark interest among the Unitarians, with Max's help? That would also interest me. All international and social service work is what I do best. I have furnished proof of this and I have available abundant written references, in all languages.

Another question: would Dubina not want to take me into the Franco-Czechoslovak Association, in view of my past and recent experience in service of the Czechoslovak cause—when it was dangerous to defend that cause? But I do not want to enter by "the back door", as if I were just anyone. You will find me immodest, but I owe it to the memory of those whom I have helped, who are dead.

If you think I should make the move from Paris, tell me frankly. I would like very much, with your consent, to see your Consul-Général and Minister. I would even urge very strongly that I see these two men. Could you provide me accommodations (a bed) for the necessary period?

Excuse me for speaking to you so freely and opening up my heart and its profound despair. But doing so, makes my pain less heavy to bear.

I believe I can count on your effective and prompt support and, with this hope, I sign off cordially and affectionately.

With best wishes from all of us, P.-C. Toureille[22]

A few months before writing this letter, Toureille began an exchange of letters with a Czech contact, Pastor J. Krenek, that demonstrated the warmth on both sides in his relationship with Czechoslovakia. The pastor had written to Toureille in September 1945, thanking him profusely for his work with Czechoslovak refugees during the war—in the Czechoslovak

Aid Center, in the aid network at the University of Montpellier, and in the many talks Toureille gave on their behalf. "We admire the fearlessness with which you continued this work when it became illegal after the 1940 armistice. . . . We hope that your friendship with our country and our mutual attachment will be expressed in a visit from you to Czechoslovakia."

Toureille replied in December 1945 by sending Pastor Krenek a detailed report of his wartime activities for the Czechoslovak refugees in France, to which Krenek answered on January 26, 1946, with an expression of "true joy at your love for our country, proved by your fatiguing but incessant aid work." He invited Toureille to visit Prague, give some talks on his war rescue work, and deliver the sermon at a French-language Protestant service that Krenek would organize for him.

In February 1946 Toureille accepted Krenek's invitation for May, adding that Czechoslovakia was his "second homeland." On March 1 Krenek replied that they were "extremely glad" he was coming and that they would find an apartment for him in the Huss House and arrange for him to give the sermon at the Hussite Church in Prague. In a further response to Toureille's requests for this visit, Krenek arranged for Toureille to meet with Pastor Robert Smith of the Scottish Church, "to discuss in particular the question of the Czech Jews."

Some months after making these contacts, and writing his desperate letter to Fišera, Toureille followed through on his desire to go back to Czechoslovakia. Besides Krenek's invitation, he was also asked by a local bishop to visit the Lutheran Slovak Church in Bratislava. The bishop described himself and his parishioners as "very grateful" and "very much obligated" to Toureille for all he did during the war years of oppression. It was probably this contact that led to a fellowship for Toureille from the Czechoslovak government to study for a doctorate at the Lutheran Faculty of Theology at the University of Bratislava.

After two years in Czechoslovakia, upon receiving his degree, Toureille emigrated with his family to the United States and took the position of pastor of the French Reformed Church in Washington, D.C. This was his break from the war years in France and from his past. He did not return to France as a permanent resident until fifteen years after the war, in September 1960, where, for the next and last fifteen years of his life, he remained an evangelist, teaching and lecturing about his missionary experiences in Africa and Europe.

In 1947, Toureille published an article in a Prague journal edited by

Prague 1946, in front of John Huss statue; Toureille, center, talking to unidentified man and woman.

Josef Fišera, explaining the lifetime attachment he, and the many French he represented, had for the Czechoslovak peoples ("Des Liens Renforcés" or "Strengthened Ties," *Calendrier*, Kalich Publishing, 69–74). He represented that attachment by describing his wartime activities, many of which were devoted to helping Czechoslovak refugees.

The depth of his feeling toward Czechoslovakia was obvious from the very beginning of the article. The Munich Pact was foremost on his conscience. He begins: "'Forgive us for Munich!' We cannot begin any other way, as Frenchmen and as Christians." He did not intend to defend French policy but wanted his readers to know that now, after the war, the French were taking account of where the Munich Pact led them:

Leprosy Mission, Morges, Switzerland, 1971. Toureille and his wife, Délie.

It is enough to look around and reflect: More than two million French soldiers taken to Germany as prisoners of war, many coming back with their health ruined; 2,800,000 French men and women sent to forced labor in Germany; 600,000 French knew the horror of the concentration camps; 300,000 citizens, principally women and children, succumbed to bombardments; 100,000 French soldiers fell on the battlefields of France, Africa, Italy and Germany.

Our material losses are equally important. Our cities and large industrial centers were bombed. All our ports, in The Channel, the Atlantic or the Mediterranean, were destroyed in the liberation in 1944. All our railroad stations, all our bridges are in ruins. One fifth of our buildings, principally those near the battlefields, carry the marks of war. Because of the mistakes of certain individuals, the French nation in its entirety had to pay dearly for the errors of Munich.

Toureille concluded, in the introduction, "In the name of all this suffering written on our hearts and our being, I take it upon myself, on behalf of my people, to ask your pardon." He extended the apology, in the same heated language, that many of his compatriots wanted to say to the Czechoslovak people, "looking you right in the eyes, with a heart beating to the same rhythm as yours: 'We remain faithful to Czechoslovakia!'"

After reviewing his wartime experience in aiding Czech refugees, he finished the article by predicting that the French and the Czechoslovak peoples would establish ties in the future: The French people hoped for the rebuilding of Czechoslovakia, and between Czechoslovak and French Protestants, there evolved a new historical tie—the latter's aid to Czech refugees during the war. There were three major bonds holding them together, he asserted: A common past of suffering, persecution, and torture because of their religious beliefs; the symbol of the képi, the military cap of a French general, that appears also on the heads of statues of Czechoslovak heroes in their cities and towns, their homes, their castles, and on their money; and, above all, the unifying bond of the cross, "symbol of our suffering and our resurrection."

Then, a return to the burden of Munich: "The French Protestants, who as a body did not accept Munich and stayed faithful to the cause and to the Czechoslovak Republic, send you a cordial 'Nazdar'! May God be with you always."

Postwar Tributes

That Toureille collected letters and tributes from those he had saved during the war showed that he wanted to maintain his connection to them and to the spiritual powers their plight evoked in him. However, his reaction to postwar tributes from governments and organizations was more begrudging. He at first objected to the suggestion that he propose himself as one of the Just, an award by the Israeli foundation Yad Vashem (Remembrance of Martyrs and Heroes) to those non-Jewish individuals who saved Jews during the war. His objection was not an uncommon one among rescuers; he felt that he was fulfilling his duty and that it would be inappropriate and arrogant to accept an award for doing what he had to do. He was finally persuaded that it was appropriate, as an identification with his church and a group of people important to him, and he would take his place with other French pastors (like André Trocmé, Marc Boegner, Joseph Bourdon, Charles Guillon, and André Morel) with whom he had worked during the war.

He then began a long correspondence, often contentious on his part, with the Yad Vashem Commission, beginning on June 14, 1971, until he finally received the award on July 25, 1974. As he negotiated with the Commission over affidavits from witnesses to his rescue work, his sense of personal dignity played a part in the prickliness of his tone.

The initial issue between Toureille and the Yad Vashem representatives in Jerusalem, and the reason for his contentiousness, was apparently the requirement under Israeli law that he provide signed testimonials from each individual whom he was claiming to have saved. He took personal offense at this, although the explanation from the Yad Vashem representative seemed appropriate and exactly what would have been expected of an agency giving such an award. Toureille's side of the correspondence revealed that he felt the process was an insult to his dignity. Perhaps this was a residual bitterness stemming from his traumatic uprooting at the end of the war—his period of despair, the feeling that he had lost his ties and his mission, his leaving the French Church, and finally, his emigration to the United States.

The earliest letter from Yad Vashem, dated September 27, 1971, was a reply to Toureille's original letter of inquiry about the award to the Just. In this September letter, the Yad Vashem representative assumed, based on Toureille's letter, that he had heard about the award through publicity about André Trocmé as one of the designees. That publicity included some misinformation on exactly what data the Yad Vashem Commission required. Under Israeli law, the Commission had to ask for a stringent set of documents, namely testimonials from the individuals saved. The letter continued politely: Toureille should therefore provide the Commission the names and addresses of such individuals, and, in a line that might have struck Toureille as officious, "I presume you have kept a list of the false baptismal certificates that you mercifully provided."

Toureille took a long time to reply. It was not until July 1972 that he wrote: "I must tell you frankly that your letter took my breath away. It is not because the departed Pastor André Trocmé received an award from Israel, that I wrote to you. What Pastor Trocmé did for the persecuted Jews has absolutely nothing to do with my actions, as Chief Chaplain of internees and refugees in France, and above all, as Vice-President, then Acting President of the Committee of Coordination of Nîmes, helping the refugees and internees in France."

He then proceeded to comply with the Yad Vashem requests. He listed the wording of the honors given him by the French, Czechoslovak, and German governments and wartime organizations, in addition to ten individuals who could testify to his rescue work. He returned to his personal reaction to the process, showing that he considered it important that he be recognized as one of a group who had served France: "I must say very frankly that I find it extraordinary that the Israeli government has not yet done anything in my favor, when just in the past year, a good number of French, who have done much less than I, have received this distinction."

He mentioned that his oldest son, whom he would soon visit, had been working as a volunteer for two-and-one-half years on an Israeli kibbutz. Then he added a final testy paragraph: "I am perfectly willing to provide more information if you so desire and I hope fervently that the State of Israel will finally do something concrete on my behalf, after so many years. The persecuted Jews who knocked at my door without cease, did not ask for so many details and explanations."

Yad Vashem acknowledged this letter with a brief thank-you and said that they would contact the names he provided and submit his case to their Commission as soon as they had received all the material. Toureille replied, more than a month later, with a thank-you in return and the promise to send more names and references. Over the next year, more names were sent; there were some surprised reactions from Toureille at the long delay in processing his documents. Toureille lost his temper again when informed that the depositions needed to be signed before a functionary at an Israeli consulate: "If I have to ask the survivors to sign their deposition in my favor, before an Israeli consular officer, the majority of them will be unwilling to do it."

The next letter in Toureille's personal papers, jumping the gap of a year, is the actual granting of the award, dated July 25, 1974: "I have the honor to inform you that the Commission of the Just, of the Commemorative Institute Yad Vashem, has decided, after a preliminary inquiry, to confer on you a Certificate of Honor and to authorize, if the happy opportunity brings you to Israel, the planting of a tree in your name in the Avenue of the Just on the Mountain of Memory in Jerusalem, for the valor and human solidarity you demonstrated in saving Jews, at the peril of your life under the German occupation."

Toureille never planted the tree himself. He might have been too ill to travel by then, or might have chosen to avoid such ceremonies. His son Marc planted the tree in his father's name in February 1988, twelve years after his father died. Marc's letter to Yad Vashem set a tone that would probably have pleased his father:

My family and I wish to express our greatest gratitude to you and to the State of Israel for allowing us to plant a tree in the Avenue of the Righteous in honor of my late father, Dr. Rev. Pierre Toureille. We were deeply impressed by the sad beauty of Yad Vashem and especially the Children's Memorial in which we could feel the presence of their spirits and souls. It was a sad reminder of the past places in which I spent a good part of my childhood.

We thank you for the kind words you spoke about my father and the French Protestants. Because of the religious persecutions we had to endure and because of our religious education which was strongly based on Jewish history as told in the Bible, we French Huguenots always had a close sense of kinship for the Jews— even more so in my case, as my mother had that "one ounce of Jewish blood" that you spoke about. We were fortunate that she was not required to fill out a *"déclaration raciale"* until late in the course of the war, and that we were saved by the Liberation.

Again, we want to thank you for such a moving experience. We shall not forget it.

Other postwar tributes to Toureille come from colleagues and fellow rescuers attesting to the broad scope and inspirational quality of his activities. (See Appendix for the full texts of these tributes.) Of special interest because it came from a German source, was the tribute by the Consul-General of the German Embassy in Bern, Switzerland, who made a formal proposal, on September 11, 1968, for decorating Pierre-Charles

Toureille with a Medal of Honor, the *Grosses Verdienstkreuz*, Highest Level:

Pastor Dr. Pierre Charles Toureille was, from 1940 to 1945 in France, Head Protestant Chaplain for foreign refugees, camp internees, and those deported for forced labor. In this capacity, he looked after approximately 40,000 persons (by the end of the war) with devotion and at the risk of his life. According to his own estimations, about 20,000 were German-speaking. These persons consisted not only of "Non-Aryans" who fled to France and had been deported, but also political opponents of the Nazi regime. He held this office on behalf of the World Council of Churches and the Protestant Federation of France.

His activities went far beyond pastoral care. His task was, to a large degree, to distribute money, clothes, food, books, and other donations. He provided his "parishioners" jobs and education and helped them in their critical situation, in every respect. In many cases he could save persons entrusted to him, from the clutches of the Gestapo. He hid them in new hiding places and helped them to escape over the Swiss border. In this way, Pastor Toureille saved many lives. His headquarters were in Lunel near Montpellier where he employed a total of nineteen persons over that period. The Gestapo put him under surveillance, summoned him and interrogated him seven times. Pastor Toureille still has warm feelings for Germany in spite of all his experiences and is still in close contact with many of his former parishioners. He is still, as he was at that time, fully ready to make sacrifices and is filled with charity.

[An attachment to this letter, from the German Consul-General in Geneva:] It is clear that Pastor Toureille has worked for many years, especially from 1940–1945, in close contact with the former Secretary-General of the World Council of Churches, Dr. Willem Visser't Hooft, who has known Mr. Toureille for forty-seven years. He spoke to the Consul-General in a very positive way about Toureille and remembered him as a courageous and tireless friend in need who was guided by genuine Christian ideals of humanity and never showed himself as embittered toward Germany in spite of the continuous harassment by the German Occupation authorities in France.[23]

Epilogue

The Riga ghetto in Latvia was formed after thousands of Jews had been shot in the Bikernieki Forest. . . . In Latvia, Lithuania and Poland, nine out of ten Jews were killed.

—*The World Must Know*

Everything we do, all the things we go through, seem to us a necessary evil, a temporary hardship, so that we may reach our goal and fulfill our duty: to keep on going, and to keep spinning the golden thread of the eternal glory of Israel, in order to prove to the world the will of our people to live under any conditions and situations. These goals supply us with the moral strength to preserve our lives and to ensure the future of our people.

—Avraham Tory, *Surviving the Holocaust: The Kovno Ghetto Diary*

Lunel

Lunel, the center of Pastor Toureille's rescue operations, has much in its past that reverberates in his own story. Lunel was a place of refuge for Jews almost 2000 years ago when, after the Romans' destruction of the Second Temple and sacking of Jerusalem in 70 A.D., the Jews of Palestine fled to north Africa and across the Mediterranean to southern Europe, including the shores of southern France.[1] At the mouth of the Rhône River, east of Lunel at Orgon, a stone oil lamp was found that experts date, at the latest, to the second half of the first century A.D. In the central medallion of the lamp, encircling the hole into which the oil was poured, are two seven-branched candelabra—the Jewish *menorah*—and olives symbolizing the source of the oil. The travel guide published by the Lunel Tourist

232

Office tells of the founding of Lunel by these Jewish refugees from Palestine, the writer fancifully combining history and legend:

> The wind is favorable, the ships leave that evening, sailing straight into the sunset. After two long months of sailing, after passing Sicily, going east of the Isle of Cyrnos and avoiding Massilia, the fugitives sight a flat and sandy shore and, through the openings in their boats, the muddy waters of a large river that flows into the sea. They follow the shoreline west for a day, gazing at this new country of ponds and marshes, woodlands and wild game, with its purple mountains across the northern horizon. The next morning, after taking stock of their condition and expressing their gratitude to the Eternal, they drop anchor near the mouth of a river, where the ibis of Egypt and the black bulls remind them of the land of Moses.
>
> The evening of the next day, after following this small river, they arrive at a plain, soft and damp but fertile, with hillsides covered with pine and oak trees. It is October 1, the beginning of the Jewish New Year, Rosh Hashanah. They stop and as the full moon rises over the marshes, they sacrifice a young goat, according to the rites of Abraham. . . . The Council of Elders decides that, in this place, they will build the new Jericho and call it Luna. The exodus is over.
>
> The little river that the exiles followed was the Vidourle. The new Jericho was the small town that we call Lunel. The crescent of Astarte and Isis still appears in our coat of arms and our inhabitants still identify themselves by the symbolic name "Pescaluna," because they are the "fishers of the moon" (*Pêcheurs de lune*) of Languedoc.[2]

During the medieval period, Lunel became one of the most important regional centers for Jewish scholarship. This group of scholars—like their most distinguished representative, Maimonides, the twelfth-century Spanish Jewish philosopher, physician, and theologian—combined the learning of the ancient classical and contemporary Moslem worlds. Benjamin of Toledo, another twelfth-century scholar, included Lunel in his travels through this area of France, commenting in his travel notes that the Jewish community of Lunel numbered about 300 families and was "a holy community of Israel bending over the Torah day and night. . . . The community gives these students aid and clothing for as long as they remain at the school."[3]

A Jewish medical school was founded in Lunel in the twelfth century. Its physicians performed the first surgical operation in Europe, according to local tradition,[4] and this school was the basis for the later establishment of the University of Montpellier Medical School. The building where this medical school was housed, identified as "the synagogue" to tourists, remains only in the ornate stone doorway. Its rounded columns and roofed lintel are set into the front wall of the building, and the decorative bands around the columns suggest a Moorish influence, with deep carvings forming hieroglyphic patterns.

The front of the Protestant temple a few streets away has a similar pointed roof and columns set into the wall but is clearly classical Renaissance in its origins. At the very top, under the roof edge, is a relief carving of an open book. On the left hand page are carved the words *La Sainte Bible* (The Holy Bible), and on the right page, *Sondez les Ecritures* (Probe the Scriptures).

Nearby is the Toureilles' former home during the war, an elegant white stone three-story building with light blue shutters that now houses law offices. The Chaplaincy office was on the second floor and on the third was Marc's room, which had been occupied by the Wehrmacht. The Ford garage next door, also requisitioned by the Germans, is now an insurance company. The family home of Micheline Toureille, Marc's wife, is a few blocks away.

During the war, the Chaplaincy office was moved to a three-story building with a roof veranda. Pastor Toureille's office was directly over the entrance, and his office manager, Mr. Parlier, sat in the room to the left. There are now flowerpots on the window ledges and a shop on the ground floor with the sign "New Baby" (in English) painted on the awning. Across from the former Chaplaincy office is an important looking building that was first the City Hall, then the municipal library. Jacob Barosin did research there when he was a refugee in Lunel. In the plaza in front was a statue of a nineteenth-century military hero, which was stolen by the Germans during the war and afterward returned.

Lunel put on a festive face for visitors in July 1996, with preparations for the running of the bulls festival; there were gleaming white buildings and flowers, and clusters of people eating and drinking at sidewalk cafes. There are two reminders of the war in evidence to a casual stroller. One is in the public park, Parc Jean Hugo, named after a former resident and grandson of Victor Hugo. This park features a memorial plaque to Jean Moulin, who was sent to France during the war by General DeGaulle to organize the FFI (French Forces of the Interior) and who was arrested and tortured, and who died in prison. The second is the Lunel railroad station, which is a war reminder only in the old postcards and photographs that show how it looked in the 1940s. Since then, the central engine roundhouse was torn down, and the building housing the ticket office and passenger waiting area has been remodeled.

But the walk into Lunel from the station must be the same as it was during the war, when refugees stepped down the sloping sidewalk into town, along a gray stone retaining wall and past some old gray houses with orange tile roofs, and second-story, wrought-iron balconies that bulge out from closed, blue-shuttered windows.

Nîmes

In a sunny plaza in central Nîmes is a bronze statue of Ernest Denis, the prominent historian and champion of Czechoslovakia, born in Nîmes in 1849. He is standing at a lectern and looking straight ahead, his face neatly bearded and mustached, his hands resting on several books. Below are the figures of two barefoot women, carved in relief; the one on the right, France's Liberty, her hand and arm clasped by the woman on the left, who is dressed as a Slav peasant. On the side is a plaque quoting Denis: "France has always been a great liberator. . . . She marches in a cortege of friends. Of these friends, Czechoslovakia is one of the most cherished." And on the back of the statue: "The union between Bohemia and France is a natural one. . . . It is, in essence, a union rooted in the history and the soul of the two nations."

At the top of the hill overlooking the city is the ruin of a stone tower built by the Romans and later part of a medieval fortification. A Roman arena sits at the city's heart, with charging bulls carved over its gates. A few blocks away is the Nîmes synagogue, a three-story building with the Ten Commandments carved over the central doorway. Its large arched stone door and window frames and classical facade testify to the cultural importance of the medieval and Renaissance Jewish communities of Provence. In the Nîmes municipal library are eighteen ancient manuscripts written in Hebrew.

Mende

The train from Nîmes to Mende climbs slowly up into the Cévennes mountains, through dominantly Protestant areas that were the villages of refuge to which Toureille sent people to hide. On the train, a young theology student and future priest talked eagerly, and in excellent English, about the war, the Résistance, and his own liberal "Républican" political views. He drew distinctions, as he saw them, among Catholicism, Protestantism, and Judaism, apologizing for oversimplifying: The Catholic church provides "transforming grace" from God to all, including those who do evil, while in the Protestant church, God is more removed, less forgiving, with good and evil actions all predestined. "Authoritarianism in a religion—in Catholicism—doesn't necessarily mean severity," he said. He remembered the first time he studied the Old Testament—he was overwhelmed by how personal and intimate was the love between God and Israel, "and therefore, all of us."

The Cévennes mountains rise gradually, stony and green, with periodic tunnels bursting onto high plateaus that allow the watchful traveler to see across miles of spiky gray-green pine, low brush, sunflower fields and stone walls and farm houses with orange-red roofs. The city of Mende sits on a high plateau, small, stony and compact, surrounded by farmland. At the railroad station was a billboard with a variety of announcements and posters dominated by religious references: "Jesus is truly risen"; "God exists, speaks to us, loves us, warns us. . . . Come hear the good news"; "Save the babies. Abortion: no!"; "Which came first, the chicken or the egg? Who made the chicken?"; "The Bible tells us that God created man in His Own Image (Gen. 1:27)."

A Last Glimpse

Marc Toureille has a videotape of his father taking a summer walk in 1961 near his own mother's house in Cournonterral, to visit the ruin of a medieval chapel. Toureille is accompanied by his wife and by Marc and Micheline and their children. There are several scenes in which Pastor Toureille is the central figure: in the black interior of the chapel where he is barely visible, sitting at a stone table, on a stone bench; in dark glasses, turning to wave at the camera, first the left hand, then the right; hands on hips, back to camera and posture erect, explaining the golden lichen on the stone walls; walking back to the car, a Ford station wagon.

His grandson plays on a dry riverbed. His mother, eighty years old, waves from the balcony of the three-story stone villa built by her father. She is dressed in black, her hair in a bun. In the background is the

Mediterranean countryside, sunny and gray-green, the trees and bushes making spiky outlines on the horizon.

In the final shot, Pastor Toureille is walking slowly down a road, hands clasped behind him, his back to the camera. He is followed by his wife, who is fixing her hair, and then his two grandchildren. There are dark green cypress trees in the distance, and a dog comes barking at them from the side. As the pastor recedes into the distance, he stops, looks back at the camera, and then waves, first lifting his left hand, then his right.

In the final paragraphs of his tribute to his friend, R.-R. Lambert, the French Jewish aid director who perished at Auschwitz, Toureille memorialized the bond he as a Protestant rescuer felt with this Jewish rescuer. Both men had dual loyalties to religious and national identities, both faced criticisms from colleagues and friends for the choices they had made, and both inspired others with the courage to take risks for a just cause:

Jewish and French, French and Jewish 100 percent, R.-R. Lambert knew how to make people devote themselves to the causes he defended. His detractors (There are some, alas, in spite of the fact that he paid with his life and his family's for his loyalty to the position he accepted of his own free will)—his detractors must well know that it is because of men like him that many Christians, of whom I am one, who are susceptible of being not much more than philo-Semites, took to heart his defense of the Jewish cause, to the point of risking their lives and the lives of their families. Because human beings everywhere and always will devote themselves to causes that certain ones among us have identified with, and lived.

It is because the memory of men like R.-R. Lambert remains so vivid and survives in spite of time passing, in spite of everything, yes, in spite of everything— that some of us would be ready again to run the same risks, and others, too, if necessary, in defense of the Jews.[5]

Appendix

Postwar Tributes and Awards

Postwar Tributes

Jean Cadier, former Dean of the Faculty of Theology, Montpellier, wrote, a few months after Toureille's death:

Pierre Toureille, . . . a man of vast erudition, speaking a dozen languages, gifted with an engaging eloquence . . . He worked at the side of Dietrich Bonhoeffer, a martyr of Nazism, whose theological writings have had such a powerful influence on our time. . . . [In his work for the European Leprosy Mission], he visited numerous churches and gave lectures of high quality, often with remarkable films that aroused interest in all regions of France, particularly in Alsace. During eight years of incessant work, sometimes in serious ill health, he informed a great number of French and European Protestants about this mission and sustained among them a spirit of prayer and generosity. Having followed this work very closely, I extend to him now my profound gratitude.[1]

Herbert Stein-Schneider was a member of Toureille's clandestine network during the war, and pastor at the French Protestant Church in Washington, D.C. after the war, replacing Toureille. Stein-Schneider wrote, upon Toureille's death:

Orator, lecturer without equal, extraordinary organizer and activist, he gave our church a new breath of life after so any harsh years of war. There are many throughout the world who owe their lives to this deeply humane pastor, courageous to the point of temerity, a witness of Christ in the darkest hours of French history.

Traveling day and night, . . . he succeeded in snatching men, women and children from the grip of the Gestapo, from deportation and from the crematorium. He organized entire convoys of illegal passengers to Switzerland where other Christian organizations cared for them. With an untiring hand, he wrote long letters so revealing of his character. He gave courage and comfort, he preached and organized at the same time. For hundreds of refugees in France, Pastor Toureille became the symbol of hope and faith.[2]

Oldrich Dubina, former Director of the Czechoslovak Center for Aid in Marseille during the war, wrote in 1973: "I can certify . . . that Pastor Toureille was Vice-President of the executive committee of the Center for Aid to Czechoslovakia from its foundation in September 1940. In carrying out the duties of this position, he helped many Czech citizens, especially those of Jewish origin. He saved many from deportation, often at the risk of his own liberty. These persons, by being placed in children's homes or on farms set up by our Center for Aid, were able to survive the war."[3]

Slavomir Brzak, Acting Director of the Czechoslovak Relief Centre in France during the war, wrote in 1974 "Pastor Toureille used all his energies and exceptional organizational talents to help people persecuted by the Nazis. While I know mainly what he did for the Czechoslovaks, which was only one sector of his activity, I can show that Pastor Toureille helped to save the lives of dozens of people, the majority being Jews."[4]

The Consul-General of the German Embassy in Berne, Switzerland, who made a formal proposal, on September 11, 1968, for decorating Pierre-Charles Toureille with a Medal of Honor, the Grosses Verdienstkreuz, Highest Level:

Pastor Dr. Pierre-Charles Toureille was, from 1940 to 1945 in France, Head Protestant Chaplain for foreign refugees, camp internees, and those deported for forced labor. In this capacity, he looked after approximately 40,000 persons (by the end of the war) with devotion and at the risk of his life. According to his own estimations, about 20,000 were German-speaking. These persons consisted not only of "Non-Aryans" who fled to France and had been deported, but also political opponents of the Nazi regime. He held this office on behalf of the World Council of Churches and the Protestant Federation of France.

His activities went far beyond pastoral care. His task was, to a large degree, to distribute money, clothes, food, books, and other donations. He provided his "parishioners" jobs and education and helped them in their critical situation, in every respect. In many cases he could save persons entrusted to him, from the clutches of the Gestapo. He hid them in new hiding places and helped them to escape over the Swiss border. In this way, Pastor Toureille saved many lives. His headquarters were in Lunel near Montpellier where he employed a total of 19 persons over that period. The Gestapo put him under surveillance, summoned him and interrogated him seven times.

Pastor Toureille still has warm feelings for Germany in spite of all his experiences and is still in close contact with many of his former parishioners. He is still, as he was at that time, fully ready to make sacrifices and is filled with charity.

[An attachment to this letter, from the German Consul-General in Geneva:] It is clear that Pastor Toureille has worked for many years, especially from 1940–1945, in close contact with the former Secretary-General of the World Council of Churches, Dr. Willem Visser't Hooft, who has known Mr. Toureille for 47 years. He spoke to the Consul-General in a very positive way about Toureille and remembered him as a courageous and tireless friend in need who was guided by genuine Christian ideals of humanity and never showed himself as embittered toward Germany in spite of the continuous harassment by the German Occupation authorities in France.[5]

Attestation from Yad Vashem, July 1, 1974 (The memorial tree was planted by Marc Toureille on February 9, 1988.): "The present document attests to the fact that at its meeting of November 6, 1973, the Commission of the Just at the Commemorative Institute for Martyrs and Heroes, Yad Vashem, has decided, on the testimony it has received from witnesses, to render homage to Reverend Dr. P. C. Toureille, who, at the peril of his life, saved Jews during the era of extermination, and authorizes the planting of a tree in his name in the Avenue of the Just on the Mountain of Memory in Jerusalem."

Walter Oppenheim, saved by Toureille during the war and Consul-General for West Germany in Marseille in 1973, wrote to Yad Vashem that same year:

I owe him my life because he helped me escape to Switzerland, saving me from deportation from the southern French camps (March 1943). Dr. Toureille had set up an organization for the care, warning, and escape of those persecuted by the Nazis. . . . His helpers, some secret, some official, were Protestant Boy Scout groups as well as theology students at Montpellier. I knew that he had stopped numerous denunciations, house searches, interrogations, and threats and that during that time he himself had escaped arrest by the Gestapo and deportation only by going underground at certain times. . . .

The accounts of the help given by Dr. Toureille to the victims of persecution

interned in the camps, also to refugees enduring forced delays, would fill volumes.
It would please me greatly if Dr. Toureille, while he is still alive (he is ill), could
receive the recognition he deserves.

Jean Boisset, the President of the Executive Committee of Toureille's
Chaplaincy, in a postwar tribute to Toureille, summarizes how Toureille
coordinated the Chaplaincy with the aid organizations:

At first, in October 1942, the office of the Chaplaincy, which employed six
people, was part of the Toureille home. The office was then installed in another
place to allow Pastor and Madame Toureille to have a more normal family life.
After the events of June 1940, as successor to Pastor Forell who had to flee to the
United States, Pastor Toureille received one list of Protestant refugees in France,
comprised of only about 20 names. Upon leaving the Chaplaincy in September
1945, he left several lists and a folder containing several thousand names and addresses. The work and organization required to achieve this, was accomplished in
extremely difficult and often dangerous conditions.

M. Toureille, with great fidelity, visited the internment camps in France and
North Africa, the Groups of Foreign Workers, the aid centers, the isolated and
those in hiding, carrying to the Christians in the churches belonging to the World
Council of Churches, moral and necessary material aid and comfort. This meant
incessant moving around, in all seasons and by all means of transportation (even
going by bicycle and on foot were made difficult by the administrative formalities
required in this period). . . . The considerable fatigue that resulted was exacerbated by the regulations on the opening hours of restaurants and hotels. M. Toureille had to skip meals and spend the night in station waiting rooms, or on public
park benches. Pastor Toureille's task was facilitated by his profound knowledge of
several languages and by his great memory. . . . He presided regularly at the religious services held in the most diverse and remote communities. . . .

Several thousand books were collected in a circulating library. The benefits of
this literature in all languages were incalculable for a population almost entirely
dominated by the psychosis of fear. . . . A very heavy correspondence required
that the Chaplaincy employ 12 people, which allowed M. Toureille to devote himself to administration. In the course of the summer of 1942, the anti-Semitic measures became more and more grave, and M. Toureille, since a great number of his
parishioners were racially Jewish, worked hard to protect them, contacting other
aid organizations for help, in France and abroad.

Pastor Toureille had to undergo surveillance from the Vichy police and from
the Gestapo. His home and his office were searched in his presence and his absence. He was even required to report to the authorities in Montpellier on two occasions, although it would have been possible for him to take refuge in Switzer-

land—he had a permanent permit to do so. By this choice, he showed openly that he would not abandon those for whom he was the ONLY connection to life. . . .

Thus, to foreigners of all nations who fled to France, M. Toureille devoted himself to showing them "the true face of France," and to those French inexperienced about foreigners, he made them known, and often, loved.

Following is an attestation by his correspondent of ten years and sponsor, Adolf Freudenberg, of the World Council of Churches:

M. Toureille was in charge of putting the Chaplaincy on its feet. The group of people assigned to him grew rapidly and soon, through direct contact by personal visits, or by letter, he was in touch with thousands of people who had lost everything and who were left to the mercy of arbitrary treatment by the Vichy and occupying authorities. . . . The Chaplaincy could work among tens of thousands of internees, foreign workers, and those refugees authorized to live on their own in the "southern zone". . . .

The difficulties [in providing funding and supplies to the refugees] increased daily and, from the end of 1942, the menace of the French concentration camps and then of deportation to Germany weighed almost continually on M. Toureille. The varied searches conducted in the Chaplaincy headquarters are a conclusive proof of that.

He always took the greatest interest in the smallest details of the often complicated situations that his parishioners presented to him. Gifted with rich and numerous talents, such as an extraordinary memory and several languages, M. Toureille, in consecrating himself with zeal and devotion to his task, has accomplished a remarkable work of charity and of Christian witness.

Awards

FFL (*Forces françaises libres*) medal, August 1945, insignia #36339, through Antoine Rybak, head of Franco-Czech resistance network, Rossi-Rybak.
La Médaille de la résistance française, May 17, 1946.
C.S.L. Vojenska Medaila za Zásluhy, I, Stupne, the Czechoslovak government, July 16, 1946.
Czech White Lion, from President Bénès, January 3, 1947. Highest government award.
Das Grosse Verdienstkreuz, upon proposal of Chancellor W. Brandt of West Germany, May 16, 1969. Highest civilian award that can be given to a non-German.
Yad Vashem award to the Righteous, July 1, 1974.
Tree planted posthumously in his honor by Marc Toureille, Avenue of the Righteous, Yad Vashem, Jerusalem, February 9, 1988.

Notes

Prologue

1. To sample the range and some of the perspectives of studies on rescuers, see the following:

Gay Block and Malka Drucker, *Rescuers: Portraits of Moral Courage in the Holocaust* (New York: Holmes & Meier Publishers, 1992). The authors consider their subjects—rescuers across Europe—as individual cases, heroes who acted independently of their communities, a minority among a majority of bystanders.

Philip P. Hallie, *Lest Innocent Blood Be Shed* (New York: Harper & Row, 1979). This study of Le Chambon-sur-Lignon explores the communal factors that motivated a whole network of villages in southern France to be rescuers.

Kristen Renwick Monroe, "John Donne's People: Explaining Differences between Rational Actors and Altruists through Cognitive Frameworks." *Journal of Politics* 53, no.2 (May 1991): 394–433. The study tested the significance of factors commonly considered important among rescuers—including religion, role models, personal honor, feeling good—and concluded that the only common factor was a sense of "shared humanity."

S. P. Oliner, and P. M. Oliner. *The Altruistic Personality: Rescuers of Jews in Nazi Europe* (New York: Free Press, 1988). Oliner and Oliner argue that rescuers are motivated by "the ethics of care."

Mordecai Paldiel, *The Path of the Righteous. Gentile Rescuers of Jews during the Holocaust* (Hoboken, N.J.: KTAV Publishing House, 1993). Paldiel agrees with the Oliners' perspective on the altruistic character.

Pierre Sauvage, *Weapons of the Spirit* (Los Angeles: Pierre Sauvage Productions and Friends of Le Chambon, 1988). This documentary film on the rescue milieu of Le Chambon-sur-Lignon includes extensive interviews of villagers.

André Stein, *Quiet Heroes. True Stories of the Rescue of Jews by Christians in Nazi-Occupied Holland.* New York: New York University Press, 1988. Stein found no pattern uniting these rescuers, except that they all acted effectively, in a small and local way.

Nehama Tec, *When Light Pierced the Darkness: Christian Rescue of Jews in Nazi-Occupied Poland* (New York: Oxford University Press, 1986). Tec found no pattern in the background of rescuers, except for personal characteristics like universalistic response to the needy.

1. Pierre-Charles Toureille, 1900–1976

1. All the biographical information and documentation on Toureille in this chapter are from the family papers collected by his son, Marc Toureille. In subsequent chapters, the family papers and photographs continue to be the sources for biographical information about Toureille, unless otherwise referenced.

2. To Be a Huguenot

1. The visitor was M. De Boufflers, whose description of the Tower is quoted in Baird, *The Huguenots*, 452–53. Baird notes that this description is often quoted in Huguenot histories.

2. Told to the author by Pierre Toureille's son, Marc.

3. See "Saint Bartholomew's Day, Massacre of, " *Encyclopedia Britannica* 10 (1998). This article states that estimates of the total number who perished in this conflict range from 2,000 by "a Roman Catholic apologist" to 70,000 by the contemporary Huguenot, the Duke de Sully.

4. Fontaine, *Memoires*. The page numbers in parentheses in the text refer to the 1994 edition translated by Ann Maury. The most recent French edition is *Memoires d'une famille huguenote: Victime de la révocation de l'édit de Nantes*, introduction and notes by Bernard Cottret (Montpellier: Presses du Languedoc, 1992).

5. All the information in this section on the Camisards is taken from Bastide, *Pages d'histoire Protestant*.

6. Sauvage, *Weapons of the Spirit*.

7. The documents excerpted below, in this section, are from Marie Brottes's dossier at Yad Vashem, Jerusalem.

8. This version of "Cevenol Hymn" was given to the author by Marie Brottes and translated by the author.

9. See Ely Ben-Gal, in *Le Plateau Vivarais*, 319–20.

10. Ibid.

11. Above population figures are taken from *Statistical Abstract*, 2d ed., 1994.

3. Pierre Toureille's Early Years and the Ecumenical Movement of the 1930s

1. Toureille's thesis on John Huss is on file in the library of the Faculty of Protestant Theology, Montpellier, France.

2. Marc Toureille remembers: "My father had a good sense of humor. When he was a theology student, he and his friends played jokes, sang hymns with made-up words, did dirty tricks. Once they were on a small train and filled goat skin flasks with water, then squirted people going by, out the windows of the train. The conductor was upset and shouted at them, 'The train will tip over with all of you hanging out one side!' And once they went to visit a parishioner who had a trap door to a wine cellar in his kitchen. My father hid under the trap door to take the man by surprise. He even went once with friends to a Catholic church, confessed to a priest and then said, 'Father, you have just confessed a Protestant!'"

3. Bethge, *Dietrich Bonheoffer*, 152.

4. Ibid., 84.

5. Ibid., 150.

6. In the library of the SHPF (Société de l'Histoire du Protestantisme Français), (Paris, no date and no journal title), 1–46.

7. The World Alliance documents in this chapter are taken from the archives of the World Council of Churches in Geneva, the Toureille folder. The documents are in no particular order and are identified only by date and title, by which they will also be referenced in the present text. Copies of these documents are in the possession of the author.

8. Bethge, *Dietrich Bonhoeffer*, 183.

9. Ibid., 188.

10. Ibid., 211.

11. W. M. Macartney, *Life and Work: The Record of the Church of Scotland*, November 1933, archives of the World Council of Churches, Geneva.

12. Bethge, *Dietrich Bonhoeffer*, 245.

13. Ibid., 246.

14. Ibid., 394.

15. Encrevé, *Les protestants français*, 53.

16. Ibid., 141.

17. Toureille, "Des Liens Renforcés," 69–74.

4. The War Years, an Introduction

1. Grynberg, *Les camps de la honte*, 25.

2. Marrus and Paxton, *Vichy France and the Jews*, 35.

3. Ibid., 36.

4. Grynberg, *Les camps de la honte*, 19.

5. Ibid., 9.

6. Ibid., 12.

7. The numbers given in the following paragraph are taken from Marrus and Paxton, *Vichy France*, 372.

8. November 1944 report, American Committee, OSE (Oeuvre de secours aux enfants), filed at the Leo Baeck Institute, New York: Nîmes Committee, "France Concentration Camp collection," AR3987, B24/8.

9. Marrus and Paxton, *Vichy France*, 176.

10. Encrevé, *Les protestants français*, 54. Here is an example of one Protestant's letter to a Nîmes newspaper protesting against the Vichy Jewish Statutes: "I am Christian and Protestant. One question has been weighing heavily on my conscience as a Frenchwoman, for several weeks: that of the Jewish Statute . . . , because the day of its promulgation was, for many of us, a day of sadness and shame. . . . I don't deny that there is presently a Jewish problem in France, with the rise of Jews to certain positions, and, above all, with the increased foreign immigration. . . . [But] I am ashamed for my country, when I see around me so many Jews whose careers have been completely destroyed" (François Boulet, "Juifs et Protestants (1940–1944)" in Encrevé, *Les protestants français*, 369.

11. Joutard, *Cévennes*, 134–35.

12. Encrevé, *Les protestants français*, 371.

13. See Joutard, *Cévennes*, 211–25, in which P. Cabanel, J. Poujol, and M. Donadille discuss the factors that promoted the building of this Protestant church rescue network.

14. Ibid., 222–23.

15. Ludwig, "Christians Cannot Remain Silent," 479.

16. The information and quotations in this section, unless otherwise referenced, are taken from D'Aubigné, Mouchon, and Mouchon, *Les Clandestins de Dieu*, 37–57.

17. Ludwig, "Christians Cannot Remain Silent," 481.

5. The War, 1939–1940

1. The chronology aligned on the left margin, which gives the wider context of the war, is taken from *Teaching about the Holocaust*, with my additions. The indented chronology, which refers to events within France, is taken from F. Boulet, "Juifs et Protestants (1940–1944)" in *Les protestants français*, ed. Encrevé, 368–80, with my additions. The chronologies that begin chapters 6 through 8 were taken from the same sources.

2. The information and quotations in this chapter, which refer to Toureille's work with the World Alliance and the WCC, are taken from the library archives of

the World Council of Churches in Geneva, unless otherwise identified. These documents are collected in a folder marked "Toureille" in the WCC archives, in no particular order and without identifying numbers. In the present text each document is identified by date. The author has copies of these World Council of Churches documents.

3. Since the summer of 1936 Toureille had already been helping German Jewish refugees, by setting up a network of theology students from Montpellier, who joined forces with village pastors to pass these refugees through the Cévennes area into Switzerland. One of these *passeurs*, Pastor L. Olivés, described how he and another student at the time, J. Bourdon, were approached by Toureille: "I was a theology student for four years at Montpellier. Already, in 1936, under the Popular Front government, I had made contact with Pastor Toureille. He was receiving young people from Germany fleeing because their mother or father were Jews. . . . I took care of them (the dean never knew and I don't know what his reaction would have been) in my student quarters. With Bourdon, we set up a motorcycle service that took these young people to Switzerland, to the refugee agency there. We never knew what happened to them afterwards. . . . I never asked where these people came from. I knew later that some came from Belgium, and other places. I came to know the Cévennes region well—I could find places for these people." Joutard, *Cévennes,* 241.

4. Toureille, "Des Liens Renforcés," 69–74.

5. Ibid.

6. In a letter dated June 19,1941, Toureille announced to Freudenberg an important new position he had just taken on with the Committee of Nîmes: "I have the duty to inform you that, as a result of the departure of Dr. Donald Lowrie, of the YMCA, for Lisbon (from where he will probably leave in a month for the U.S.A.), I have been serving, since June 12, as President of the Committee of Coordination. That requires my presence in Marseille at least one day a week. If that increases my work load, it also increases my opportunity for action. I can have, as a result, one assistant in my office. I have become, therefore, the liaison among ALL the private aid organizations (Christian, Jewish or others) and Vichy." A handwritten note here by Freudenberg adds: "According to Guillon, Toureille is now the President of the Committee of Coordination of Nîmes, works with the Czechs and is the chief Protestant chaplain in Vichy."

7. Leo Baeck Institute archives, New York. The Committee of Nîmes (partial list): International YMCA/Alliance universelle des unions chrétiennes de jeunes gens (Donald Lowrie; Charles Guillon; Tracy Strong); AFSC (Roswell McClelland; see his account of the 1942 deportations from French camps, in chapter 7); American Friends of Czechoslovakia; American Joint Distribution Committee (Jewish); Centre d'aide tcheque (O. Dubina); CIMADE; Commission centrale des organisations juives d'assistance en France (Jewish); Commission des camps

des oeuvres israélites d'assistance aux refugiés (Jewish); Comité d'assistance aux refugiés (CAR/Jewish; R.-R.Lambert); Red Cross/Croix Rouge—American, French, and Polish; Catholic Church of France; European Aid to Students; Federation of Protestant Church of France (M. Boegner); HICEM (Jewish emigration association of three organizations); ORT (Organisation pour la reconstruction et le travail; Jewish vocational training); OSE (Oeuvre de secours aux enfants, Agency for Aid to Children; Dr. Joseph Weill); Service social d'aide aux emigrants (SSAE); Unitarian Aid Committee (Noel Field); Rabbis Hirschler (Grand Rabbi of Strasbourg), Kapel, Salzer, Schilli; Abbé A. Glasberg

8. Toureille's personal papers, letter of attestation regarding his wartime activities. In the possession of Marc Toureille.

9. Toureille was well aware of the dangers involved, especially in making mistakes—which he sometimes did. In his memoir, *The Hunted Children*, Lowrie told one story about Toureille that demonstrated the constant tensions under which the aid groups worked and the danger in making mistakes, especially because of the precariousness of balancing legal with clandestine operations (93). Identified in Lowrie's book as "the pastor who was one of the vice-presidents of the Nîmes Committee," Toureille once, on a train, left his briefcase full of financial and some secret information about the Committee's organization. The Vichy police ransacked his home and office but luckily didn't investigate further any of the other organizations with which he was working.

10. All the following quotations are taken from Grynberg, *Les camps de la honte*, 343.

11. Ibid., 196, 367.

12. Archives of Centre de documentation juive contemporaine, Paris, No. CCCLXIII-90, n.d., translated by Marc Toureille.

13. R.-R. Lambert's war diary, "Carnet d'un témoin, 1940–1943," quoted in Grynberg, *Les camps de la honte*, 113.

14. Ibid., 328–29.

15. Encrevé, *Les protestants français*, 253.

16. Ibid., 256–57.

17. Ibid., 255.

18. Ibid., 117.

19. Ibid.

20. D'Aubigné, Mouchon, and Mouchon, *Les clandestines de Dieu*, 12 ff.

21. Encrevé, *Les protestants français*, 162ff.

22. Joutard, *Cévennes*, 219–21.

23. Lowrie, *The Hunted Children*, 58–59.

24. Joutard, *Cévennes*, 239–40.

25. Leo Baeck Institute, New York, minutes of Committee of Nîmes, archives.

26. Leo Baeck Institute, New York, archives on French internment camps.

27. See Grynberg, *Les camps de la honte*, 12; Marrus and Paxton, *Vichy France*, 166.

28. Marrus and Paxton, *Vichy France*, 176.

6. The War, 1941

1. Encrevé, *Les protestants français*, 226.

2. Committee of Nîmes minutes referred to in this chapter are in the Leo Baeck Institute archives.

3. See, for example, Varian Fry's *Assignment: Rescue* (New York: Scholastic Inc., 1968), for an account of his successful attempts in 1941 to provide emigration to refugee artists and intellectuals under Vichy. Some, but not all, of his rescue activities were clandestine, through networks operating out of Marseille.

4. Joutard, *Cévennes*, 82.

5. Toureille, "Des Liens Renforcés."

6. Lowrie, *The Hunted Children*, 122–23.

7. Toureille, "Des Liens Renforcés."

8. The following story was told to the author by Joseph Fišera.

9. Encrevé, *Les protestants français*, 645–47. The following information and quotations concerning Fišera were taken from this article. The author also interviewed him in July 1996, during which he verified what he had written in the article.

10. Lowrie, *The Hunted Children*, 160.

11. Ibid.

12. Ibid.

13. All Committee of Nîmes minutes refered to in this chapter were obtained from the Leo Baeck Institute, New York.

14. Here and throughout the rest of the manuscript, when individual cases are referred to and have not been published previously, I have used random initials instead of the real names, to protect the person's privacy.

15. Joutard, *Cévennes*, 139.

16. All Committee of Nîmes minutes referred to in this chapter were obtained from the Leo Baeck Institute, New York.

17. Marc Toureille commented: "G. was brought to Cournonterral to raise rabbits on my grandmother's property, namely the building on the north side of the garden. It consisted of a former winery, three stalls for horses, and a four-room apartment. G. arrived with his wife and a four-year-old daughter. He was still wearing his GTE [forced labor group] uniform. At first they lived in a small two-room house outside of town. It had been built by my great-grandfather as a meeting place for his friends and fellow poets. G. had to wait for the apartment to be vacated by its tenant."

18. In June, Toureille became president of the Committee of Nîmes, although

it is not clear whether this remained his permanent position in 1941, since Lowrie did return to France for committee meetings up to December 1941, the date the United States entered the war. In a letter to Freudenberg, dated June 19, 1941, Toureille announced his new position as president of the Committee of Nîmes: "I have the duty to inform you that, as a result of the departure of Dr. Donald Lowrie, of the YMCA, for Lisbon (from where he will probably leave in a month for the U.S.A.), I have been serving, since June 12, as President of the Committee of Coordination. That requires my presence in Marseille at least one day a week. If that increases my work load, it also increases my opportunity for action. I can have, as a result, one assistant in my office. I have become, therefore, the liaison among ALL the private aid organizations (Christian, Jewish or others) and Vichy." A handwritten note by Freudenberg, attached to the letter, adds: "According to Guillon, Toureille is now the President of the Committee of Coordination of Nîmes, works with the Czechs and is the chief Protestant chaplain in Vichy."

19. Archives and Documentation, Ministry of Foreign Affairs, Paris, Guerre 1939–1945, Vichy État français, C administrative volume 150.

20. Toureille file, World Council of Churches archives.

21. Encrevé, *Les protestants français,* 256.

22. Holzschuh, *Le Village sur la Montagne.* Excerpts from the French edition, Geneva, 1939, in the possession of the author.

23. See F. Boulet, "Juifs et Protestants (1940–1944)," *Les protestants français,* ed. Encrevé, 340–41, for this account.

24. Encrevé, *Les protestants français,* 171.

25. Ibid., 174.

26. Grynberg, *Les camps de la honte,* 12.

7. The War, 1942

1. All information on Committee of Nîmes meetings in this chapter was obtained from the Leo Baeck Institute archives, unless otherwise referenced.

2. Doc. No. I.479, ADL 2W3179, S.C.T. Vichy, Insp. Régionale, Préfet Lozère, Archives.

3. Marc Toureille commented: "The Wehrmacht paid rent, 100 Francs per month, which, of course, came out of the cost of Occupation paid by the Vichy government."

4. The minutes of the Chaplaincy meetings are filed in the archives of the World Council of Churches in Geneva. Copies are in the author's possession.

5. Contrôle postal, S.C.T. Vichy, Insp. Régionale, Préfet Lozère. Archives. ADL 2W3179.

6. Joutard, *Cévennes,* 232. ADL liasse VI M2 21, la Lozère.

7. Contrôle postal, S.C.T. Vichy, Insp. Régionale, Préfet Lozère. Archives. ADL 2W3179.

8. D'Aubigné, Mouchon, and Mouchon, *Les Clandestins de Dieu*, 17.

9. Ibid., 17–18.

10. Ibid., 18–19.

11. Ibid., 20–21.

12. Ibid., 21–22.

13. Ibid., 22.

14. Bolle, "Toureille, Pierre-Charles," 180–81.

15. D'Aubigné, Mouchon, and Mouchon, *Les Clandestins de Dieu*, 25–26.

16. Ibid., 54. All references to Freudenberg's memoir in this and the following paragraphs are taken from the chapter "Across the Border," 37–57.

17. Ludwig, "Christians Cannot Remain Silent," 480.

18. D'Aubigné, Mouchon, and Mouchon, *Les Clandestins de Dieu*, 127–28.

19. McClelland, "An Unpublished Chapter," Reel XX, F XX, 41 pp.

20. Bolle, *Le Plateau Vivarais-Lignon*, 175–76.

21. See Yves-Marie Hilaire's comments during this discussion, *Les protestants français*, ed. Encrevé, 303–4.

22. Quoted as a survey response by historian Pierre Bolle, *Le Plateau Vivarais-Lignon*, 305.

23. Joutard, *Cévennes*, 242–44.

24. Ibid., 244–45.

25. Ibid., 263.

26. Encrevé, *Les protestants français*, 305.

27. Ibid.

28. In the archives of the World Council of Churches, Geneva.

29. Hallie, *Lest Innocent Blood Be Shed*, 99–103.

30. Bolle, *Le Plateau Vivarais-Lignon*, 378.

31. Ibid., 369.

32. Ibid., 396.

33. Ibid., 293.

34. Hallie, *Lest Innocent Blood Be Shed*, 142–45.

35. Leo Baeck Institute archives.

36. U.S. Holocaust Memorial Museum archives.

37. Leo Baeck Institute archives.

38. Leo Baeck Institute archives.

39. The following account is taken from Donald Lowrie's report of August 1942 and from Marrus and Paxton, *Vichy France*, 266–69.

40. Ibid., 267.

41. Leo Baeck Institute archives.

42. Toureille, "Des Liens Reforcés."

43. Lowrie, *The Hunted Children,* 247.

44. Toureille, "Des Liens Reforcés."

45. Ibid.

46. The following story is based on Anna Sperber's memoir, Toureille dossier, Yad Vashem archives.

47. The following information is taken from the Papets' testimony on behalf of Toureille's candidacy for the Medal of the Just, Toureille dossier, Yad Vashem archives.

48. Toureille dossier, Yad Vashem archives.

49. Barosin, *A Remnant.*

50. Ibid., 59.

51. Letter written on CIMADE letterhead, Nîmes. Given to the author by Jacques Poujol and marked CCXX-94.

52. Archives Nationales, Commissariat général aux questions juives, AJ 38 292.

8. The War, 1943–1945 and After

1. Bolle, "Toureille, Pierre-Charles," 182.

2. Archives of the World Council of Churches, Geneva.

3. Ludwig, "Christians Cannot Remain Silent," 481.

4. Lowrie, *The Hunted Children,* 247–48.

5. Toureille, "Des Liens Reforcés."

6. Ibid.

7. Ibid.

8. Letter to the author, July 1996.

9. Toureille, "Des Liens Reforcés."

10. Toureille dossier, Yad Vashem archives.

11. Marc Toureille provided additional information: "This Gypsy from Lunel was François Pascucci. He was 47 years old. Lunel had been designated by the authorities as a site of forced residence for Gypsies as a first assembly point before their internment and deportation. Luckily for them and for reasons unknown, neither internment nor deportation materialized. Unlike the majority of Gypsies, the Pascucci family had given up their wandering and settled in Lunel before the war. They had a successful scrap iron business and were well known and respected."

12. According to Marc Toureille, "'Die beste Kompagnie,' a Wehrmacht marching song, was heard too often, as they all were. Each group would alternate that line with one identifying the number of their own unit. The first group would sing 'Die erste K,' the second, 'Die zweite K,' and so on. My mother used to say that the German soldier was ordered to sing while marching to keep him from thinking."

13. Marc Toureille commented: "The FFI finally blew up the Pont de Lunel so the U.S. Air Force would not bomb it for the third time. They completely missed it twice while killing many civilians. And both times, they bombed days after the Germans had already retreated and the bridge had lost its strategic importance. So much for the stupidity of war!"

14. Arlette Gauthier, as told to and translated by Micheline Toureille.

15. Toureille's writings in this section are all in manuscript form, unpublished unless otherwise described. They are in the possession of Marc Toureille.

16. Tory, *Surviving the Holocaust,* 168.

17. Encrevé, *Les protestants français,* 259.

18. Given to the author by Jacques Poujol.

19. Cadier, *Le Calvaire d'Israël.*

20. The following case information was taken from Toureille's own manuscript and from Joutard, *Cévennes,* 120–22.

21. Joutard, *Cévennes,* 122.

22. Given to the author by Josef Fišera.

23. Toureille dossier, Yad Vashem archives. Translation by Albrecht Funk, visiting professor, University of Pittsburgh.

Epilogue

1. The following information on ancient and medieval Jewry in the Lunel area is from Iancu and Iancu, *Les Juifs du Midi,* 21–39.

2. M. Chauvet, *Terres de Prestige,* Lunel Tourist Bureau.

3. Ibid., 23.

4. See *Encyclopedia Judaica,* 566.

5. Archives of the Centre de documentation juive contemporaine, Paris, No.CCCLXIII-90, n.d.. Translated by Marc Toureille.

Appendix

1. "En souvenir du Pasteur Pierre-Ch. Toureille," *Le Christianisme au XXe siècle,* January 24, 1977.

2. In the possession of Marc Toureille.

3. Toureille dossier, Yad Vashem archives, 1973.

4. Toureille dossier, Yad Vashem archives.

5. Toureille dossier, Yad Vashem archives. Translation by Albrecht Funk, Visiting Professor, University of Pittsburgh.

Selected Bibliography

Books and Articles

Baird, Henry M. *The Huguenots and the Revocation of the Edict of Nantes.* New York: Charles Scribner's Sons, 1895.

Barnes, Kenneth C. "The German Church Struggle and the Oxford Conference," In *Holocaust and Church Struggle: Religion, Power and the Politics of Resistance.* Edited by Hubert G. Locke and Marcia Sachs Littell. Studies in the Shoah. Vol. 16. pp 139–55. Lanham, Md.: University Press of America, 1996.

Barosin, Jacob. *A Remnant.* New York: Holocaust Library, 1988.

Bastide, Samuel. *Pages d'Histoire Protestante: Les Camisards.* Cévennes: Musée du Désert, n.d.

U.S. Holocaust Museum. *The World Must Know: The History of the Holocaust as Told in the United States Holocaust Memorial Museum.* Edited by Michael Berenbaum. Boston: Little, Brown, and Co., 1993.

Bethge, Eberhard. *Dietrich Bonhoeffer: A Life in Pictures.* London: SCM Press Ltd., 1986.

———. *Dietrich Bonhoeffer: Man of Vision, Man of Courage.* New York: Harper & Row, 1970.

Block, Gay, and Malka Drucker. *Rescuers: Portraits of Moral Courage in the Holocaust.* New York: Holmes & Meier Publishers, 1992.

Bolle, Pierre. "Toureille, Pierre-Charles." *Dictionnaire du Monde Religieux dans la France Contemporaine: 5. Les Protestants.* Paris: Beauchesne (n.d.)

———, ed. *Le Plateau Vivarais-Lignon, Accueil et Résistance 1939–1944.* Actes du Colloque du Chambon-sur-Lignon. Le Chambon-sur-Lignon: Société d'Histoire de la Montagne, 1992.

Cadier, Henri, avec le concours de R. Benoit, H. Manen, Monique M., P. Toureille, A. Freudenberg. *Le Calvaire d'Israël et la Solidarité Chrétienne.* Geneva: Les Éditions Labor et Fidès, 1945.

Cadier, Jean. Doyen de la Faculté de Théologie, Montpellier. "En souvenir du

Pasteur Pierre-Ch. Toureille." *Le Christianisme au XXe siècle,* (January 1977).

D'Aubigné, Merle, Jeanne Mouchon, and Violette Mouchon. *Les Clandestins de Dieu.* Paris: Librairie Arthème Fayard, 1968. Translated by William Nottingham and Patricia Nottingham under the title *God's Underground* (St. Louis: Bethany Press, 1970).

Encrevé, André, and Jacques Poujol, eds. *Les protestants français pendant la seconde guerre mondiale. Actes du colloque de Paris, Palais du Luxembourg, 19–21 Nov. 1992.* Paris: Société de l'Histoire du Protestantisme Français, 1994.

Encyclopedia Judaica. s. v. "Lunel." Jerusalem: Keter Publishing House Ltd., 1971.

Fontaine, Jacques. *Mémoires d'une famille huguenote, victime de la révocation de l'Édit de Nantes.* 1838. Translated by Ann Maury under the title *Memoirs of a Huguenot Family* (Baltimore, Md.: Genealogical Publishing Co., Inc., 1994).

Greenbaum, Masha. *The Jews of Lithuania. A History of a Remarkable Community, 1316–1945.* Jerusalem: Gefen Publishing House Ltd., 1995/5755.

Grynberg, Anne. *Les camps de la honte: les internes juifs des camps français 1939–1944.* Paris: Éditions La Découverte, 1991.

Hallie, Philip. *Lest Innocent Blood Be Shed: The Story of the Village of Le Chambon and How Goodness Happened There.* New York: Harper & Row, 1979.

The Holy Bible. King James version. New York: American Bible Society, 1986.

The Holy Scriptures, According to the Masoretic Text. Philadelphia: The Jewish Publication Society of America, 1954/5714.

Holzschuh, Peter (racontée par). *Le Village sur la Montagne: Tableau de l'Église Fidèle sous le Régime Nazi,* Transcrit par Johan Maarten. Traduction de Hilde Hoefert. Geneva: Éditions Labor, 1939.

Iancu, Daniele, and Carol Iancu. *Les Juifs du Midi, Une histoire millénaire.* Avignon: Éditions A. Barthélémy, 1995.

Joutard, Philippe, Jacques Poujol, and Patrick Cabanel, eds. *Cévennes, terre de refuge 1940–1944.* Presses du Languedoc/Club Cévenol, 1994.

Klima, Ivan. *The Spirit of Prague.* London: Granta Books, 1994.

Lowrie, Donald. *The Hunted Children.* New York: W.W. Norton, 1963.

Ludwig, Hartmut. "'Christians Cannot Remain Silent about This Crime': On the Centenary of the Birth of Adolf Freudenberg." *Ecumenical Review,* vol. XLVI, no.4 (1994): 475–85.

McClelland, Roswell. "An Unpublished Chapter in the History of the Deportation of Foreign Jews from France in 1942." Washington, D.C.: United States Holocaust Memorial Museum archives, RG-43.002.01.

"La Maison d'Accueil Chrétienne pour Enfants [MACE] à Vence," (brochure, July 22, 1941). In possession of J. Fišera.

MacIntyre, Alasdair. *After Virtue,* 2d Edition. Notre Dame: University of Notre Dame Press, 1984.

Marrus, Michael R., and Robert O. Paxton. *Vichy France and the Jews.* Stanford, Calif.: Stanford University Press, 1995. First published in French: *Vichy et les juifs.* Paris: Calmann-Levy, 1981.

Resnick, Daniel P. *The White Terror and the Political Reaction After Waterloo.* Cambridge, Mass.: Harvard University Press, 1966.

Sauvage, Pierre. *Weapons of the Spirit.* Pierre Sauvage Productions and Friends of Le Chambon, Inc., Los Angeles, 1988, 1990. Film.

Stein-Schneider, Herbert. "À la Faculté de Théologie de Montpellier: Sur le banc des accusés se trouve le régime nazi, son racisme obscène, sa brutalité sans raison, son terrorisme aveugle." *Reforme,* 4 juillet 1987.

———. "In Memoriam." (1976). In possession of Marc Toureille.

Teaching about the Holocaust: A Resource Book for Educators. U.S. Holocaust Memorial Museum, 1996.

Tory, Avraham. *Surviving the Holocaust. The Kovno Ghetto Diary.* Cambridge: Harvard University Press, 1990.

Toureille, Marc, joint author. Letter to the Editor, sent to national newspapers, on burning of Black churches, Summer 1996.

Toureille, Pierre. "Au temps du maquis et depuis la liberation." *Le Calvaire d'Israël et la Solidarité Chrétienne* (1945): 128–36.

———. "Des Liens Renforcés." *Calendrier Evangélique.* Edited by J. Fišera. (Prague: Kalich Publishing, 1947), 69–74.

———. "Le problème des minorités en Europe." *L'Avant-Garde, Journal populaire du Christianisme Social,* (November 1937). [Expanded version in World Council of Churches archives, Toureille file, Geneva.]

———. "Les protestants de l'Europe centrale et les missions en terre païenne." Société de l'Histoire du Protestantisme Français (Paris), [n.d.].

———. "Masaryk." *L'Avant-Garde* (November 1937).

Wilks, Mark. *History of the Persecutions Endured by the Protestants of the South of France, and more especially of the Department of the Gard during the years 1814, 1815, 1816, etc., including a Defence of Their Conduct from the Revolution to the Present.* London: Longman, Hurst, Rees, Orme & Brown, 1821.

Primary Sources

Manuscripts by Pierre-Charles Toureille

These manuscripts were originally written in French. All of them are in the possession of Marc Toureille.

"Aid to Protestant refugees." March 1, 1945.

"Béziers, 1961: Speech on Missions Day."

Curriculum Vitae.

"German retreat from Lunel." August 13–September 3, 1944.

"The lure of Paris." March 1, 1945.

"On the function of our library." March 27, 1945.

"The reason for loyalty certificates." April 27, 1945.

Sermon, given on November 11, 1925, upon his consecration to ministry, Cournonterral, Hérault.

"Some difficult cases." [n.d.]

"Some of the children under our care." April 5, 1945.

Survey questionnaire to refugees. 1945.

Thesis, Bachelor in Theology, Faculty of Protestant Theology, Montpellier, 1924. *Jean Hus: Les Débuts de la Crise Religieuse Actuelle de la Nation Tchécoslovaque.*

"Tribute to R.-R. Lambert." Centre de documentation juive contemporaine, Paris, CCCLXIII-90. (n.d.) Translated by Marc Toureille.

"Witnesses." (Parishioners' testimonials of faith, n.d.)

Correspondence

Freudenberg, A. Letter to Pierre Toureille. Geneva, April 5, 1946. Toureille file, World Council of Churches archives, Geneva.

Krenek, Pastor (President of the Synod of the Evangelical Church of Czech Brothers, Prague). Letters to Pierre Toureille. September 1945, January 26, and March 1, 1946. Translated by George Pistorius, Professor Emeritus, Williams College, Williamstown, Mass.

Saussine, Jacques (nephew of Pierre Toureille). Letter to Rabbi Kappel. August 25, 1942. Provided by J. Fišera.

Toureille, Pierre-Charles. Correspondence with Adolf Freudenberg and other directors of refugee aid at World Council of Churches (and World Alliance for Promoting International Friendship through the Churches), Toureille file, World Council of Churches archives, Geneva.

———. Correspondence with Yad Vashem and testimonials to Toureille. In Toureille's personal papers, in the possession of Marc Toureille.

———. Letter to Josef Fišera, January 10, 1946. In possession of Fišera.

———. Letters to M. et Mme. A. Seckel-van der Maulen, May 7, 1942; Pastor J. Bourdon, September 30, 1942, and October 10, 1942. Mende, la Lozère departmental archives, Vichy contrôle postal files.

———. Letter to Pierre Toureille, grandson. Postcards from England, May 1966, and France, September 1967. In possession of Marc Toureille.

Documents, Minutes, and Reports

Archives Nationales, Commissariat Général aux Question Juives, AJ 38 292. S.E.C. de Vichy Rapport no. 543, Montpellier, 26 octobre 1942. Objet: activité de Pierre Toureille. Provided by François Boulet, Paris.

Déclaration Raciale (en vue de l'application de la loi du 2 juin 1941 portant status des juifs).

Lowrie, Donald A. Reports to international leaders on the deportations from French internment camps, August 1942. "France, concentration camp collection." The Leo Baeck Institute, New York. AR3987, B24/8.

Meetings of the Committee of Coordination of Nîmes, 1940–1943. Includes reports and statements by Toureille and his letter to Vichy official concerning conditions in internment and forced labor camps. "France, concentration camp collection." The Leo Baeck Institute, New York. AR3987, B24/8.

Minutes from Committee of Coordination of Nîmes, statements by Toureille. April 15, 1942. Provided by Jacques Poujol, Paris.

Minutes from Toureille's Chaplaincy meetings. 1941–1943. World Council of Churches archives, Toureille file, Geneva.

Sicherheitspolizei (SD), Montpellier. May 8 and August 18, 1943. Summons to Pierre Toureille.

Wehrmacht Oberleutnant und Batterie-Chef ; Mayor of Lunel: requisition of Marc Toureille's room.

Wulman, Dr. American Committee of OSE (Oeuvre de secours aux enfants; Agency for Aid to Children). October 26, 1944. Report on Jewish children lost during the German occupation of France. "France, concentration camp collection." The Leo Baeck Institute, New York. AR3987, B24/8.

Yad Vashem archives, Jerusalem, dossier on Pierre Toureille. Correspondence with Toureille, and letters and testimonials from those he rescued.

Yad Vashem archives, Jerusalem, dossier on Marie Brottes. September 10, 1990. In possession of the author.

Interviews by Author

Barosin, Jacob. New York, June 1996.

Boulet, François, historian. Paris, July 1996.

Brottes, Marie. Le Chambon-sur-Lignon, May 6, 1994.

Fišera, Josef, historian. Paris, July 1996.

Gauthier, Arlette. Lunel, July 1996.

Lichtenstein, Jean (Toureille). By letter. April and May 2001.

Kessler, Anne-Marie (Toureille). By letter. July and August 1996.

Poujol, Jacques, historian. Société de l'Histoire du Protestantisme Français, Paris, July 1996.

Toureille, Marc, Micheline Toureille, and son, Pierre. Williamstown, Mass., 1995–1998.

Index

Administrative Committee of the Chaplaincy of Protestant Foreign Refugees or Internees in France. *See* Chaplaincy

Agde camp, 185

Aged, in internment camps, 97, 109, 135

Agriculture: jobs in, 119, 147, 218; by refugees, 78–79, 114–15, 131–32, 196, 214

Aid centers, 68, 97, 147–48, 195–96

Aid organizations, for refugees and internees, 5, 151; conflict over helping in internment camps, 82–83; control of funding for, 70–71; cooperation among, 71–73, 79–80, 129, 133, 242; French Jews in, 84–88; goals of, 96–97, 107, 117, 119–20, 160, 178; and religion, 67, 151; response to deportations, 82–83, 176–77; Toureille in, 6, 119–20; Toureille's dissatisfactions with, 119–20, 124–25, 133–34; and Vichy government, 73–74, 77–78, 99, 117, 140, 145. *See also* Jewish organizations

Aid Society for Pastors of France, 150

Allied armies, 175–76, 178, 199

Alsace, minorities in, 58

American Bible Society, 129

American Friends Service Committee, 67, 162, 177–78

Ammundsen, Bishop, 48–49, 51–52

Andrews, C. F., 48

Anti-Semitism, 161; French, 64, 69; Nazi, 77, 90; opposition to, 69, 90–91; Vichy, 64–65, 67–69, 90–93

"Appeal to All French Protestants" (Toureille), 203–5

Archbishop of Canterbury, 194–95

Arnou, Father, 144, 145

Astier, Gabriel, 17

Austria, 60, 64

Balkans, Protestant minorities in, 53

Baltic states, minorities in, 58

"Banality of Good, The" (Ben-Gal), 32

Barosin, Jacob and Sonia, 185–86, 234

Barot, Madeleine, 126, 130

Barth, Karl, 60, 72, 109, 195

Barthian wing, of Confessing Church (German), 43

Bastide, Samuel, 17–19

Baville, Intendant, 17–18

Belgian Congo, Toureilles as missionaries in, 7, 211

Belgium, 63, 180, 205

Benedite, Daniel, 84

Benès, President, 6, 179

Bertrand, A.-N., 156–57

Bible Institute (Albany, N.Y.), 7

Bibles, 99, 133; for distribution in internment camps, 101, 108, 130

Boegner, Marc, 76, 138; on Church's role, 90–91, 172; coordinating aid, 61, 79, 133, 150, 152; and Final Solution, 156–58, 163–64; influence of, 89–90; and Protestant conferences, 159; protesting deportations, 176, 178; protesting oppression of Jews, 67, 93, 135–36, 163; and rescue activities, 70, 124, 159, 228; style of, 71–72, 89; and Toureille's and Freudenberg's relations, 126–27; Toureille's relations with, 70–71, 99, 133–34

Bohemia, 60. *See also* Czechoslovakia

Boisset, Jean, 81, 150, 152, 242

Boisson, Louis, 24–25

Bolle, Pierre, 91, 159

Bonhoeffer, Dietrich, 3–4, 72; on Nazis, 50, 51–52; and World Alliance, 41–42, *49*, 51–53, *52;* in Youth Commission, 45, 47–50, 53–55

Bourdon, Joseph, 228
Brinon, F. de, 156–57
Britain, 60; immigrants to, 120, 216; reports
    on Final Solution to, 160, 194–95
Brottes, Marie, 27–31
Brozik, 117
Brunner, Emil, 195
Brzak, Slavomir, 240
Bulgaria, 58, 59, 219

Cadier, Jean, 88, 202, 239
Calas, Jean, 20
Calvin, John, 11–12
Calvinism, 11–12
Cambodia, 117
Camisards, 16–20
Canteens, at internment camps, 100
Cardier, Jean, 135
Carême conference, 90
Catholicism, conversion to, 11, 13–17
Catholics: protesting treatment of Jews, 157;
    relations with French Protestants, 12–13,
    20, 33, 69; rescue efforts by, 67, 153–54;
    Slavs as, 36–37; and Vichy government, 67,
    70. See also Gerlier, Cardinal
Cavalier (Camisard leader), 19
Censorship, 99
Center for Czechoslovak Aid (CCA), 4, 6, 78–
    79, 179, 196, 224, 240
"Certificates of loyalty," from Chaplaincy,
    219–20
Cevenol Hymn, 31
Chaillet, Father, 178
Chamby, Switzerland, Youth Commission
    conference in, 53–54
Chaplaincy: coordination with other organiza-
    tions, 133, 151–52; finances of, 150–51,
    152–53; need for help from, 209–10; or-
    ganization of, 149, 151–53; postwar activi-
    ties of, 215–16, 219–20; rescue activities
    through, 81, 182, 192, 208–9, 242–43;
    staff of, 134, 152–53, 183–84, 192, *193*,
    194; tasks of, 149, 201; and Toureille,
    155–56, 242–43; in Toureille's home,
    78, 234
Charles IX, 13
Chasseur, Juillerat, 22–25
Chayla, Abbé du, 18
Children, 210; attempts to save, 68, 97, 177–
    79; deportations of, 66, 178; in internment
    camps, 127, 139; Jewish, 66, 177–79; liber-

ating from internment camps, 97, 112, 116,
    124, 145
Christian Home for Children. See MACE
Christian Socialist movement, 60
Christian World Conference on a Just and
    Durable Peace, 202–4
Christianity, 36, 148; Bonhoeffer's develop-
    ment in, 41–42; on minorities, 51, 59; right
    of sanctuary in, 157–58
Church, 157; opposing governments' steps
    toward war, 45–46; in postwar assimilation
    of refugees, 219; and racism, 90, 93; role in
    spiritual resistance, 166, 169–73; Tou-
    reille's, 98–99; warning about death camps,
    160–61. See also Catholics; French Protes-
    tant Church; Protestants
Church of Christ, separating from German
    Evangelical Church, 50
Church-state relations: Eight Theses of
    Pomeyrol on, 137–38; French Protestant
    position on, 89–90; and Le Chambon-sur-
    Lignon's spiritual resistance, 169–70; sepa-
    ration of, 25, 43; Toureille's writings on,
    201–7
CIMADE, 5, 159–60; in coordinated aid
    efforts, 79, 126, 133; Toureille's relations
    with, 130, 134, 150–52
Civil liberties: after French Revolution, 20;
    Huguenots', 12–13, 19
Civil war of 1620, 13
Clothing/shoes: for internees, 68, 101, 108–9,
    128–29; for refugees, 152, 154
Cohen, Asher, 69, 166–67
Collaborators, 200, 212–15
Commission on Minorities (World Alliance),
    50–51, 53–54
Committee for Ecumenical Aid to Refugees
    (WCC), 70–71, 78–80, 133, 195, 208, 215
Committee of Assistance to Refugees (CAR),
    85–86, 100
Committee of Coordination of Nîmes, 6, 85;
    difficulty of choices in rescue efforts, 73–
    74, 102, 162; and foreign labor groups,
    120–21, 123–24, 146–49; goals of, 67, 83–
    84, 120; helping Czech refugees produce
    food, 114–15; and liberation, 97, 110, 112,
    123–24, 177–79; Lowrie on, 135, 144; or-
    ganization of, 132, 152; reaction to depor-
    tations, 173–77; rescue activities by, 117,
    177–79; response to internment camps,
    82–83, 109; Toureille's reports to, 94–95,

146–49; Toureille's role on, 78, 80, 97, 135, 146; and Vichy government, 144, 145; work with internment camps, 109, 127, 145

Concentration camps, 91–92, 114. *See also* Death camps; Internment camps

Confessing Church (German), 43, 55

Conscientious objectors, French, 53

Conversions: to Catholicism, 13–16; of refugees, 94, 208, 210–11

Council of Constance, 38

Cournonterral, Hérault, 103

Couronne, M., 200

Craske, W. T., 45, 48

Czechoslovak Center for Aid. *See* Center for Czechoslovak Aid (CCA)

Czechoslovakia, 6, 59; France's bond with, 34–35, 45, 60–61, 227, 235; Germany invading, 60–61, 63; minorities in, 53, 58, 59; Munich Accords sacrificing, 4, 60–61; Protestants in, 44–45, 53; Toureille in, 2, 7, 224; Toureille's attachment to, 6, 44–45, 222–27

Czechs, 39, 54, 56, 90, 176; at Christian Home for Children, 113–14, 178–79, 196–97; as foreign workers, 114–15, 148; in internment camps, 94, 103, 112; refugees in France, 78–79, 114–15, 222–24

D'Angoulême, Duke, 21

David, Mrs., *193, 194*

De Villars, le Maréchal, 19

Death camps, in Poland and Eastern Europe: deportations to, 156, 161, 195; German explanations of, 158; knowledge of, 160–61, 164–67; Nazi research on killing efficiency at, 167–68; refugees fleeing, 159–60

Deborah, Israelite prophetess, 30

Denis, Ernest, 34–35, 235

Denmark, 54, 63

Deportations, 71, 123, 207; aid organizations' response to, 82, 159–60, 162, 173–77, 187; and Committee of Nîmes, 80–81, 173–77; conditions of, 161–63; exemptions from, 174, 176; explanations for, 164–69, 173–74, 175; from foreign workers groups, 212–13; of foreigners in French and Allied armies, 175–76; from French camps, 65–66, 68, 161, 171; of French Jews, 85, 88; of Jews, 77, 140, 178; in Nazis' Final Solution plan, 110, 144, 156–57; protests against, 163, 170, 176, 195; response to, 67–70; secrecy about, 173, 175

Depression, Great, 64

Dietrich, Suzanne de, 60–61

Dietrich Bonhoeffer circle, of Confessing Church (German), 43

Disarmament, as World Alliance goal, 45–48, 50

Diseases: in foreign workers groups, 147–48; and internment camps, 68, 98, 108–9, 111, 135, 145; of Toureille family, 104

Djelfa camp (Algeria), 108

Doctors, 108, 121–23

Dominican Republic, 96

Donadille, Marc, 164

Doussau, Commandant, 144

Dragonnades system, 13, 15

Du Ferre (or Du Serre), 17–18

Dubina, Oldrich, 78, 179, 223, 240

Duke of Berwick, 19

Dumas, André, 83

Durand, Marie, 9–10, 88

Eastern Orthodox Church, 151

Economy, 45–46, 48–49, 63–64

Ecuador, 96

Ecumenical movement, 41–42, 55

Edict of 1787, restoring Protestant rights, 20

Edict of Nantes, 13–15

Edict of Pacification (1561), 14

Education, 121; in internment camps, 127, 139; for refugees, 54, 210; of Toureille children, 113, 141–42; Toureille's, 1–2, 34–39, 224; Toureille's teaching, 7

Eight Theses of Pomeyrol, 137–38

Emigration: aid organizations trying to arrange, 68, 71, 96–98, 174; Jews hoping for, 65–66, 177–78; obstacles to, 96, 110, 120–21; postwar, 206; by Toureille family, 224; Toureille trying to expedite, 82, 95–96, 110–11, 123

Encrevé, André, 69

Evangelical Confessing Church (Germany), 71

Evangelical Leprosy Mission, 7

Evangelical Reformed Church of France, 41

Evangelism, Toureille's, 208, 210–11

Evian Conference, on refugee problem, 161

Fascism, 42, 64

Fédération Protestante de France. *See* Protestant Federation of France (PFP)

Fišera, Joseph, 112–16, 196, 222–23

Final Solution, Nazis', 144; beginning of, 156–57; knowledge of, 160, 163–67, 173–77; response to, 161, 167–69, 173–77

Finland, 219

Fischer, Franz, 46–47

Fontaine, Jacques, 14–16

Food: Czech refugees producing, 114–15; sent to internment camps, 68, 101, 128–29

Food shortages: in France, 96, 100, 107, 119, 123; in internment camps, 99–101, 154; of Toureille family, 104–5, 141–42

Forced labor battalions, 68, 144, 209; accusations of collaboration in, 212–13; as alternative, 120–22; and Chaplaincy, 149, 151–52; liberation from, 123–24, 145; makeup of, 78, 102, 176; worsening conditions in, 146–49

Foreign workers groups. See Forced labor battalions

Foreigners, 6, 63–64, 65, 102, 210. See also Jews, foreign vs. French; Refugees

France, 33, 53, 85; armed vs. spiritual resistance in, 66–69; and Czechoslovakia, 4, 34–35, 45, 60, 225, 227, 235; division of, 5, 64; emigration from, 12–13, 16, 121; food shortages in, 96, 104–5, 107, 119; handling postwar refugee issues, 205–7, 219; and Huguenots, 9–10, 16–20; medals and honors awarded to Toureille by, 6–7; Nazis in, 63, 198–99, 207; Nazis occupying southern, 159, 163, 171, 178, 189; Protestant population of, 13, 25, 33, 69–70; refugees in, 63–64, 77, 96, 215–20; refugees traveling to, 179–80; WWII devastation to, 227. See also French army; Occupied Zone, France; Vichy government

Franco, Francisco, 63

Franco-Czech resistance network. See Réseau Rossi-Rybak

Franco-Czechoslovak Association, 223

Free French forces, 199–200

Free Zone. See Vichy government

Freemasons, persecution of, 32, 88

French: in World Alliance, 43, 47, 50. See also Jews, foreign vs. French

French army, 109; foreigners in, 175–76, 183–85; Toureille in, 3–5, 41; trying to protect Huguenots, 21–24; volunteers from foreign workers groups for, 147–48

French Army of Africa, 199–200

French Forces of the Interior (FFI), 234

French Foreign Legion, 102, 208

French Militia, 199–200

French Protestant Church, 42–43, 71, 89, 128; aid to refugees, 79, 149–52, 219; evangelism by, 206, 210–11; heritage of resistance in, 10, 135; inspired by *The Village on the Mountain*, 136–37; meeting at Mialet, 182–83; population of, 13, 25, 33, 69–70; protesting forced labor to Germany, 193–94; protesting oppression of Jews, 26, 67, 69; relations with state, 90–91, 202–4; reorganization of, 25–26; and spiritual resistance, 135–36; Toureille's dissatisfactions with, 7, 203–4, 207, 222–23; of Washington, D.C., 7, 192, 224. See also Huguenots

French Protestant Committee for Aid to the Czech Churches, 61

French Reformation, 11

French Reformed Church. See French Protestant Church

French Revolution (1789), 19–20

Freudenberg, Adolph, 5–6, 72, 151, 195; and aid to internment camps, 94–95, 98–99, 102–3; appreciation for Toureille's work, 128, 243; background of, 71–72; conflict in relationship with Toureille, 110, 119–20, 124–25; and coordination of aid, 72–73, 79, 133; direct contact with internees and refugees, 125–26, 154–55; and emigration, 95–98, 159–60; and the Final Solution, 160–61, 165; goals of, 70, 107, 132–33; and liberation, 97–98, 110–20; sending materials to internment camps, 108, 128–29; and Toureille, 111, 139, 145–46; Toureille's correspondence with, 82, 99, 125–27, 129–32, 140, 150–52, 195–96; Toureille's relations with, 70–71, 79–80, 128–29, 134, 139; Toureille's reports to, 96–97, 121–22, 124–25, 135

Freudenberg, Elsa Liefmann, 71

Freund-Valade, Marc, 116, 178

Friedrich, Ernst, 214–15

Fund for Allocations to Families, 150

Funds, 145; for Chaplaincy activities, 150–52; Freudenberg reviewing, 128–29; lack of, 146, 150–51; for liberation from internment camps, 121, 123, 155; from Switzerland, 101, 132–33; Toureille distributing,

99, 124–25, 132; Toureille pleading for, 99, 132–33

General Union of Jews in France (UGIF), 85
Gerlier, Cardinal, 152; asked to intervene for Jews, 166–67; protesting deportations, 158, 176, 178; protesting treatment of Jews, 157
German Church, at World Alliance meetings, 76
German Commission of Control, 96–97
German Evangelical Church (DEK), 43, 50, 52
German Protestant Church, response to fascism, 43, 55, 69
Germans, 29, 59; expectations of Nazis, 76–77; in French internment camps, 68, 98, 102–3; in World Alliance, 43, 47, 50–51
Germany, 64, 71, 77, 123, 157; domination of Catholic Church by, 36–37; forced laborers sent to, 193–94; military expansion by, 5, 59–61, 63; minorities in, 54, 58; Nazification of, 42–43, 50–51; postwar tribute to Toureille, 6, 230–31, 240–41; refugees from, 56, 63–64, 94–96, 102, 212–16, 219; and religion, 41, 72, 76, 95–96; *The Village on the Mountain* set in, 136–37. *See also* Nazis
Gerstein, Kurt, 168
Gestapo, 171, 178, 196, 198; German refugees accused of collaboration with, 213–14; interrogating Toureille, 6, 88, 197–98; surveillance of Toureille, 82, 192
Goldschmidt, Mr., *193*
Gothie, Pierre, 182
Gounelle, Elie, 93
Gourfinkel, Nina, 83
Grand Rabbi of France, 136
Greece, 59
GTE (*Groupes de travailleurs étrangers*). See Forced labor battalions
Guillon, Charles, 133, 164, 228
Gurs camp, 71, 98, 100, 103, 129, 135, 145; administration of, 127–28, 144; conditions in, 72, 107; deportations from, 174, 178; liberation from, 110, 178

Heating shortages, 109
Henriod, Henri-Louis, 50, 71, 133; and conflict over liberating internees, 97–98; and Freudenberg-Toureille meeting, 127, 129;

on Nazi repression of minorities, 51–52; Toureille's relations with, 133–34
Henry of Navarre (Henry IV), 13
Hirschler, Grand Rabbi, 176–77
History of the Persecutions Endured . . . (Wilks), 21, 24–25
Hitler, Adolf: appeasement of, 4, 60; plot to assassinate, 3, 42
Holocaust: failure of Church to stop, 42; and Jewish populations, 58–59. *See also* Death camps; Final Solution
Huguenots: affinity with Jews, 31–33, 136, 183, 230; beliefs of, 14, 143; character of, 26–27; churches of, 12–13, 20; forced conversion of, 13–16; heritage of rescue, 29–32; history of, 11, 16–19, 183; imprisonment of women, 9–10; maintaining identity, 10–11; persecution of, 12–15, 17–18, 20–25, 136; resistance by, 10, 135. *See also* French Protestant Church
Hull, Cordell, 177
Hungarians, 62
Hungary, 53, 58, 195, 219
Hunted Children, The (Lowrie), 83–84
Huss, John, 1–2, 34–39

Identity papers, false, 28, 192, 197–98; Toureille getting for refugees, 5–6, 149, 183–84
Ilbak, Ella, *194*
Industry, need for labor in, 218
Informers, Résistance shooting, 29–30
Intellectuel engagé ethic, 70
Intergovernmental Committee for Refugees, 160
Internees, 5, 151, 216; Freudenberg's direct contact with, 124–26; letters of tribute to Toureille from, 207–8; Toureille's questionnaire for, 220–21; Vichy treatment of Jewish, 64–65
Internment: of Committee of Nîmes members, 80–81; following Statute for Jews, 94
Internment camps, 124–25, 127, 171, 174, 179–80; aid for, 68, 100–101, 128–29; aid organizations working in, 77–79, 145, 151–52; conditions in, 72, 98, 100, 102, 107–8; conflict over response to, 71, 74, 82–83, 109; deaths in, 68, 100; distribution of packages in, 107–8, 128–29; food shortages in, 99–101; French response to, 67–69,

Internment camps (*continued*)
205; identification of people at, 127–28; leaves from, 121–23; medical care in, 108, 111, 187; moving of refugees among, 129–30; obstacles to aid in, 111–12; populations of, 102, 121, 135; religion in, 109, 138–40; Toureille's work in, 99, 132–35, 242; Vichy government asking for help with, 77–78; Vichy plans for, 109, 135, 144–45. *See also* Deportations; Liberation
Israel, and Yad Vashem awards, 228–29
Italian army, 179
Italian Zone (in France), 179, 196
Italy, 54–55, 77

Jean-Faure, André, 144–45
Jewish organizations, 67, 87, 94–95, 101, 110, 117, 140, 206
Jews, 54; in aid organizations, 84–88; at Christian Home for Children, 112, 114, 116; in concentration camps, 91–92; conversion of, 94, 208–11; Czechs, 90, 116, 240; deportations of, 70–71, 77, 140, 176, 195; foreign *vs.* French, 66, 85, 87, 94, 136, 170; in foreign workers groups, 147–48; German refugees, 53, 77; history in Lunel, 232–34; Huguenots' affinity with, 30–33, 136, 230; in internment camps, 65, 102; lack of world response to news of Final Solution, 161; numbers being killed, 167–68; persecution of, 6, 136; populations of, 33, 58–59; postwar tributes to Toureille from, 7, 241–42; protected by Le Chambon, 28–29, 170–71; Protestant principles on, 51, 73, 137–38, 158–59; protests of persecution of, 26, 51, 88, 90, 136; Red Cross's wariness in aiding, 72–73; as refugees, 63–64, 93–94; refugees without documents assumed to be, 155; rescue efforts for, 6, 166–67, 171, 177–79; roundups of, 156–58, 171, 174, 185; taken to Switzerland, 117, 159; Toureille and, 138–40, 188, 205–7, 237; under Vichy government, 5, 64–69; and Yad Vashem awards, 27–29, 228–30. *See also* Anti-Semitism
Joy, Charles, 110
Justice, 89–90, 203–4

Kapel, René Samuel, 82–83
Kaplan, Grand Rabbi, 166–67
Krenek, Pastor J., 223–24

Kristallnacht, 64
Kundt Commission, 96–97

Lagarde, Général, 21–25
Lambert, Raymond-Raoul, 85–88, 117, 237
Lamirand, George, 169–70
Languedoc, Camisards in, 16–20
"*L'Antisémitisme païen . . . et chrétien*" (Martin), 91–92
Laporte, Pierre (Roland), 19
Laval, Pierre, 66, 158, 173–74, 177–78
L'Avant-Garde (journal), 55–59
Le Chambon-sur-Lignon, 27–31, 169–71
League of Nations, 46, 194
Leenhardt, Henri, 192
Legal, A., 61
Les Milles camp, 68, 135, 144, 178
Les Protestants de l'Europe Centrale et les Missions en Terre Païnne (Toureille), 44–45
Les protestants français pendant la seconde guerre mondiale, 163
Liberation: aftermath of, 154–55, 214; of children from internment camps, 97, 112, 116, 124, 145; from foreign labor groups, 123–24, 147–48; from internment camps, 72, 82, 96–98, 109–11, 123, 145, 178, 214; public negativity about, 119–20
Liberation committee, running Lunel, 199
Lichtenstein-Warnery, Délie. *See* Toureille, Délie Lichtenstein-Warnery (wife)
Lindenkopf, in *The Village on the Mountain,* 136–37
Lodging shortages, 96, 120
Loiseau-Chevalley, Suzanne, 161–62
Louis XIV, 13, 16, 20
Lowrie, Donald, 6, 78, 102, 117, 127, 135, 144; and Christian Home for Children, 112, 114–15, 179; and Committee of Nîmes, 80, 83–84, 173–77; and Vichy officials, 145–47
Lunel, 200, 232–35; Chaplaincy office in, 81; Toureille family home in, 6, 234; White Terror in, 20–25
Lutheran wing, of Confessing Church (German), 43
Luxembourg, 63

MACE (Maison d'accueil chrétienne pour enfants—Christian Aid Home for Children), 6, 112–15, 142, 178–79; evacuation of, 116–17, 196–97

Macedonia, minorities in, 58
Management Committee (of World Alliance), 46–47
Marignan, M., 200
Martin, Jacques, 91–92, 164–65
Martyrdom, 12, 17–19, 37–38
Masaryk, Tomáš, 2, 35, 44, 55–56, 112
Mautner family, 28–29
Mazel, Abraham, 18–19
Media, reports on internment camps, 107
Medical care, in internment camps, 68, 108, 111, 187; sick leaves from, 121–23, 145
Medici, Catherine de, 13
Mende, 235–36
Mexico, 117, 177
Mialet, French Protestants meeting at, 182–83
Military chaplain, Toureille as, 5
Minorities: Nazi repression of, 51–52; Toureille's article on, 55–59; World Alliance work on, 51–53, 76
Missionaries, Toureilles as, 7, 44, 211, *226*
Missions Society of Paris, 44
Money. *See* Funds
Monier, Henriette, *194*
Monnier, Jean, 2
Morel, André, 228
Mortality rate, in internment camps, 98, 100, 102, 107
Munich Accords, 4, 60–61, 63, 225–27

Napolean, 20
National Council (of Reformed Church of France), 89
Nationality, of Jews, 58
Naturalization, postwar, 206
Nazis, 30, 76, 87, 94, 196; anti-Semitism of, 77, 90; armed *vs.* spiritual resistance to, 66–69; and deportations, 65–66, 68; and Final Solution, 144, 156, 161; internees trying not to offend, 124–25; occupying southern France, 159, 163, 171, 178, 189; repression of minorities, 51–52; retreat in France, 198–99, 207; rise of, 42–43, 46, 50–51
Netherlands, 63
Niemöller, Martin, 50
Nîmes, 235
Noé camp, 107–9, 135, 145
North Africa, 178; internment camps in, 121, 123, 134–35
Norway, 54, 63

Occupied Zone, France, 145–46, 156–57, 163
Office of Joint Aid (WCC), 128
Oppenheim, Walter, 241–42
Oradour-sur-Glane, destruction of, 30
ORT *(Organisation pour la reconstruction et le travail)*, 127
OSE *(Oeuvre de secours aus enfants)*, 178

Pacificism, 42–43
Pact of Paris of 1928, 46
Pajer, Karol, 196–97
Papet, Robert and Thérèse. *See* Parlier, Robert and Thérèse
Paris, postwar refugees in, 216–18
Paris synod of 1559, 12–13
Parlier, Robert and Thérèse, 183–85, *193, 194*, 197–98, 234
Partisans, Czech, 196
Pastors, 70, 153, 209; and aid for internment camps, 108, 126, 129, 133; knowledge of Final Solution, 164–65; meetings of, 90, 93, 182–83; repression of German, 51, 72, 76; rescue activities of, 29, 182; Toureille's vocation as, 39–41
Peace treaties, from WWI, 46–47, 50, 57
Pétain, Marshal, 5, 64; Boegner protesting treatment of Jews to, 156–57; and Committee of Nîmes, 145, 174; support for, 70, 90–91, 138, 169–70. *See also* Vichy government
Poland, 54, 63; death camps in, 66, 68; justifications for deportations to, 173, 175; minorities in, 58–59
Poles, 148, 176
Police: looking for Jews, 28; Vichy, 171, 192, 197–98. *See also* Gestapo
Politics, 55; mixed with religion, 21, 38–39, 56, 70; within World Alliance, 43 *See also* Church-state relations
Pomaret, Charles, 1
Pomeyrol conference, 158–59, 164–65
Portugal, 107, 110, 129
Pou, Mr. and Mrs., *193*
Pouget, Irène, *193*
Poul, Captain, 18
Predestination, in Calvinism, 11–12
"Problem of the Minorities in Europe, The" (Toureille), 55–59
Protestant Federation of France (FPF), 4–5, 25–26, 99, 194; Boegner in, 70, 89; and coordination of aid organizations, 133, 150, 152

Protestants, 53; aid to refugee and interned,
72, 93–94, 139–41, 150, 153–54; Czech,
44–45, 103, 115, 227; emigration from
France, 13, 16; English, 20–21; evaluating
rescue activities of, 163–64; in foreign labor groups, 123–24; in internment camps,
99, 103, 138–39, 154; and Nazis' Final Solution, 156, 163–67; principles concerning
Jews, 51, 73, 137–38, 158–59; relations
with Jews, 90, 92–93, 136. *See also* French
Protestant Church; Huguenots; Switzerland; World Alliance; World Council of
Churches
Purge trials, 212–15

Quakers, 67, 98, 110, 151, 174
Quervain, Alfred de, 109

Racism, the church and, 51, 90
Ravenel (Camisard leader), 18
Récébédou camp, 107, 109, 138–39, 187
Red Cross, 67, 71–73, 98, 129
Reformation, 11, 37
Reformed Church of France. *See* French
Protestant Church
Refugees, 54, 110, 146; aid for, 72, 93–94,
124–25, 131–32, 150, 172; and aid organizations, 70–72, 77–80, 84; Czech, 61, 78–
79, 222–24; emigration for, 95–96; French
attitudes toward, 67–69, 119–20, 160–61,
210; German, 53, 56, 63–64, 77, 94–96,
102, 212–16, 219; Jews as, 28–31, 77, 91–
92, 156–57; Jews as, *vs.* French Jews, 85,
87, 136; mistreatment of, 61–62; needs of,
96, 98, 154; outside internment camps,
153–55; postwar, 205–7, 219–20; postwar
purge trials of, 212–15; Sperber family as,
179–82; Switzerland not accepting, 123,
159–61; Toureille's correspondence with,
128, 153; Toureille's proposals for, 205,
215–20; Toureille's work with, 5, 99, 132–
33, 154; tribute to Toureille from, 207–8,
227–31. *See also* Internees; Internment
camps
Religion, 43; comparison of, 236; determination of, 94, 155–56, 186; in distribution of
aid, 151, 193; and politics, 21, 38–39, 56,
70; resistance and rescue as duties of, 27,
72, 207; services in internment camps, 108,
138–39, 152; of Slavs, 36–37; thanks for

Toureille's inspiration, 207–8; Toureille's, 8,
211. *See also* Bibles; Pastors
Religious materials, for internees, 108, 152.
See also Bibles
Religious tolerance, in France, 13, 19–21
Rescue activities, 165; choices in, 73–74, 102,
162; costs of, 166, 221–22; Huguenot heritage of, 26, 29–32; increasing, 159, 207;
for Jewish children, 177–79; motivations
for, 27–31; obstacles to, 81–82; postwar
tributes to Toureille for, 6–7, 207–8, 222–
24, 227–31, 239–43; Protestants evaluating
afterward, 163–64; through Chaplaincy, 81,
192–93, 208–9; Toureille's, 5–6, 159, 172–
73, 179–86, 201–2; Toureille's evangelism
through, 208, 210–11; Trocmé's and Le
Chambon's, 170–73
Réseau Rossi-Rybak, 6
Resistance, 116; armed, 66–67, 116; as religious duty, 27, 72. *See also* Spiritual resist-
ance
Resistance, the, 29–30, 156, 194
Revue du christianisme social, 77, 91–92
Rivesaltes camp, 139, 154, 178
Romania, 53, 59
Rotkirsh, Mr., *193*
Rumania, 219
Russia, refugees from, 61–62
Russier, M. and Eva, 28

Salièges, Archbishop, 178
Salzer, Grand Rabbi, 147
Sanctuary, right of, 157–58
Saussine, Jacques, 187
Schwartz, Israel, 136
Schwartz, Joseph J., 109
Schweitzer, Mr. and Mrs., *194*
Scottish Church, in Czechoslovakia, 224
Serbs, as minority, 76
Sicardie, Corbière la, 17
"Silence is impossible" (Boegner), 89–90
Slavic, Toureille studying, 2
Slavs, 1, 34–36
Slovakia, refugees from, 61–62
Smith, Robert, 224
Sochor, J. B., 61–62
Social Christianity, 204
Socialist government, in France, 64
"Song of Deborah, The," 30
South America, 177

Soviet Union, 58–60
Spain, 55, 63, 96
Spanish Civil War refugees, 63, 94, 102
Sperber, Anna and Ferdinand, 179–82
Spirit, power of, 202
Spiritual resistance, 5, 66–67, 71–72; beginnings of, 88–93; Church's role in, 166, 169–73; influences on, 135–37; Papets in, 184–85
St. Bartholomew's Day Massacre (1572), 13
Statutes for Jews (Vichy), 65, 94; explanation of, 92–93; of foreign *vs.* French Jews, 85, 136; racial declaration of, *118;* response to, 67, 91, 93
Stein-Schneider, Herbert, 192–93, 208–9, 239–40
STO *(Service du travail obligatoire),* 194
"Strengthened Ties" (Toureille), 224–27
Stricker, Miss, *193*
Stricker, Mr., *193*
Strong, Tracy, 54, 173–77
Sudetenland, 76
Sweden, 54, 96, 151–52
Swiss Committee of Protestant Churches, 205
Switzerland, 11, 54, 107; aid to refugees from, 72, 111–12, 130–31, 149–50; Bibles for internees from, 99–100; and Chaplaincy, 152, 193; and French Protestants, 70, 128; Huguenots fleeing to, 18–19; not accepting refugees, 123, 159–61, 205; refugees going to, 117, 178, 193; Toureille's interactions with, 6, 100–101, 132–33
"Synod of the Desert," 20

Tassigny, General de Lattre de, 200
Tavernier, Colonel, 146–47
Thurneysen, Eduard, 72
Tory, Avraham, 201
Totalitarianism, 46, 88
Touat, Pierre du (Toureille alias), 77
Toureille, Anne-Marie (daughter), 3, 189; at Christian Home for Children, 6, 112–14, 142, 196–97; on father's work, 104–5, 201
Toureille, Délie Lichtenstein-Warnery (wife), 2, 40, *194,* 198, 230, 236; and children, 3, 105; death of, 8; illness of, 104, 113, 141; as missionary, 7, 211, *226;* retirement of, 7–8
Toureille, Etienne Charles (father), 1, *3,* 39
Toureille, Francine (daughter), 3, 113

Toureille, Léonie Bastide (mother), 1, *3,* 11, 40
Toureille, Marc (son), 3, 104, 113, 189, *193,* 198, 199, 236; on father's rescue activities, 221–22, 230; on Huguenots and Jews, 31–32; rescue activities of, 192
Toureille, Micheline (daughter-in-law), 236
Toureille, Paul (great-grandfather), 1
Toureille, Pierre-Charles (personal), 1–6, *4, 194, 225;* appearance of, 8, 236–37; childhood of, 1, *2, 3;* honors and tributes awarded to, 6–7, 207–8, 227–31; as missionary, *226;* as student, *35;* at World Alliance meetings, *49, 52. See also* Writings, Toureille's
Toureille, Simon (son), 3, 104, 113, 200
Toureille family, 189; education of children, 141–42; emigration to United States, 7, 224; food shortages of, 141–42; during war, 103–4, 221–22
Toureille homes: Cournonterral, Hérault, 103; in Lunel, 142, 234; Montpellier, 141; Papets sharing, 183–84; Wehrmacht requisitioning room in, 149, 234
Toureille Lichtenstein, Jean (son), 3, 6, 112–14
Toureille sisters, *3*
Tower of Constance, 9–10, 18
Transportation, lack of, 96, 120
Trocmé, André, 29, 71, 158, 169–73, 228–29
Trocmé, Jacques, 172
Tuck, H. Pinkney, 177
Turkey, Jewish population of, 59

Unitarians, 67, 151
United States, 101, 107–8, 152, 176–77; Freudenberg trying to expedite emigration to, 96, 98; immigrants to, 120, 178, 216; reports about Final Solution in, 160, 194–95; Toureille family's emigration to, 7, 224
U.S. National Council of Churches, 194–95
U.S. State Department, 102

Vélodrome d'Hiver, 156
Vichy government, 64, 70, 86–88, 88, 90; and aid organizations, 99, 117, 146–48, 173, 179; aid organizations helping with refugees, 68–69, 77–78; aid organizations working in internment camps, 73–74, 79, 82–83; and aid to refugees, 73, 100, 131–32; anti-Semitism of, 32, 64–66, 90–93; and

Vichy government (*continued*)
Christian Home for Children, 112, 178–79; and Committee of Nîmes, 80, 84, 132, 144, 174; concerns about emigration of Jewish children, 177–78; and conditions for foreign workers, 120–21, 146–48; and deportations, 65–66, 158, 173–74, 176; deportations protested to, 158, 174; and internment camps, 65, 71, 98, 109, 124–25, 127, 144–45; and liberation from camps, 97, 109; protests to against treatment of Jews, 6, 26, 136, 163; refugee policies of, 5–6, 80, 94, 119–20; resistance to, 30–31, 66–69; roundups of Jews by, 171, 185; support for, 90, 169–70; surveillance of Toureille by, 82, 140, 155, 187–88, 192; and Toureille, 6, 145–46, 148. *See also* Statutes for Jews
Vichy police, 171, 192, 197–98
Village on the Mountain: Portrait of the Church Faithful under the Nazi Regime, The, 136–37
Vincent, Isabeau, 17
Visas, 117, 120, 134–35, 177
Visser't Hooft, W. A., 72, 127, 133, 159, 195; and Nazis' Final Solution, 164–65, 167–69; spiritual resistance of, 137–38; and Toureille, 93, 133–34
Vlassov's Army, 196
Vogt, Paul, 195
Voltaire, 20, 38

Wannsee Conference, Nazis planning Final Solution at, 144, 156
Washington, D.C., French Protestant Church in, 7, 192, 224
Weapons of the Spirit (documentary film), 27
Weill, Joseph, 83, 110, 146
White Terror, 20–25
Wilks, Mark, 20–21, 24–25, 26–27
Women, 146–47; aid for, 131, 209–10; imprisonment of Huguenot, 9–10
Work, 127; for Czech refugees, 78–79, 114–15; forced labor sent to Germany, 175, 193–94; by refugees, 119, 215–18; Toureille looking for, 222–23. *See also* Forced labor battalions
World Alliance for Promoting International Friendship through the Churches, 3, 41–42, 50, 203; conferences of, 48–49, *49*, 51–53, *52*, 76; disarmament as goal of, 45–46; on minorities, 52–53; on revision of WWI peace treaties, 46–47; Toureille in, 43–45, 54; and WCC ecumenical committee, 71, 79. *See also* Youth Commission
World Council of Churches (WCC), 5, 89, 110; aid to refugees and internees by, 73, 93–95, 109, 133; and Chaplaincy work, 6, 150–51; and Nazis' Final Solution, 160–61, 163–69, 194; refugee commission of, 71–72; and Toureille, 6, 93–94, 98–99, 183, 186–87; and Visser't Hooft, 93–94, 137–38. *See also* Committee for Ecumenical Aid to Refugees
World Jewish Congress (WJC), 160, 163, 168, 194
World War I, effects on European dynamics, 57
World War II: chronologies of, 75–76, 106–7, 143, 190–91; devastation to France from, 227
Writings, Toureille's, 201–7; on Czechoslovakia, 224–27; on postwar purge trials, 212–15; questionnaire for internees, 220–21; style of, 11, 36

Xenophobia, French, 64

Yad Vashem awards, 116; meaning for Protestants in relation to Jews, 32–33; for Toureille, 7, 228–30, 241–42; for village of Le Chambon, 27–29, 31, 171
Yellow star, 156–57, 163
YMCA, 6, 54, 67, 71, 101, 108
Youth Commission (of World Alliance for Promoting International Friendship through the Churches), 3; Bonhoeffer in, 41, 53–55; conferences of, 47–50, 53–54; Toureille in, 41, 45, 47–50